Perl 6 Deep Dive

Data manipulation, concurrency, functional programming,
and more

Andrew Shitov

BIRMINGHAM - MUMBAI

Perl 6 Deep Dive

First published: September 2017

Production reference: 1060917

Published by Packt Publishing Ltd.
Livery Place
35 Livery Street
Birmingham
B3 2PB, UK.

ISBN 978-1-78728-204-9

www.packtpub.com

Credits

About the Author

Andrew Shitov has been a Perl enthusiast since the end of the 1990s, and is the organizer of over 30 Perl conferences in eight countries. He worked as a developer and CTO in leading web-development companies, such as Art. Lebedev Studio, Booking.com, and eBay, and he learned from the "Fathers of the Russian Internet", Artemy Lebedev and Anton Nossik.

Andrew has been following the Perl 6 development since its beginning in 2000. He ran a blog dedicated to the language, published a series of articles in the *Pragmatic Perl* magazine, and gives talks about Perl 6 at various Perl events. In 2017, he published the *Perl 6 at a Glance* book by DeepText, which was the first book on Perl 6 published after the first stable release of the language specification.

Acknowledgements

Through the course of writing this book, I contacted many people who helped me clarify many dark corners of Perl 6. First of all, thanks to the reviewers of this book, Liz Mattijsen, who is also the core developer of the Perl 6 compiler, and Alex Kapranoff, who has helped me promote Perl 6 for more than a decade already.

I would also like to thank the whole Rakudo compiler team, who worked hard to make things happen even when almost nobody believed that Perl 6 would become a reality. So, primarily, thanks to Jonathan Worthington for not only working on the compiler, but also for his talks, which I found on YouTube and used for reference. Also, thanks to the rest of the team.

Special thanks go to Wendy van Dijk, who has done great work to change the image of the Perl language and has personally helped me promote my books.

And of course, thanks to the author of Perl, Larry Wall, and his wife, Gloria, for the years of patience and enthusiasm; they made Perl 6 fly in the end.

This book has also been possible due to the number of other Perl 6 books that appeared this year; so, I want to thank the authors of those books as they indirectly stimulated me to write faster and more.

Finally, this book took its shape with the efforts of the editors at Packt, Lawrence Veigas, who guided me through the writing process, and Mehul Singh, who joined at the last stage of the publishing process and provided many suggestions on how to make the book better and more useful for the readers.

About the Reviewer

Alex Kapranoff studied software engineering in one of the smaller Russian cities and then worked in the internet industry for about 20 years in roles ranging from software developer to CTO to technical manager. Having written production code in many programming languages, he still considers Perl his one true love. Perl 6 is a huge step forward for the language, for the ecosystem, and, maybe even for programming language theory.

Agava, Inline Technologies, Rambler.ru, and Yandex are companies that provided Alex with the opportunities to be his best and write impactful code in Perl on a day-to-day basis throughout his career.

Alex has worked on a number of books about the performance-oriented web server software, Nginx, and published his own take on *Nginx Troubleshooting* with Packt Publishing.

I am very grateful to the whole worldwide Perl community – an amazing group of people using and constantly improving the language that we all love and have the most impact with.

www.PacktPub.com

For support files and downloads related to your book, please visit www.PacktPub.com. Did you know that Packt offers eBook versions of every book published, with PDF and ePub files available? You can upgrade to the eBook version at www.PacktPub.com and as a print book customer, you are entitled to a discount on the eBook copy. Get in touch with us at service@packtpub.com for more details.

At www.PacktPub.com, you can also read a collection of free technical articles, sign up for a range of free newsletters and receive exclusive discounts and offers on Packt books and eBooks.

https://www.packtpub.com/mapt

Get the most in-demand software skills with Mapt. Mapt gives you full access to all Packt books and video courses, as well as industry-leading tools to help you plan your personal development and advance your career.

Why subscribe?

- Fully searchable across every book published by Packt
- Copy and paste, print, and bookmark content
- On demand and accessible via a web browser

Customer Feedback

Thanks for purchasing this Packt book. At Packt, quality is at the heart of our editorial process. To help us improve, please leave us an honest review on this book's Amazon page at `https://www.amazon.com/dp/178728204X`.

If you'd like to join our team of regular reviewers, you can email us at `customerreviews@packtpub.com`. We award our regular reviewers with free eBooks and videos in exchange for their valuable feedback. Help us be relentless in improving our products!

Table of Contents

Preface

Perl 6 is a new programming language in the Perl family. It has come a long way from the start of its development in 2000 to the current state, when the language is production ready.

Although the initial project of the language was a next version of Perl 5 to trim some edges, get rid of legacy, and add features that were requested by the community, it instead turned out to be a shiny language that holds the spirit of Perl, offers us a variety of modern mechanisms, and allows you to follow paradigms such as functional and reactive programming.

The great thing about today's Perl 6 is that all these new things are already built into the language and no external libraries are needed to start working with them. For example, take one of the most difficult topics: concurrent and parallel programming. Perl 6 has support for it so that the programmer can start using it right away without thinking about how to organize spawning new threads or implement inter-process communication and access shared data.

One of the goals that we had while writing this book was to show that Perl 6 is a great tool you can consider for your daily practice.

This book contains 15 chapters that cover everything from the basics to more complex themes such as functional programming.

What this book covers

Chapter 1, *What is Perl 6?*, talks about the reasons why Perl 6 appeared, briefly describes the changes that happened since Perl 5, and explains how to install the compiler and run the first program, "Hello, World!".

Chapter 2, *Writing Code*, prepares you to write a Perl 6 code and explains how the source code is organized. It gives an overview of the Unicode support that Perl 6 offers to a programmer.

Chapter 3, *Working with Variables and Built-In Data Types*, takes you through the built-in types of the language and teaches you how to work with variables, such as simple scalars, arrays, and hashes, as well as composite data types.

Chapter 4, *Working with Operators,* covers the dozens of built-in operators in Perl 6 and introduces you to concepts such as meta-, cross-, and hyper-operators, which may be new for the Perl 5 programmers.

Chapter 5, *Control Flow,* explains the main elements to control the flow of programs in Perl 6, such as conditional checks and loops.

Chapter 6, *Subroutines,* covers the work with subroutines in Perl 6. It explains how to create and call a subroutine, how to describe its arguments and return types, and how to deal with anonymous and nested subroutines.

Chapter 7, *Modules,* talks about the topic of organizing code into modules and the ways of importing the module in a program.

Chapter 8, *Object-Oriented Programming,* introduces the concepts of inheritance, roles, and introspections, and gives information about using an object in code. It also discusses the object-oriented facilities of Perl 6.

Chapter 9, *Input and Output,* is devoted to input and output in a console application and working with files and directories.

Chapter 10, *Working with Exceptions,* talks about exceptional situations that the program can face, for example, disk failure or broken connection to a database. Also, it shows how to create your own exceptions to control the behavior of the program.

Chapter 11, *Regexes,* describes the redesigned regular expressions, which was one of the keystones of Perl 5 and has become even more powerful in Perl 6.

Chapter 12, *Grammars,* introduces the new built-in tool that helps create a parser, a translator, or a compiler; a domain-specific language or even a programming language; or even a parser that can work with human languages.

Chapter 13, *Concurrent Programming,* describes that Perl 6's built-in support of the concepts, which makes it easy to create an application that supports parallel and concurrent programming, such as threads, junctions, promises, and channels.

Chapter 14, *Functional Programming,* shows the ways in which you can use the functional programming style with Perl 6, including recursion, reduction, higher order functions, closures, currying, and lazy evaluations.

Chapter 15, *Reactive Programming,* talks about a particular topic of functional programming--event-driven programming. It explains how to work with supplies and taps and how to filter and transform the data streams.

What you need for this book

This book can, of course, be read without a computer at hand, in which case, you need nothing more than the book itself. However, to follow the examples in the book, you need a compiler of Perl 6, which you can download from
`http://rakudo.org/how-to-get-rakudo/` (more details on installing it are in `Chapter 1`, *What is Perl 6?*). The Rakudo Perl 6 compiler works on a variety of platforms--Windows, macOS, and Linux. You will also need your favorite text editor to write programs in.

Who this book is for

This book is intended for different groups of people--first of all, to the current developers that use the Perl 5 programming language and are willing to switch to Perl 6 in the near future or simply want to know what's new in the world of Perl. Second, this book will suit the needs of software developers who are interested in broadening the horizons of their tools and want to be familiar with a new handy programming language that offers built-in support of many programming paradigms. The content of this book is built in such a way that references to Perl 5 are avoided as much as possible, so both people with and without a Perl 5 background can read this book with ease. Finally, this book is written with the hope that it will become a textbook for the educational courses of Perl 6.

Conventions

In this book, you will find a number of text styles that distinguish between different kinds of information. Here are some examples of these styles and an explanation of their meaning.

Code words in text, database table names, folder names, filenames, file extensions, pathnames, URLs, user input, and program output are shown as follows: "If the file does not exist, the `$fh handle` will be set to a `Failure` object."

A block of code is set as follows:

```
say 0.7 * (@street ==>
grep {.number %% 2} ==>
grep {.colour eq 'red'} ==>
grep {.renovation-year < 2013} ==>
map {.area * 3} ==>
reduce {$^a + $^b});
```

Any command-line input and output are shown in bold as follows:

```
$ perl6 -v
This is Rakudo version 2017.07 built on MoarVM version 2017.07
implementing Perl 6.c.
```

New terms and **important words** are shown in bold.

Reader feedback

Feedback from our readers is always welcome. Let us know what you think about this book—what you liked or disliked. Reader feedback is important to us as it helps us develop titles that you will really get the most out of.

To send us general feedback, simply email `feedback@packtpub.com`, and mention the book's title in the subject of your message.

If there is a topic that you have expertise in and you are interested in either writing or contributing to a book, see our author guide at `www.packtpub.com/authors`.

Customer support

Now that you are the proud owner of a Packt book, we have a number of things to help you to get the most from your purchase.

Downloading the example code

You can download the example code files for this book from your account at `http://www.packtpub.com`. If you purchased this book elsewhere, you can visit `http://www.packtpub.com/support` and register to have the files e-mailed directly to you.

You can download the code files by following these steps:

1. Log in or register to our website using your e-mail address and password.
2. Hover the mouse pointer on the **SUPPORT** tab at the top.
3. Click on **Code Downloads & Errata**.
4. Enter the name of the book in the **Search** box.
5. Select the book for which you're looking to download the code files.
6. Choose from the drop-down menu where you purchased this book from.
7. Click on **Code Download**.

Once the file is downloaded, please make sure that you unzip or extract the folder using the latest version of:

- WinRAR / 7-Zip for Windows
- Zipeg / iZip / UnRarX for Mac
- 7-Zip / PeaZip for Linux

The code bundle for the book is also hosted on GitHub at `https://github.com/PacktPublishing/Perl-6-Deep-Dive`. We also have other code bundles from our rich catalog of books and videos available at `https://github.com/PacktPublishing/`. Check them out!'

Errata

Although we have taken every care to ensure the accuracy of our content, mistakes do happen. If you find a mistake in one of our books—maybe a mistake in the text or the code—we would be grateful if you could report this to us. By doing so, you can save other readers from frustration and help us improve subsequent versions of this book. If you find any errata, please report them by visiting `http://www.packtpub.com/submit-errata`, selecting your book, clicking on the **Errata Submission Form** link, and entering the details of your errata. Once your errata are verified, your submission will be accepted and the errata will be uploaded to our website or added to any list of existing errata under the Errata section of that title.

To view the previously submitted errata, go to `https://www.packtpub.com/books/content/support` and enter the name of the book in the search field. The required information will appear under the Errata section.

Piracy

Piracy of copyrighted material on the Internet is an ongoing problem across all media. At Packt, we take the protection of our copyright and licenses very seriously. If you come across any illegal copies of our works in any form on the Internet, please provide us with the location address or website name immediately so that we can pursue a remedy.

Please contact us at `copyright@packtpub.com` with a link to the suspected pirated material.

We appreciate your help in protecting our authors and our ability to bring you valuable content.

Questions

If you have a problem with any aspect of this book, you can contact us at
questions@packtpub.com, and we will do our best to address the problem.

1
What is Perl 6?

In this chapter, we will examine the reasons why Perl 6 appeared and follow the history of the development of the language. You will see some examples of changes that have happened since Perl 5, and you will learn how to download and use the compiler, where to find the documentation, and how to run your first program in Perl 6.

In this chapter, we will cover the following topics:

- Origins of Perl 6
- Differences from Perl 5
- Perl 6 resources
- Compilers
- Working with Rakudo Star
- Writing our Hello World program

Origins of Perl 6

Perl 6 is a programming language from the Perl family. Perl itself emerged in 1987 and since then, it is constantly evolving: its current stable version is 5.26, which was released in May 2017. In 2000, Larry Wall, the creator of Perl, proposed to start working on the next version of the language—Perl 6.

There were a few reasons for that. First, a language should continue developing to reflect the new requirements of developers. Second, it may change the perception of Perl in the non-Perl community. The version 5.0 appeared in 1993 and despite that, the language has continued developing. The major version number was still 5 and in the eyes of many people, it meant that Perl was stalled since 1993. The new major version update would refresh the perception.

The idea was to make Perl 6 "the community rewrite of Perl". Larry asked the community to share what bits of Perl they wanted to change. That call for changes resulted in 361 RFC (Request for Comments) documents, which are published at `https://perl6.org/archive/rfc/`. These documents are only of historical interest as of today.

Later, the various proposals were systematically analyzed, grouped together by similar topics and published as a series of Synopses. The naming and numbering principle behind those documents were to keep the structure of the chapters of the Programming Perl book.

Later, Synopses were once again summarized and explained in a set of documents called Apocalypses and Exegeses. All these papers are available today at `http://design.perl6.org`, but again, they are not the final specification of the language, only a collection of historical documents.

Another important idea about Perl 6 was about the way compilers are created. In Perl 5, the language rules are indirectly defined by the single available compiler. Some bugs, or not obvious behavior of the compiler, may be considered as part of the language standard. In Perl 6, it was decided to have a clear language specification, and no reference compiler. There can be more than one compiler. The main requirement for them is implementing the specification and passing the set of tests.

Differences from Perl 5

Let's briefly look at some of the changes that happened on the way to Perl 6. In the following sections, you will see a few examples of code in Perl 5 and 6. They are intended for a general understanding of how Perl 5 transforms to Perl 6, but you are not expected to understand every bit of it. All the details about the syntax of Perl 6 will be explained later in this book.

Sigils

One of the most difficult things for the newcomers to Perl are sigils. A sigil is a character in front of the name of variables in Perl that denotes the structural type of a variable. For example, $ for scalar values, @ for arrays, and % for hashes.

The problem arises when you access an element of an array or hash. Let's consider the following lines of code as an example in Perl 5 of an array with the first few Fibonacci numbers:

```
my @fibonacci = (0, 1, 1, 2, 3, 5, 8, 13);
print $fibonacci[4];
```

First, a @fibonacci array is created. The name of the variable includes the @ character as a sigil. In the second line, we access one of the elements of that array and use another sigil, $, this time. This is because a single element of an array is a scalar, and scalars use $ as a sigil. For those who learn Perl, this small change in sigils is a big problem in understanding the basics of the language.

In Perl 6, sigils are unified and are part of the variable names. You do not change it independently, whether you access an element of an array or an array as a whole. The preceding example will look like this in Perl 6:

```
my @fibonacci = (0, 1, 1, 2, 3, 5, 8, 13);
print @fibonacci[4];
```

In both lines, the same sigil is used for the @fibonacci array and for its @fibonacci[4] element. This approach is much more consistent and easier for a beginner.

Signatures

In Perl 5, you had to extract the values of the arguments of a function yourself by using either the built-in shift function, or from the default @_ array.

Let's see this in the following example, with a function to calculate the sum of its two arguments. In Perl 5, you had to do some additional work to get the actual passed parameters.

First, get the argument values with shift in Perl 5:

```
sub add {
    my $x = shift;
    my $y = shift;
    return $x + $y;
}
```

Then, by using the @_ array:

```
sub add {
    my ($x, $y) = @_;
    return $x + $y;
}
```

Unlike many other programming languages, it was not possible to declare a list of the function's formal parameters directly. For instance, this is how you do it in C or C++:

```
int add(int x, int y) {
    return x + y;
}
```

In Perl 5, it is possible to restrict the number of arguments and their structural types with the help of prototypes. Sigils are used there to tell Perl the type of the argument. The preceding function for addition may look like this in Perl 5:

```
sub add($$) {
    my ($x, $y) = @_;
    return $x + $y;
}
```

Using function prototypes will make the compiler complain when the function is used with the different number of arguments (say, one or three instead of two), but you still have to get their values yourself.

Perl 5.20 introduced *function signatures.* So, now, you may benefit from declaring the arguments in one go. The following code gives an example of such approach. Both $x and $y arguments are declared in the function header.

```
use v5.20;

use feature qw(signatures);
no warnings qw(experimental::signatures);

sub add($x, $y) {
    return $x + $y;
}

say add(4,5);
```

You will notice that you need to instruct Perl to use the features of Perl 5.20 by mentioning the minimal version number in the script. You will also notice that you must activate the corresponding feature by a separate instruction. However, even more, because signatures are an experimental feature, you have to manually disable the warning message to get a clean output.

In Perl 6, *function signatures* are allowed from the very beginning, so you may directly use it:

```
# This is Perl 6
sub add($x, $y) {
    return $x + $y;
}
```

Actually, signatures in Perl 5.20 are an example of backporting features from Perl 6 to Perl 5. So, despite the fact that Perl 6 was meant to be the next version of Perl 5, Perl 5 still gets some elements that were designed in Perl 6 to make Perl better.

Classes

To make the user experience better, let's take a look at another important example of where the syntax of Perl changes in Perl 6.

Traditionally, object-oriented programming is done in Perl 5 with the help of the so-called **blessed hashes**. Data members of an object are elements of the hash, and the blessed reference to that hash may be used to call a method on an instance of the class. The following example shows you what to do to define a class and create an instance of it in Perl 5:

```
package MyClass;

sub new {
    my ($class) = @_;
    my $this = {
        counter => 0
    };
    bless $this, $class;
    return $this;
}

sub inc {
    my ($this) = @_;
    $this->{counter}++;
    return $this->{counter};
}

1;
```

So far, the class named `MyClass` has two methods—`new`, to create a new instance, and `inc`, to increment the counter and return the new value. When dealing with Perl 5's classes, don't forget to return a true value at the end of the module, and that is the goal of the `1` in the last line of the file.

In the main program, you can use `MyClass` by creating an instance and calling methods on the variable as follows:

```
use MyClass;

my $var = MyClass->new;

print $var->inc, "\n";
print $var->inc, "\n";
print $var->inc, "\n";
```

The implementation of the object-oriented things in Perl 5 was another obstacle for newcomers who may have had an experience of working with classes in other languages but were confused by the way Perl 5 created them.

Classes in Perl 6 are way more familiar to developers who have worked with other object-oriented programming languages.

This is how you define the same class, as shown in the preceding example, in Perl 6:

```
class MyClass {
    has $!counter;

    method inc() {
        $!counter++;
        return $!counter;
    }
}
```

As you see, the whole class is defined within the pair of braces. Its data members are explicitly declared with the `has` keyword, and there's no need to return `1` at the end of the file.

Now, create an object of the class and increment the internal counter three times, like we did in the Perl 5 example earlier. This is how you do it in Perl 6:

```
my $var = MyClass.new;

say $var.inc;
say $var.inc;
say $var.inc;
```

Do not focus on the details yet because it will all be explained in later chapters.

So far, we've seen three examples of where it was desired to improve the syntax of Perl 5.

To see more examples of changes between Perl 5 and Perl 6, you may refer to a few articles grouped under the title 'Perl 5 to Perl 6 guide' in the documentation of Perl 6 at `https://docs.perl6.org/language.html`, which is dedicated to that specific topic:

`5to6-nutshell`	Perl 5 to Perl 6, in a nutshell—How do I do what I used to do?
`5to6-perlfunc`	Perl 5 to Perl 6 guide—functions
`5to6-perlop`	Perl 5 to Perl 6 guide—operators
`5to6-perlsyn`	Perl 5 to Perl 6 guide—syntax
`5to6-perlvar`	Perl 5 to Perl 6 guide—special variables

Compatibility with Perl 5

Existing Perl 6 compilers cannot execute Perl 5 programs without modifications in the source code. Perl 5 and Perl 6 are sometimes called sister languages. Both share the same spirit of Perl, and, in many cases, it is possible to convert the program from Perl 5 to Perl 6.

One of the biggest advantages of Perl 5 is the **CPAN** (**Comprehensive Perl Archive Network**). It contains a myriad of modules for the immense number of areas. Most probably, your task is already solved by some author of CPAN. To use this useful heritage in your programs in Perl 6, you may want to use the `Inline::Perl5` module, which allows using an existing Perl 5 module without modifying the source code.

For example, let's take one of the most popular modules in Perl 5, `Text::CSV`, and embed it in our program in Perl 6.

```
use Inline::Perl5;
use Text::CSV:from<Perl5>;

my $csv = Text::CSV.new;

$csv.parse('First name,Last name');
say $csv.fields.join("\t");

$csv.parse('Astrid,Lindgren');
say $csv.fields.join("\t");
```

With `Inline::Perl5` enabled, the `:from<Perl5>` suffix loads the `Text::CSV` module from Perl 5 module directory. That module must be installed as a regular Perl 5 module from CPAN.

The rest of the program uses the $csv object, which is an instance of Text::CSV. Notice that you have to follow Perl 6 syntax, so, for instance, instead of creating the object with Text::CSV->new use Text::CSV.new. The same applies to calling the parse method: in Perl 5 it would be $csv->parse(), while in Perl 6 you use dot: $csv.parse(). Working with objects in Perl 6 is described in Chapter 8, *Object-Oriented Programming*.

Luckily, there is already a module Text::CSV for Perl 6. You can find it on the http://modules.perl6.org page. Using Inline::Perl5 can be very useful for those modules on CPAN, which do not yet have equivalents or replacement, written in Perl 6. For example, the following example taken from the module documentation shows how to connect to the database (of course, you need PostgreSQL to be installed to test the example):

```
use Inline::Perl5;
use DBI:from<Perl5>;

my $dbh = DBI.connect('dbi:Pg:database=test');
my $products = $dbh.selectall_arrayref(
    'select * from products', {Slice => {}}
);
```

The Inline::Perl5 module is available at https://github.com/niner/Inline-Perl5.

Perl 6 resources

Perl 6 has a long history and many documents were created during that time, for instance, language ideas, draft specifications, and compiler documentation. Many enthusiasts wrote articles and blog posts about Perl 6. Some of that is outdated and does not reflect the current state of the language. In this chapter, I will give you a brief list of materials that are up-to-date and that you should use in your practice of working with Perl 6.

Documentation

The main entry point for documentation of the Perl 6 programming language is the Documentation section of Perl 6's site (http://docs.perl6.org). It contains a few sections with a comprehensive description of the types, operators, and built-in classes that are available in Perl 6. As the language is still developing, you may sometimes find places in the documentation where it does not reflect the current state of the language. In this case, you may consult the community of language developers or check the files from the test suite.

Test Suite

Perl 6's test suite, called Roast, can be found in the repository at `https://github.com/perl6/roast`. It contains thousands of tests covering many corners of Perl 6. The test suite is also a good place to look if you want to see ways you can write programs in Perl 6. It may be a long read sometimes, but many tests are checking the features from all possible angles.

In Roast, the tests are grouped in directories with names such as `S32-io`. These names correspond to the numbers of the Synopses, and are split into thematic sections. For example, for the Synopses 11 'Compilation Units', there exist three directories in tests—`S11-compunits`, `S11-modules`, and `S11-repository`.

STD.pm

`STD.pm` is a huge file describing the formal Perl 6 grammar. The grammar of Perl 6 is written in Perl 6 itself. The repository of `https://github.com/perl6/std` contains the grammar and the `viv` utility that translates the grammar into the Perl 5 code. We have mentioned the `STD.pm` grammar because it may be interesting for those readers who want to dig deeper into the internal structure of the grammar. In the rest of this book, we will explain the grammar based on examples of code in Perl 6.

Community

The developers of Perl 6 traditionally use IRC for communication. You may also join the `#perl6` channel to ask questions about the language or execute a piece of Perl 6 online.

To join the channel, follow the instructions listed on the `https://perl6.org/community/` page.

If you want to run the code in IRC, refer to the `rakudo` bot as follows:

```
<me> rakudo: say "Hello, World!"
<+camelia> rakudo-moar cb8fa0: OUTPUT: «Hello, World!␤»
```

In the output, you can see that `Rakudo` is using the MoarVM backend by default. The string that was printed by the program is displayed after the `OUTPUT` keyword.

Use this feature carefully as the result of your requests will be visible to the whole room and also be logged. The best use case is to show the behavior of the compiler when you find a bug or when you see a different result from what is said in the documentation. The Perl 6 developers are always present in the IRC channel and will advise on what is wrong or will aim to fix the bug and make the documentation correct.

If you are on Facebook, visit the Perl 6 group here:
`https://www.facebook.com/groups/1595443877388632/`

In the offline, you will see many people who love Perl 6 at various conferences. Go to the Perl Conference (previously known as **YAPC**, (**Yet Another Perl Conference**)), which is held every year in Europe and in the USA. You may find more about them on `http://theperlconference.org` and `http://www.yapc.eu`. For many years, there were work Perl booths at the big open-source conferences like **OSCON** and **FOSDEM**. There are also many local conferences, workshops, and local group meetings. Find the closest group to your location at `http://pm.org`.

Compilers

During the process of Perl 6 development, a number of compilers were created. Some of them were just a playground to test some ideas, whereas some were more mature. Among the most important, we should mention the following four projects:

- Parrot
- Pugs
- Perlito
- Rakudo

There were more attempts to create a Perl 6 compiler, which were less successful or less complete. We will go through the preceding list to see the highlights of each project and then focus on Rakudo, which is the compiler you should use today.

Parrot

Parrot is the first virtual machine aimed to be the base of the Perl 6 compiler. The initial design of the language suggested that the source code is compiled to the bytecode, which is executed by the virtual machine. Parrot's goal was to create a virtual machine suitable for handling all the needs of Perl 6 from simple data types, such as integers, to more complicated structures, such as classes, with the ability to call methods on objects and follow the object hierarchy.

The project is available at `parrot.org`. After some time, Parrot started supporting other programming languages, such as Lua or Python, and the virtual machine became less focused on Perl 6 itself. For example, the Ponie project was an attempt to create a compiler that would execute Perl 5 programs using Parrot.

Parrot became one of the virtual machines inside another project, Rakudo. However, before we go to Rakudo, let's follow the historical path and talk about Pugs.

Pugs

Pugs (Perl User's Golfing System) is a Perl 6 compiler written in Haskell. It was started in 2005 by a sole developer and soon attracted more people to the team. Pugs was the most sophisticated compiler of its time. It was difficult and very time consuming to compile the project, the execution speed was low, but the quality of the compilation and the coverage of Perl 6 specification were outstanding.

Pugs main role in Perl 6 as of today is the vast test suite. It was created to test Pugs itself, but turned out to be an official test suite for Perl 6. A compiler that claims to call itself a Perl 6 compiler must pass the test suite tests.

Pugs are not developing anymore, but its source code is available on GitHub at `https://github.com/perl6/Pugs.hs`.

Perlito

Perlito is another very interesting example of a project of building a Perl 6 compiler. It was aimed at cross-compiling Perl 5 or Perl 6 to one of these languages—JavaScript, Java, Go, Python, Ruby, or Lisp. You can find the project's repository at `https://github.com/fglock/Perlito`.

Perlito offers a web interface to compile the subset of Perl 6 in the browser. It compiles the code in Perl 6 to JavaScript and executes it immediately. This page is available at `http://fglock.github.io/Perlito/perlito/perlito6.html`. This project covers the Perl 6 specification only partially, but it may still be used to create various online educational systems for both Perl 5 and 6.

Rakudo

Rakudo is a compiler initially built on the Parrot virtual machine. Later, it started using the **Java Virtual Machine (JVM)**, but in the end, the developers of Parrot created their own virtual machine, **MoarVM** (**Metamodel on a Runtime Virtual Machine** (`www.moarvm.org`)). Currently, the support of JVM is limited, and the main virtual machine is MoarVM.

Rakudo itself is a Perl 6 compiler. For us, the most useful compiler is Rakudo Star, which is a distribution including the compiler as well as a number of Perl 6 modules and a few command-line tools, such as a module installer. In this book, we will use the Rakudo Star compiler to run programs in Perl 6.

Rakudo's website is `rakudo.org`.

Working with Rakudo Star

Rakudo is the most complete compiler available today. It supports the biggest subset of the Perl 6 language, and it would not be a mistake to say that Rakudo is the only compiler you should use to learn Perl 6.

Downloading and installing Rakudo Star

There are a few ways of installing Rakudo Star on your computer. You can either download the source code and compile it or download an installer for your platform. Rakudo Star is available for all major platforms, namely, Windows (both 32- and 64-bit versions), Mac OS X, and Linux.

The main download page of Rakudo Star is `http://perl6.org/downloads`. On that page, you will find links to the latest versions of the Rakudo Star distributions for different platforms and instructions on how to install them.

On Windows, the process is extremely simple. Just download the most recent version of the MSI installer, run it, and follow the instructions.

On Mac OS X, you either download a `.dmg` installer, or use the `brew` manager, as shown here:

```
$ brew install rakudo-star
```

On Linux, you have to install Rakudo Star from the source files.

After you have installed Rakudo Star, you will find the `perl6` executable file in its `bin` directory. Make sure to add the path to that directory to your system-wide PATH variable so that you can type `perl6` from any location.

In the rest of this book, we will assume that Rakudo Star is installed, and we will use the `perl6` executable to run programs.

Command-line options

The Perl 6 compiler of Rakudo Star accepts a few command-line options. Let's take a look at some of them.

The -c command

The `-c` command-line checks the syntax of the program and exits. It also runs the BEGIN and CHECK blocks in the program, which are discussed in the section Phasers of `Chapter 2`, *Writing Code* later in this book. This command-line option is useful if you only want to check that there are no syntax errors in the code and don't want to execute it, with the exception being the code in the BEGIN and CHECK code blocks.

In the case of correct programming, it prints the following output:

```
Syntax OK
```

If there were compile-time errors, the compilation will stop at the first error and will display it on the console, mentioning the line number where it found an error.

The error message contains the description of the error and indicates the exact place in the code with the help of the eject character (⏏). If your console supports colors, the fragment of the code before the eject character is green, and the rest of the line is red.

Here is an example of a program that misses the closing quote for the string:

```
say "Hello;
```

Run it to check the syntax, as shown here:

```
$ perl6 -c err.pl
```

The program did not compile, and this is what the compiler prints:

```
===SORRY!=== Error while compiling /Users/ash/code/err.pl
Unable to parse expression in double quotes; couldn't find final '"'
at /Users/ash/code/err.pl:2
------> <BOL>⬧<EOL>
    expecting any of:
        argument list
        double quotes
        term
```

The --doc command

The --doc (notice the double hyphen) command-line extracts the documentation from the program and prints it. Here, the so-called **Pod** documentation is meant. We will cover the Pod syntax in Chapter 2, *Writing Code*.

Let's see the small program that includes the documentation inside itself:

```
=begin pod
=head1 Hello, World program
=item This program prints "Hello, World!"
=end pod

say "Hello, World!";
```

Run it with the --doc command-line option as follows:

```
$ perl6 --doc pod.pl
```

It will print only parts of the documentation. The code itself will not be executed:

```
Hello, World program

  * This program prints "Hello, World!"
```

The -e command

The -e option allows you to pass the whole program in a command line. This is useful for short programs that do a few actions or, for example, for small tests when you check how things work in Perl 6.

Run it with the program enclosed in quotes:

```
$ perl6 -e'say "Hello"'
```

And this is the result you will see:

```
Hello
```

The -h and --help commands

The -h and --help commands print the text with a list of available command-line options.

The -n command

The -n command-line option creates a loop so that the program is executed once for every line of the text submitted to the input of the program.

It may be, for example, a one-line utility that prints the first letter of the strings from the STDIN input:

```
perl6 -n -e'print $_.substr(0, 1)' < file.txt
```

It will print the line composed from the first characters of the lines in file.txt.

The -p command

The -p command-line option acts like the previously described -n option, but it also prints the value of the default variable $_ at the end of each line. We will see the meaning of the default variable in the following chapters.

The -I and -M commands

The -I and -M options are used to load modules into the program. The module's name is passed to the -M option and if necessary, the path to the module should be passed in the -I option.

The -v and --version command

The `-v` and `--version` options print the version of the current Perl 6 compiler as follows:

```
$ perl6 -v
```

At the time of writing, I am using Rakudo Star version 2017.01, and this is what the output looks like:

```
This is Rakudo version 2017.01 built on MoarVM version 2017.01 implementing
Perl 6.c.
```

The important thing here, apart from the version itself, is the virtual machine that is used to execute Perl 6 (MoarVM, as shown earlier) and the version of the Perl 6 language specification (it is 6.c in this example).

The Rakudo Star versioning scheme uses the year and the month of the release date of the distributive. Rakudo is rapidly developing, so check the `rakudo.org` site regularly to get updates.

The --stagestats command

The `--stagestats` is a command-line option that is more Rakudo-specific than the others we have described earlier. It prints the time spent by the compiler at different stages of compiling and executing the program.

The output differs depending on whether you are running a program or checking its syntax with the `-c` command-line option. Let's first take a look at what is printed when the `-c` option is used:

```
$ perl6 --stagestats -c hello.pl
```

The output is as follows:

```
Stage start      :    0.000
Stage parse      :    0.107
Stage syntaxcheck: Syntax OK
```

Without the `-c` option, you will see more statistics, because the program will not only be compiled but also executed, as shown here:

```
$ perl6 --stagestats hello.pl
```

The regular output of the program is printed:

```
Stage start      :    0.000
Stage parse      :    0.327
Stage syntaxcheck:    0.000
Stage ast        :    0.000
Stage optimize   :    0.003
Stage mast       :    0.008
Stage mbc        :    0.000
Stage moar       :    0.000
Hello, World!
```

Writing our Hello World program

So far, as we have installed the Rakudo Star compiler, it's now time to create the first program in Perl 6. It will print Hello, World! and exit.

The program is really easy. All you need is a single line with the only instruction to call the built-in say function. It takes the string, prints it to the console, and adds a new line after it.

This is how the whole program looks:

```
say 'Hello, World!'
```

Save the code to the file, say, hello.pl, and pass it to the compiler as follows:

```
$ perl6 hello.pl
```

It will compile the program and immediately execute it. The result is the desired string on the screen:

Hello, World!

Notice that the output ends with a new line. This is the behavior of the built-in say function. Alternatively, we could use another method of printing the output, using the print built-in function. Unlike say, it will not add the new line at the end of the output, so you have to do it yourself by adding the special symbol \n:

```
print "Hello, World!\n"
```

Notice that this time, a pair of double quotes is used. Double quotes treat special characters such as \n differently compared to single quotes. Inside double quotes, the \n converts to a new line character. That will not happen in single quotes, and, in that case, \n will appear on the screen as a sequence of two characters, and \n.

Because the program contains only one line of code, it is not necessary to end it with a semicolon. However, you can always do that:

```
say "Hello, World!";
```

This program produces exactly the same output as before.

Summary

In this chapter, we looked briefly at what kind of programming language Perl 6 is and how it differs from its sister language, Perl 5. We looked at the history of Perl 6 and at different projects of the Perl 6 compilers. Finally, we installed Rakudo Star, the best compiler tool of today and created the first 'Hello, World!' program.

In the following chapter, we will look at how to organize the code in the program.

2
Writing Code

This chapter will prepare you to write Perl 6 code. Before we examine variables, data types, object orientation, and other important topics, let's learn more about how the source code is organized in Perl 6. There are many elements that differ from other programming languages, and it is worth spending time getting used to it.

In this chapter, we will cover the following topics:

- Using Unicode
- Whitespaces and unspaces
- Comments
- Creating Pod documentation
- Phasers
- Simple input and output

Using Unicode

The default assumption is that the source of a Perl 6 program uses UTF-8. It gives you the power of the whole spectrum of characters without worrying if it will work. In Perl 5, for example, you had to add special instructions in order to inform the interpreter that you are using non-ASCII characters in the source code. In Perl 6, this is much easier.

First, Unicode characters may be freely used in strings. For example, let's try some Greek and Chinese graphemes, as shown in the following lines of code:

```
say 'C = 2πr';      # Circumference of a circle
say '日 + 月 = 明';   # 'Sun' and 'Moon' give 'bright'
```

The preceding two lines of code will print the corresponding strings as expected:

```
C = 2πr
日 + 月 = 明
```

Alternatively, it is possible to refer to the Unicode codepoints by their names. For example, consider the following line of code:

```
say "Perl 6 is c[FLEXED BICEPS]";
```

The preceding line of code prints the following output with a muscle emoji:

```
Perl 6 is 💪
```

Using Unicode in Perl 6 is not limited to the strings, content only. Characters outside of ASCII may be used in the names of variables and functions. Let's return to the example of the add($x, $y) function from Chapter 1, *What is Perl 6?*, and rename it and its arguments using Greek letters:

```
sub Σ($α, $β) {
    return $α + $β;
}

say Σ(8, 9); # 17
```

Furthermore, some Unicode characters can be used to express simple actions instead of more conventional code. For example, here are the characters with rational fractions:

```
say ½;      # prints 0.5
say ½ + ¼; # 0.75
```

Non-ASCII Unicode digits are also allowed, but it is perhaps not a good idea to use them in a regular code without special needs:

```
say ४२; # Prints 42
```

Superscripts such as ^{2} or ^{3} may be used instead of calling a function to calculate the power of a number, as shown in the following lines of code:

```
say 7²;  # 49
say 2⁷;  # 128
```

Another example of using Unicode characters is the list of mathematical operations over sets, such as ∈ or ∪.

In the next example, the Unicode versions of simple arithmetical operators are used instead of the regular * and / characters that are traditionally used:

```
say 10 × 4;   # 40
say 100 ÷ 4;  # 25
```

In Perl 6 programs, you may often see a few other Unicode characters. Let's take a look at the most frequent of them.

The French quotes « » can be used in place of a pair of quotes to create lists. For example, in the following code, an `@array` gets the sequence of Fibonacci numbers. We've seen this example in Chapter 1, *What is Perl 6?*. Let's first update it to use the quoting syntax to creating arrays, as shown in the following lines of code:

```
my @fibonacci = <0 1 1 2 3 5 8 13>;
say @fibonacci[4]; # 3
```

We will see that kind of syntax in detail in Chapter 3, *Working with Variables and Built-in Data Types*; however, let's now see how to use the French quotes to enclose the list of values:

```
my @fibonacci = «0 1 1 2 3 5 8 13»;
say @fibonacci[4]; # 3
```

For one-liners (short programs that are executed primarily in the -e command-line option), the Unicode quotes may be very helpful because they help to avoid the problem of nested single quotes. You can see how it works in the following example:

```
$ perl6 -e'say 'Hello, World!''
```

Instead of single quotes (`'`), a pair of Unicode quotes is used here (' and ').

When working with regular expressions and grammars (we will talk about them in Chapter 11, *Regexes*, and Chapter 12, *Grammars*), you will often see a pair of square angle brackets, which you may freely use in your code to quote strings, shown in the following code:

```
say ⌜Hello, World!⌟;
```

In Perl 6, the elements of the language, which can be expressed in Unicode characters, have equivalent forms written in ASCII. The ASCII characters are sometimes referred to as Texas characters. The following table lists the correspondence between the Unicode and the ASCII versions of the most common constructions:

Unicode	ASCII equivalent	Meaning in Perl 6
« »	<< >>	These quote a list of array elements, and are also used in hyperoperators (refer to `Chapter 4`, *Working with Operators*).
' ' " „ "	' ' " " "	These single and double quotes are used to quote strings. Special characters such as n are interpolated inside double quotes.
⌜ ⌟	Q/ /	This syntax is used to create a string without interpolation.
× ÷	* /	These are arithmetic operations of multiplication and division
−	−	Minus sign, used as an operator, for example (note that there is a separate MINUS SIGN character in Unicode with the 0x2212 code).

There are a few predefined constants for mathematical calculations-- π, e, and τ. There is a separate symbol to represent infinity—∞. All these symbols also have a correspondence in the ASCII representation:

Symbol	ASCII equivalent	Comment
π	pi	This is the value of π (3.14159...).
e	e	This is the value of e (2.71828...). Note that the Unicode representation is the 0x1D452 character, not the ASCII e.
τ	tau	The value of τ is 2π (6.283185...).
∞	Inf	Infinity is always bigger than any number.

Typing Unicode characters may be a separate task. Of course, you can always copy a character from Google or Wikipedia, but you will loose productivity in that case. Refer to the page *Entering Unicode Characters* in the Perl 6 online documentation available at `docs.perl6.org/language/unicode_entry`. It contains detailed instructions on how to enter the Unicode characters in different editors and IDEs.

Whitespaces and unspaces

As we just saw, a Perl 6 program can intensively use the Unicode characters outside of the conventional ASCII set. This also applies to the **whitespaces**. Whitespaces are those gaps between the elements of the program, that are traditionally represented by spaces (ASCII code 0x20), tabs (0x09), and newlines (a single line feed character 0x0A in Unix and a series of two characters, carriage return 0x0D, and line feed 0x0A in Windows). Perl 6 extends the concept of whitespaces and accepts Unicode whitespace in every place of the code where a regular space is allowed. Be careful when you work with an existing code that, for some reason, is filled with Unicode characters.

A whitespace character set in Perl 6 includes characters that have one of the following Unicode properties:

- `Zs`: Separator, Space
- `Zl`: Separator, Line
- `Zp`: Separator, Paragraph

You can find a complete list of characters from the listed categories at `https://en.wikipedia.org/wiki/Whitespace_character`. Among them are a regular space, vertical and horizontal tabs, newlines, linefeeds, non-breaking space, and thin space.

On a bigger scale, Perl 6 allows the program to be formatted as the programmer wants it. On the other hand, there are a few rules regarding where spaces can occur, which you should follow when writing a Perl 6 program.

If the language forbids having a whitespace at a particular place in the code, but you desire to format the program to make it more spacious, you can add the so-called **unspace**. This is a sequence started with a backslash placed immediately after the previous piece of code and followed by one or more whitespace characters. It resembles the backslash at the end of a Unix command-line instruction that continues on the next line.

Let's take look at the most important cases where the language rules regarding the spaces are strict and may conflict with your habits.

The first example is a function call. In Perl 6, parentheses are not required around the arguments of a function, but as soon as you use them, you cannot have a space between the name of the function and the opening parenthesis. Examine the following three calls:

```
say add 4, 5;    # OK, no parentheses
say add(4, 5);   # OK, no space
say add (6, 7);  # Error
```

The first two lines are correct, while the last one produces a compile time error, as shown here:

```
Too few positionals passed; expected 2 arguments but got 1
```

The error message may sound misleading, but remember that in Perl 6, you can pass arrays to the function. In this case, the compiler cannot guarantee that it understood the intention of the programmer correctly. The `add (6, 7)` construction may be interpreted as calling a function with a single argument that is a two-element array—`(6, 7)`.

If you still prefer visual separation of the argument list and the function name, place an unspace between them as follows:

```
say add\ (6, 7);
```

Now it is compiling with no complaints. Newlines inside the unspace are also allowed; consider the following example:

```
say add\
(6, 7);
```

It is also possible to format the code differently, leaving the opening parenthesis on the same line with the function name, as follows:

```
say add(
    6, 7
);
```

This approach may be handy when you need to pass many arguments and, for example, comment on each of them:

```
say add(
    6, # first argument
    7  # second argument
);
```

We will talk more about functions in Chapter 6, *Subroutines*. However, for now, let's return to the methods of organizing the source code.

Comments

In Chapter 1, *What is Perl 6?*, we've seen two ways of writing programs—by passing it in the -e command-line option or by saving it in a file. Of course, all big programs are stored in files. In this section, we will see how Perl 6 helps the programmer to organize the code better by adding comments.

Comments are parts of the source code, which are ignored by the compiler. Comments are intended to give additional information about the program itself. Good examples of comments are explanations of the algorithms used, or the purpose of variables, or a description of the input arguments of a function.

Perl 6 offers two ways of saving additional human-oriented information in the source code by using comments and the so-called Pod. First, we will examine the comments.

Comments are fragments of source code that a compiler does not consider as direct instructions for execution. In Perl 6, there are three ways of leaving comments:

- One-line comments,
- Multiline comments,
- Embedded comments.

Let's examine them in detail.

One-line comments

One-line comments are separated from the program source code with the # character. Everything after the # symbol is skipped by the compiler until the end of the current line.

In the following example, we take the 'Hello, World!' program from Chapter 1, *What is Perl 6?*, and add a one-line comment to it:

```
say 'Hello, World!'; # Prints 'Hello, World!'
```

This is a fully correct Perl 6 program. It has one call of the built-in say function and a comment about what it does. The part of the string, starting from the # character, is a one-line comment.

If you run that program, it prints Hello, World! and nothing more. It works exactly the same as the program with no comments at all.

One-line comments may also occupy a separate line of code. For example, let's add more comments to the same program:

```
# This is a program in Perl 6.
# It prints the 'Hello, World!' string.
# To run it, install Rakudo Star and
# run it from the command-line:
# perl6 ./hello.pl

say 'Hello, World!'; # it prints the string

# The program ends here.
```

This is also a completely valid Perl 6 program. From the perspective of business logic, the program did not change, as with the previous example, but from the perspective of future maintenance, it became much better as it explains what it does.

Another common practice of using one-line comments is to temporarily hide pieces of code. For example, during the debugging process, you want to disable some actions. Instead of removing the line of code, you can comment it out by adding the # character at the beginning of the line. Consider the following lines of code as an example:

```
say 'Hello, World!';
# print "Hello, World!\n";
```

Sometimes, you do the opposite—you add additional printing instructions to the program to see the values of different variables, and comment those instructions before making the code production-ready.

Here is an example of how you print the values that were passed to the function. I have used the addition example from Chapter 1, *What is Perl 6?*:

```
sub add($x, $y) {
    say "x = $x, y = $y";
    return $x + $y;
}

say add(4, 5); # 9
```

This program simply prints the result of the addition, but if you uncomment the first line of the subroutine code, it will also print the values of the $x and $y variables in a human-readable format which is shown in the following code:

```
x = 4, y = 5
9
```

Multiline comments

Although one-line comments may be used to provide big chunks of documentation, having to place the # character in each line makes the comments themselves difficult to maintain. For example, if you modify the text of a comment, you may also want to reflow the whole paragraph so that all the lines are more or less the same length and the whole comment is more attractive visually.

In Perl 6, multi-line comments are supported. The syntax for a multi-line comment is the following. It starts with the #` sequence (the # character, same as in one-line comments, followed by a backtick symbol). Then, the part with the body of the comment goes in. It must be enclosed into a pair of brackets.

For example, curly braces may be used like this:

```
#`{This program in Perl 6
prints the 'Hello, World!' string}

say 'Hello, World!';
```

Here, the comment resides in two lines of the source code, but there is no need to mark every line of it with the # character.

Other pairs of embracing characters may be used. For example, parentheses or square brackets:

```
#`(A multi-line comment
placed between pair of parentheses)

#`[Another multi-line comment,
this time in square brackets]
```

Although the comments are intended to be read by humans in the first place, the compiler has to understand where the comment starts and ends. In the preceding example, the closing character of the comment body is defined by the corresponding character after the #` sequence.

If it is an opening brace ({), then the compiler scans the following text and looks for the closing counterpart, the } character in this example. This also means that you cannot use the closing brace in the text of the comment, because it will be treated as the end of comment.

One of the ways to have such a character in the comment is using a different pair of enclosing symbols. For example, if the whole comment is embedded in a pair of parentheses, then it is safe to use a closing square bracket in the body of that comment, as shown here:

```
#`(A multi-line comment
in parentheses and it contains the } character inside
it)
```

Also, it will not be a problem if you use the balanced pairs of the same characters. For example, consider the following block of code:

```
#`(Function add(x, y) adds two numbers
and returns their sum)
sub add($x, $y) {
    return $x + $y;
}
```

Here, the comment is using the `#`` (...) pair of parentheses, but it contains another pair of parentheses inside: `add(x, y)`. In this case, the program is correct and the comment ends where it should end according to the intention of the programmer.

The second way of allowing the same characters in the comment is to use a sequence of more than one character to mark the comment.

For example, a pair of double braces will work like this:

```
#`{{Two characters at the beginning
let us easily include the closing } brace, for
example}}
```

Another good option is to use a combination of different characters. The closing sequence should mirror the opening one, as shown here:

```
#`([Another way of having
a closing ] character inside the comment])
```

Finally, one-line comments may appear inside the multi-line comment. In this case, they will be just a part of it, as shown in the following example:

```
#`{If you want to print the value of the variable $x,
find the following line in the code:
# say $x
and uncomment it.}
```

Embedded comments

Embedded comments in Perl 6 are comments that use the syntax of multi-line comments, but are placed inside the main code. Unlike the one-line comments, embedded comments are not propagated until the end of the line and may be terminated by the closing character.

Let's demonstrate an example of an embedded comment on the add function, shown as follows:

```
sub add($x, $y) {
    return $x + #`(this is numeric addition) $y;
}
```

The #`(this is numeric addition) comment informs the reader that the + operator expects its operands (variables $x and $y in the example) to be numeric values (unlike the concatenation of strings, for example). The whole comment is embedded into the $x + $y expression. After the comment ends, the regular code flow continues. The compiler ignores the comment and, thus, the line remains syntactically correct.

Embedded comments should be as short as possible to make the whole code easier to read. Use it to give small explanations or to temporarily disable a fragment of code during the debugging of the program.

Creating Pod documentation

Pod is a sublanguage inside Perl 6 used to write documentation. It can be considered as an extended version of comments, which allows more functionality in expressing the content. Pod in Perl 6 is the evolution of the POD (Plain Old Documentation) in Perl 5. In Perl 6, the name is not an abbreviation and thus is not capitalized. In this section, we will examine the syntax of the Pod markup language.

Pod content is placed in the same source file as the Perl 6 program itself. A Pod section is a series of lines containing some textual information. The compiler is switching between parsing Pod and Perl 6 when it sees the beginning and ending marks of the Pod section. Pod syntax is designed to express the semantics of the documentation and to help organize it in a more structured way.

Let's see how you create a Pod block. There are a few types of Pod blocks, as well as a few ways of creating them.

The =begin / =end Pod block

Pod blocks start with the = sign, which should be the first non-space character in the line (thus, you cannot start a Pod block as you do a one-line comment—next to the code on the same line).

The block is marked with the pair of =begin and =end directives, each of which must be followed by a Perl 6 identifier describing the type of the data contained in the Pod block. There are a few predefined identifiers, they are either fully lowercased or fully uppercased. Consider a few examples of the most useful Pod blocks.

```
=begin pod
This program is the first program in Perl 6.
=end pod

say 'Hello, World!'
```

Here, the Pod block begins with =begin pod and stops with =end pod. Everything outside of the block is a regular Perl 6 program.

If you simply run the program, then the Pod is ignored. Save the program in a file and run it from a command-line as follows:

```
$ perl6 pod.pl
Hello, World!
```

In Chapter 1, *What is Perl 6?*, we looked at different command-line options that the Rakudo Star compiler supports. It is time to use one of them --doc to see how the compiler extracts the Pod documentation from the program and prints it without executing the program itself:

```
$ perl6 --doc pod.pl
This program is the first program in Perl 6.
```

In the preceding example, the type of block was pod. There are other types of Pod blocks.

The table type creates a Pod with a table:

```
=begin table
    Language    Year of appearance
    C           1973
    C++         1983
    Perl        1987
    Perl 6      2000
=end table
```

You can do some minimal formatting of the table in the source code yourself, but the Pod parser and formatter (parts of Rakudo in our case) do some extra jobs to display the table nicely. This is how the table will look if you run the program with the `--pod` command-line option:

```
$ perl6 --doc pod.pl
Language  Year of appearence
C         1973
C++       1983
Perl      1987
Perl 6    2000
```

Notice that the indentation is lost and the table rows are printed from the beginning of the line. Another change is that there are two spaces between the columns while we had a bit more in the source code.

The table can optionally contain a caption, which you place in the `=begin` line using the so-called adverbial syntax, as shown in the following example:

```
=begin table :caption<History of Programming Languages>
    Language    Year of appearance
    C           1973
    C++         1983
    Perl        1987
    Perl 6      2000
=end table
```

The caption will be printed above the table:

```
$ perl6 --doc pod.pl
History of Programming Languages
Language  Year of appearance
C         1973
C++       1983
Perl      1987
Perl 6    2000
```

Before we go further into the other types of Pod blocks in Perl 6, let's learn alternative syntaxes to declare a Pod block:

- Abbreviated blocks
- Paragraph blocks

In the *abbreviated block,* the opening = sign is immediately followed by the name of the Pod block type. No closing =end directive is needed anymore, and the end of the Pod block will be the indicated by either an empty line or by the start of another Pod block.

Here is another example of the table block with the abbreviated syntax:

```
=table
    Language    Year of appearance
    C           1973
    C++         1983
    Perl        1987
    Perl 6      2000

say 'Ok';
```

The Pod block with a table ends before the empty line. After that, the compiler is switching back to parsing the Perl 6 code.

In the *paragraph block,* you start the Pod section with the =for directive, followed by the identifier. Thus, the last example may start with either =table or =for table.

This syntax is more natural for other types of Pod blocks whose content is usually short. For example, headers or items of a list. In those cases, the content of the block is supplied on the same line, immediately after the opening directive, as shown in the following example, which reflects part of the contents of the current chapter:

```
=head1 Writing Code
=head2 Comments in Perl 6
=item One-line comments
=item Multi-line comments
=item Embedded comments
```

Extracting the documentation with the --doc command-line option generates the following output:

```
Writing Code
  Comments in Perl 6
  * One-line comments
  * Multi-line comments
  * Embedded comments
```

It contains headers on two levels and a simple bullet list.

Phasers

When creating a program in Perl 6, it is important to understand that controlling the program flow is a little trickier than simply following the instructions of the code. There are special types of code blocks that are automatically called by the compiler at different phases of the compilation and the execution processes. Those blocks are called **phasers**.

We mentioned two of them, BEGIN and CHECK, in Chapter 1, *What is Perl 6?*, when we talked about the -c command-line option of the compiler. Now, let's take a look at the rest.

Syntactically, phasers are blocks of code in curly braces preceded by a phaser name. The following table summarizes the different phasers that exist in Perl 6. Some of the phasers are executed at compile-time before the rest of the program is compiled and executed. Some are called at runtime.

Phaser name	Execution stage	Actions
BEGIN	compile-time	This block is called before the main program is compiled
CHECK	compile-time	This block is called after compilation is complete and the compile-time phase is about to stop
INIT	runtime	This block is called when the program is compiled and is ready to be run
END	runtime	This block is called after the program is executed and is ready to quit

Let's expand the 'Hello, World!' program and add a few phasers to it:

```
BEGIN {
    say 'BEGIN 1';
}
END {
    say 'END';
}

say 'Hello, World!';

BEGIN {
    say 'BEGIN 2';
}
CHECK {
    say 'CHECK';
}
INIT {
```

```
    say 'INIT';
}
```

This code produces the following output:

```
BEGIN 1
BEGIN 2
CHECK
INIT
Hello, World!
END
```

In this example, please pay attention to a couple of characteristics of the phaser blocks. There are two BEGIN blocks here, and they are executed in the order they appear in the source code. Also, the actual position of the block is not always important. For example, the END block is located before the main program but is executed after it. Similarly, the second BEGIN block and the CHECK and INIT blocks are located after the main program but are called before it.

Phasers are good candidates that can do some work when the program is about to start or finish. For example, you may check if the program is running in the correct environment with the BEGIN block. In the END block, you may close all open files or print something to the log before the program quits.

In Chapter 10, *Working with Exceptions*, we will work with another two phasers—CATCH and CONTROL.

There are many more phasers in Perl 6 that help to organize hooks during the program execution, such as ENTER and LEAVE that are called when the flow of the program enters or leaves a block of code. For a detailed description of those phasers, refer to the documentation page at docs.perl6.org/language/phasers.

Simple input and output

In the previous examples, we used the built-in print and say functions to print something to the console (speaking more strictly, to the standard output attached to the program). In this section, you will learn how to perform basic reading from the standard input. This is basically how the program gets what you type onto the console.

To read the input, there are a few functions that you may use directly without loading any modules. They are listed in the following table:

Function	What it does
get	This reads one line from the input and returns it
lines	This returns the list of lines containing the data lines that came from the standard input
slurp	This returns a string that contains the whole input

The get and line functions may be used when you need to parse the input data line by line. For example, call get as many times as you need if you know the structure of the input, or create a loop and iterate over the array that is returned by lines.

The slurp function does the job in one go. You can use it, for example, to copy everything from input to output. This is the program that does that:

```
print slurp;
```

There is another useful function: prompt. Use it to make two actions at once: the function prints a text message on the screen and returns the string that the user entered. This function blocks the execution of a program until the user finishes the input with a new line.

Let's demonstrate the work of the prompt function on an example program that calculates the circumference of a circle. The following program requests the radius from the user and then prints the result.

```
say 'The circumference is ',
    tau * prompt 'Enter the radius > ';
```

The program first prints the prompt message Enter the radius > and waits until the user types a number and presses the Enter key. Then, the say function prints another message, The circumference is, and appends the value that it gets after multiplying the input value by τ, which, as we've seen in the *Using Unicode* section of this chapter, equates to 2π. We can see that in the following code:

```
$ perl6 circumference.pl
Enter the radius > 12
The circumference is 75.398223686155
```

We intentionally did not introduce any variables (we'll talk about them later in `Chapter 3`, *Working with Variables and Built-in Data Types*). Notice that the actual output happens from right to left: first, the message from `prompt`, then the text printed by `say`.

More sophisticated input and output, as well as working with files, are discussed in `Chapter 9`, *Input and Output*.

Summary

In this chapter, we looked at the way a Perl 6 program is organized. The source code is written in Unicode, and there are many Unicode elements in the syntax of the language that may be used to make the program more expressive. We also examined how to create and use comments that vary from one-line notes to bigger Pod blocks that may contain documentation about the program. We looked at that ways the parts of the source code may be placed in different phasers to change the flow of the program. And finally, you learned a method for getting input from the users.

Now, we are ready to create real Perl 6 programs. In the next chapter, we will talk about the data types in Perl 6 and how to use variables.

3
Working with Variables and Built-in Data Types

Perl 6 is a language with gradual typing. This means that you are not required to indicate the type of the variables you create: you may freely use the same variable to store data of different types. However, you may also create a typed variable and, in that case, the compiler will check the usage of that variable and make sure that the variable is only used in the operations allowed for that type.

In this chapter, we will first go through the built-in types of Perl 6 and, later, learn how to work with variables:

- Built-in data types
- Type hierarchy
- Variables
- Scalars, arrays and hashes
- Object-oriented properties of data types
- Simple and composite data types

Using variables

In any programming language, variables are named pieces of memory that you can use to store a value as well as retrieve it. In Perl 6, a variable is a container that can host a value of one of the types, either built-in in the language or created by the user.

Declaring variables

Every variable must be declared before its use in the program. You don't need to declare all the variables at the beginning of the program. From a practical perspective, the point of declaration can (and should) be as close as possible to the place where it is first used. The most practical reason to do that is to make the visibility of the variable better—if you declare too early, you force the reader of your program to think about the purpose of the variable; on the other hand, if you make changes in the code, there is a big chance of forgetting to remove the variable declaration if it is not located close to the place it is used.

To declare a variable, use the my keyword, as shown here:

```
my $x;
```

It is possible to declare a variable together with initialization:

```
my $x = 42;
```

Perl 6 also defines the concept of **constants.** These are variables whose value can only be set once in the **initializer.** To create a constant, use the constant keyword, as shown here:

```
constant $C = 10;
```

It is not possible to assign a new value to the constant.

Now, let's see what kind of variables are available in Perl 6.

Variable containers in Perl 6

There are three basic types of variable containers: scalars, arrays, and hashes. First, you will learn the basics of how to use them in code. Then, later in this chapter, in the *Using built-in data types* section, we will take a deeper look at the data types available in the language.

The structural type of the container is expressed by a special character called **sigil.** It always stands before the variable name and, in many cases, may be considered a part of it.

The name of the variable is an **identifier.** An identifier is a string of alphabetic characters, digits, underscore characters, and hyphens. The first character cannot be a digit or a hyphen. Alphanumeric characters are understood in the Unicode sense, so, together with hyphens, it is possible to create very expressive variable names. The identifiers are case-sensitive.

In the following sections, you will see examples of naming the variables. Notice that a variable is always preceded by a sigil, while bare identifiers may be function or class names, as we will see in other chapters of this book.

Scalars

A scalar is a container that can keep a single value, such as an integer, a string, or an object.

Scalar variables use the $ sigil. We have seen a few examples in the previous sections, and here are some more. Notice that the same scalar variable, if it is not explicitly declared with a data type, can host a value of different types at different moments:

```
my $x = 42;
say $x;
my $y = $x * 2;
say $y;

$x = 'Hello, World!';
say $x;
```

(Of course, it is better not to change the type of the data during the program flow.)

Inside the strings in double quotes, scalar variables are interpolated and replaced by their current values. In the following program, the process of calculating an equation is printed as a string:

```
my $a = 3;
my $b = 4;
my $c = sqrt($a * $a + $b * $b);

say "If the legs of a right triangle are $a and $b, ";
say "then the hypotenuse is $c.";
```

This code prints the following output:

```
If the legs of a right triangle are 3 and 4,
then the hypotenuse is 5.
```

Now, let's move on to the next type of variables—arrays.

Arrays

Array variables can host more than one value. The values can be of the same type, or can be of different types. Arrays are often used to keep lists of data items.

Arrays in Perl 6 are prefixed with the @ sigil. To access the elements of an array, the postfix pair of square brackets is used. For example, the second element of the @a array is @a[1]. Note that indexing starts from zero.

Let's take a look at how to create an array of integer numbers:

```
my @odd_numbers = 1, 3, 5, 7, 9, 11;
```

Alternatively, you can use parentheses or angle brackets. The following two arrays are the same as the previous one:

```
my @array2 = (1, 3, 5, 7, 9, 11);
my @array3 = <1 3 5 7 9 11>;
```

When printing it using the say built-in function, Perl 6 prints the content of the array in square brackets, as you can see here:

```
say @odd_numbers; [1 3 5 7 9 11]
```

Here is another example of an array that contains data of mixed types:

```
my @array = 1, 'two', 3E-2;
```

All the elements here are of different types (integer, string, and floating-point value), but they can easily be accessed via their index:

```
say @array[0]; # 1
say @array[1]; # two
say @array[2]; # 0.03
```

Let's take a further look at the possibilities that arrays offer in Perl 6.

Methods of the Array type

An array in Perl 6 is actually an object of the Array class. Working with classes is a subject of Chapter 8, *Object-Oriented Programming*. So far, we will discuss how we can access different properties of arrays in Perl 6 programs.

To get the length of an array, call the elems method, as follows:

```
my @a = 1, 3, 5;
say @a.elems; # 3
```

The three methods—push, pop, and append—modify the array: push adds a new element to the end of the array; pop takes the last element, removes it from the array, and returns it; append adds new elements to the end and, unlike push, can add more than one new element. Let's examine the output of the following program:

```
my @a = 1, 3, 5;

@a.push(7);
say @a; # [1 3 5 7]

say @a.pop; # 7
say @a; # [1 3 5]

my @b = 9, 11;
@a.append(@b);
say @a; # [1 3 5 9 11]
```

Alternatively, you may use functions instead of methods. The preceding program can be written differently, as shown here:

```
my @a = 1, 3, 5;

push @a, 7;
say @a; # [1 3 5 7]

say pop @a; # 7
say @a; # [1 3 5]
my @b = 9, 11;
append @a, @b;
say @a; # [1 3 5 9 11]
```

The next group, unshift, shift, and prepend, are the three methods complementary to push, pop, and append. The method unshift adds an element to the beginning of an array; shift removes and returns the first element; prepend adds new elements to the beginning. The following block of code demonstrates the effect of using these methods:

```
my @a = 1, 3, 5;

@a.unshift(7);
say @a; # [7 1 3 5]

say @a.shift; # 7
say @a; # [1 3 5]

my @b = 9, 11;
@a.prepend(@b);
say @a; # [9 11 1 3 5]
```

The `splice` method cuts the array into three parts and optionally replaces the middle one with a new list. The first two arguments of the `splice` method are the index of the first element that will be removed or replaced and the length of that fragment. For example, consider the following piece of code:

```
my @even = 2, 4, 6, 8, 10, 12, 14, 16, 18, 20;
@even.splice(4, 3);
say @even; # [2 4 6 8 16 18 20]
```

Here, three elements with indices 4, 5, and 6 will be removed from the original array.

In the next example, the same elements are replaced with the values 100 and 200:

```
my @even = 2, 4, 6, 8, 10, 12, 14, 16, 18, 20;
@even.splice(4, 3, (100, 200));
say @even; # [2 4 6 8 100 200 16 18 20]
```

The length of the replacement does not need to be the same as the removed part.

Hashes

In the array, indexes are integer numbers starting from zero. **Hashes** are another structural type of data in Perl 6 that can be treated as arrays whose indices are strings.

Hashes use the `%` sigil. Other names for hashes from various programming languages are associative arrays, dictionaries or dicts, and maps. Hashes are very useful when you need to keep a few values together. For example, take a look at the following code snippet:

```
my %city =
    name => 'London',
    country => 'gb',
    latitude => 51.52,
    longitude => 0,
    area => 1577,
    inhabitants => 8_700_000;
```

Elements of the hash are pairs, which are in turn two things—the **key** and the **value**. In this example, keys of the `%city` hash are `name`, `country`, and so on, and their values are `London` and `gb`.

The layout of the code in such assignments may be changed to align the keys and the values, as you can see here:

```
my %city =
    name         => 'London',
```

```
country    => 'gb',
latitude   => 51.52,
longitude  => 0,
area       => 1577,
inhabitants => 8_700_000;
```

In the assignment, pairs of the hash can be surrounded in parentheses, as shown here:

```
my %city = (
    name => 'London',
    country => 'gb',
    latitude => 51.52,
    longitude => 0,
    area => 1577,
    inhabitants => 8_700_000);
```

When a hash is printed (`say %city`), it is displayed in a pair of curly braces, as shown in the following lines of code:

```
{area => 1577, country => gb, inhabitants => 8700000,
latitude => 51.52, longitude => 0, name => London}
```

If there are keys with identical names, then the last one wins. Consider the following hash creation:

```
my %city =
    name => 'London',
    name => 'Paris';
say %city;
```

This program prints `{name => Paris}` only.

The information in this section is enough to continue on our way to learning types in Perl 6.

Methods of the Hash class

Let's see what methods are available for the hashes.

First, the two methods, `keys` and `values`, return lists (sequences, to be strict) containing all the keys and values of the hash.

```
my %capitals =
    Spain  => 'Madrid',
    Italy  => 'Rome',
    France => 'Paris';

my @countries = %capitals.keys;
```

```
my @cities    = %capitals.values;

say @countries; # [France Italy Spain]
say @cities;    # [Paris Rome Madrid]
```

The `kv` method returns a list of both keys and values:

```
say %capitals.kv; # (France Paris Italy
                  #  Rome Spain Madrid)
```

A similar method, `pairs`, returns a list of pairs (pairs are data types containing a key and a value):

```
say %capitals.pairs; # (France => Paris
                     #  Italy => Rome
                     #  Spain => Madrid)
```

To invert the pairs, use the `antipairs` method, as shown here:

```
say %capitals.antipairs; # (Paris => France
                         #  Rome => Italy
                         #  Madrid => Spain)
```

The size of the hash, which is actually the number of pairs in it, is returned by the `elems` method, shown as follows:

```
say %capitals.elems; # 3
```

Naming conventions

Perl 6 does not force the user to follow any specific naming conventions for variable names. Still, it is better to follow a general common sense approach. Variable names may be as short as one letter, but they can also be descriptive and contain many words.

Single-letter names are the best choice in loops, or in some calculations where all the mentions of the variable are located compactly and are clearly visible on the screen. Single-letter names, of course, may use both lower and uppercase letters. While there is no standard in Perl 6, the uppercase names are used for constants and pseudo-constants in the documentation; for example, check out `https://docs.perl6.org/language/variables#Compile-time_variables`.

Here are some examples of single-letter names:

```
constant $N = 100;
my $n = prompt('Enter a number: ');
```

```
say "You entered $n";
say 'This number is too big' if $n > $N;
```

For longer names, there are a few alternatives. Either you start with a small or capital letter, or the whole name is capitalized. Again, uppercase names such as $MAXIMUM are better to represent constants, even if you don't use the constant keyword. In general, lowercase names are preferable. Let's rewrite the previous program so that it uses longer variable names:

```
constant $MAXIMUM = 100;
my $value = prompt('Enter a number: ');
say "You entered $value";
say 'This number is too big' if $value > $MAXIMUM;
```

In many cases, even longer names are needed. In this case, there are a few ways to construct the name using two or more words. First, you can use the so-called camel case names, for example, $userValue or $valueFromInput. Second, the underscore character is a good candidate for concatenating parts of the name—$user_value or $value_from_input; this style is called snake case. Finally, Perl 6 allows extravagant names with dashes, for example, $user-value or $MAXIMUM-VALUE (kebab case). The – character is not a minus operator in this case, and is a part of the name. So, the $uservalue, $userValue, $user_value, and $user-value names are four different names. Consider the following code snippet:

```
constant $MAXIMUM-VALUE = 100;
my $entered-value = prompt('Enter a number: ');
say "You entered $entered-value";
say 'This number is too big'
    if $entered-value > $MAXIMUM-VALUE;
```

Choose your own style and try to consistently use it throughout the program.

Typed variables

In the previous examples, the type of the content that is hosted in a variable container was defined by the value that was assigned to a variable:

```
my $x;      # Declaring a variable as a container.
$x = 2;     # Now it contains an integer.
$x = 'Two'; # But now it keeps a string.
```

Perl 6 allows you to make the type of the variable container strict by specifying it together with a variable declaration:

```
my Int $x = 2;
```

Here, the `$x` variable will only be able to accept integers. An attempt to assign it to a string, for example, will result in the following error:

```
$x = 'Two'; # Type check failed in assignment to $x;
            # expected Int but got Str ("Two")
```

Similarly, Perl 6 allows elements of different types in the same array:

```
my @a = (1, 'two', 3.0);
```

Declaring an array with a type makes its element typed values. This means that you cannot assign a value of another type to it, as shown in the next example:

```
my Int @a;
@a = 1, 2, 3;
say @a;
@a[2] = 'Two';
```

The last assignment causes the type check error:

```
Type check failed in assignment to @a; expected Int
but got Str ("Two")
in block <unit> at typed-arr.pl line 7
```

Typed variables can use any of the built-in types or user-defined classes. In the next section, we will talk about the data types available in Perl 6 by default. In Chapter 8, *Object-Oriented Programming*, you will learn how to create your own classes.

Using simple built-in data types

Perl 6 comes with a number of various built-in types that cover the common range of things, such as Booleans, integers, and strings, but also offers unusual data types. We will cover them in this section. To demonstrate the built-in types, we will print them to the console using the say function, as we did in the 'Hello, World!' example.

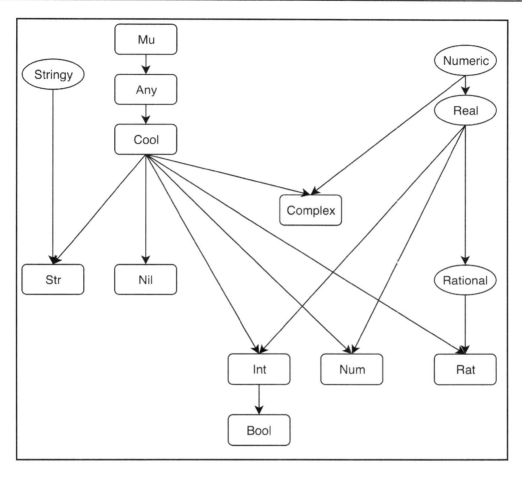

The hierarchy is built using two types of items: roles and classes. Roles are drawn in ovals, while classes are rectangle boxes. Roles are similar to interfaces in some programming languages. In this chapter, we won't focus on the details of what is a role or a class. You can learn that in detail in Chapter 8, *Object-Oriented Programming*. For now, we will assume that you have some basic understanding of object-oriented programming and will be able to understand the hierarchy of the data types.

In the following sections of this chapter, we will go through the main data types that you may use in your practice.

Integer data type

The value of the Int type is an integer value in Perl 6. The value can hold both positive and negative numbers, as well as zero, and the language does not limit the size of the number. It can be as small as one byte, for example, take a look at the following example:

```
say 42;
```

It can also be of arbitrary precision, as shown here:

```
say 239874637819093248768900298372340;
```

In the preceding examples, common decimal notation was used. Perl 6 allows using other bases; for example, 16 for hexadecimal values. To create an integer with a base other than 10, use the so-called adverbial notation, as shown in the following example:

```
say :16<D0CF11E>;
```

This will print 218951966, which is the decimal representation of the :16<D0CF11E> integer.

In the same manner, you will create values with other bases. Consider the following example:

```
say :8<755>;
say :2<10101>;
```

The preceding two lines of code will print 493 and 21, correspondingly.

The base value should not necessarily be a power of two. Other integer values between 2 and 36 are allowed, for instance, consider the following lines of code:

```
say :5<342>;
say :30<102spqr>;
```

In the first example, the base is 5, thus, the digits 0 to 4 are available in the representation of a number. The value :5<342> corresponds to 97 in the decimal form.

In the second example, we are free to use more 'digits', namely, 30 of them. Those digits are the regular Arabic digits 0 to 9, followed by 20 letters of the Latin alphabet, which are a to t. The decimal value of :30<102spqr> is 731399307.

You may have noticed that, in the preceding examples, some letter digits were in uppercase and some were in lowercase. For Perl 6, there is no difference; the integer digits, when they include alphabetical characters, are case-insensitive. So, the numbers :16<D0CF11E> and :16<d0cf11e>, as well as :30<102spqr> and :30<102SPQR> are equivalent.

Case-insensitivity indirectly defines the range of the allowed bases for integers; as we have 10 Arabic digits and 26 Latin letters, their combination gives 36 different characters.

In Perl 6, long integer values (that is, integers with many digits) may be spelled down with visual separation to groups of digits using the underscore character. The most straightforward goal of that feature is to provide the way to split the number into the groups of three digits. For example, consider the following line of code:

```
say 75_926_028;
```

Here, the notation of 75_926_028 is nothing more than giving the number of 75926028, but it lets us clearly see that the number is 75 million, 926 thousand, and 28. For the compiler, there is no difference, and both numbers are equally easy to read. For humans, it is much more easy to read a number that is split into groups.

Technically, you are not restricted to the way you split the number. This means that the following format is formally correct:

```
say 2_12_85_06;
```

This format may be suitable for phone numbers, but not for regular integers.

You cannot, however, have two underscores in a row. Neither can a number start or end with it. The following three attempts will not compile:

```
say 20__17;
```

This code will generate the compiler error:

Only isolated underscores are allowed inside numbers

```
say _2017;
say 2017_;
```

The error message in these two cases is a bit shorter, the compiler just says that it is:

Confused

Methods of the Int type

Data types in Perl 6 are represented by a number of built-in classes, which means that methods can be called on the objects of those classes. Object-oriented features of the language are described in Chapter 8, *Object-Oriented Programming*, but, for now, it is not possible to avoid some elements of it.

In this section, only the most interesting methods will be listed. The full list of possibilities can be obtained on the documentation page (https://docs.perl6.org/type/Int).

The most fundamental thing that is important now is that methods are called using the dot on either the value itself or on the variable containing the value of the corresponding type. You will see the way to call methods immediately in the next section.

Converting to a character using the chr method

Integer values can be converted to the corresponding character. The correspondence is defined by the Unicode codepoint.

In the case of values below 256, it coincides with the ASCII table. Considering the following code snippet:

```
say 65.chr; # prints A
```

Higher values produce characters from the Unicode tables, as shown here:

```
say 8594.chr; # →
```

The same result can be obtained using the hexadecimal representation, as shown here:

```
say 0x2192.chr; # →
```

Checking whether the number is prime

The is-prime method returns a Boolean value, telling us whether the number is a prime number or not, as shown here:

```
say 10.is-prime; # False
say 11.is-prime; # True
```

Executing the is-prime method on big numbers may be slow.

Generating a random number

The `rand` method returns a random number between zero and the given value. Notice that this method is inherited from the `Real` role (refer to the diagram at the beginning of the *Using simple built-in data types* section), and the return value is a floating-point number:

```
say 100.rand;
```

Running this code a few times results in different values being printed, as you can see here:

```
70.1530942429978
57.2150256026057
13.7542877975353
94.6395293813437
```

Getting the sign of the value

The `sign` method (also inherited from the `Real` role) returns either −1 or 1, depending on the sign of the value. Consider the following code snippet:

```
say 42.sign;   # 1
say -42.sign;  # -1
```

The result of calling the method on zero is 0, as shown here:

```
say 0.sign;  # 0
```

The sign method also works with infinities:

```
say Inf.sign;    # 1
say (-∞).sign;  # -1
```

Calculating the square root of the value

To calculate the square root of the value, call the `sqrt` method on it:

```
say 9.sqrt;  # 3
```

The routine is also defined in Perl 6 as a standalone built-in function. Consider the following code snippet:

```
say sqrt(9);  # 3
```

As the `sqrt` method is inherited from the `Numeric` role, the result is a floating-point value:

```
say 10.sqrt;  # 3.16227766016838
```

Getting the next and previous values

The two methods, `pred` and `succ`, correspondingly return the previous and the next values for integer arguments:

```
say 42.pred; # 41
say 42.succ; # 43
```

This method also works with non-integer values, when they add or subtract 1, as shown in the next fragment:

```
say pi.pred;    # 2.14159265358979
say (3/4).succ; # 1.75
```

The names of the methods come from the words predecessor and successor.

Getting the absolute value

The `abs` method returns the absolute value. In the following example, the method is called on a variable:

```
my $x = -42;
say $x.abs; # 42
```

To call it on a value, parentheses are needed for negative values. Otherwise, the unary minus operator (see more in `Chapter 4`, *Working with Operators*) will be applied to the result of calling the `abs` method:

```
say (-42).abs; # 42
say -42.abs;    # -42
```

Rational data type

In Perl 6, a special type `Rat` exists to store the rational numbers. In many cases, `Rat` will be used when you deal with floating-point numbers. Internally, the `Rat` value is represented by a pair of integer values, numerators, and denominators. Thus, any `Rat` number is a rational value equal to the division N/D. The integer numerator part is a value that can be arbitrarily long. The denominator part is a 64-bit integer.

Rat values appear as soon as you have a constant with the decimal point without an exponential part. Consider the following example:

```
say 3.14;
```

The 3.14 literal creates a Rat value here.

There is another syntax to create a Rat value: use the slash as in division and, optionally, enclose a number in the pair of angle brackets, as shown here:

```
say 1/2;
say <1/2>;
```

Also, you may use Unicode characters for fractions. For example, the following line will create a Rat number equal to 0.5:

```
say ½;
```

The internal structure of Rat values provides a fantastic ability for precise calculations. Unlike many other languages, where a floating-point arithmetic uses the IEEE numbers with limited precision, in Perl 6, the use of Rat numbers helps to avoid rounding errors when working with small numbers or, for example, with two numbers so close to each other that they cannot be compared precisely using the IEEE representations.

In the following examples, we will use the Rat numbers:

```
say 1/2 + 1/4 + 1/8 + 1/16;
say 0.1 + 0.2 - 0.3;
```

The last example is interesting because it prints 0 in Perl 6. Perl 6 uses Rat for calculations, and internally treats the values as 1/10, 2/10, and 3/10. Thus, the full sum of 0.1 + 0.2 - 0.3 is equivalent to 1/10 + 2/10 - 3/10, which results in a Rat value of 0/10, which is zero. In many other languages that use floating-point numbers, including Perl 5, the same calculation will not produce zero. The result would be small, but still non-zero; for example, 5.55111512312578e-17.

The advantage of using Rat for precise calculations is obvious. For example, in financial calculations, you may use Rat numbers to avoid rounding errors. (In many cases, though, in the financial calculation, you may use integers and count in cents; so, instead of keeping 9.99 € as a floating-point number, operate with 999 cents instead.)

Methods of the Rat type

The Rat method has a few specific methods and a number of methods that are inherited from its base classes or roles, such as Real or Numeric. Some of these methods were already discussed, in the *Methods of the Int type* section.

Getting the Perl representation of the value

The `perl` method returns a string that can represent the Rat value as Perl 6 understands it in the source code. The result can either contain a decimal point or a slash, depending on what is better for precise representation of the value.

Consider a couple of examples that display the preceding idea:

```
my $x = 1/3;
say $x.perl; # <1/3>

my $y = 1/2;
say $y.perl; # 0.5
```

Even more, the following code is valid Perl 6 code:

```
say 10/20.perl; # 0.5
```

Converting to an Int value

To convert the Rat value to an integer value, call the `Int` method. This is the general principle for type conversion: data types define the methods whose names repeat the names of other data classes.

```
my $x = 10/3;
say $x.Int; # 3
```

In this program, the result of `$x.Int` is 3, but you should keep in mind that `10/3` in the assignment is not a division, but a way to express a Rat number. The same can be done using a more explicit form, as shown here:

```
my $x = <10/3>;
```

Getting the numerator and denominator

To get the two parts of a Rat value, use the `numerator` and `denominator` methods. Let's take a look at how they work on the example of the value from the previous section:

```
my $x = 10/3;
say $x.numerator;   # 10
say $x.denominator; # 3
```

Methods for rounding the value

There are four different methods that convert a `Rat` value to an integer: `round`, `ceiling`, `floor`, and `truncate`.

The `round` method rounds the value according to the mathematical definition: the value is rounded towards the closest integer. We can see that in the following code snippet:

```
say 3.14.round; # 3
say 2.71.round; # 3
```

(Notice that the first dot separates the decimal part of the number, while the second dot is a method call.)

Negative values are also rounded so that the result is the closest integer number. We can see that in the following code snippet:

```
say (-3.14).round; # -3
say (-2.71).round; # -3
```

The `truncate` method just cuts the decimal part, regardless of the sign, as follows:

```
say 3.14.truncate; # 3
say 2.71.truncate; # 2

say (-3.14).truncate; # -3
say (-2.71).truncate; # -2
```

Finally, the pair of `ceiling` and `floor` methods rounds the number to the next or previous integer, as shown here:

```
say 3.14.ceiling; # 4
say 3.14.floor;   # 3

say (-2.71).ceiling; # -2
say (-2.71).floor;   # -3
```

Methods pred and succ

These two methods work similar to how they work on an integer value. The integer part is returned, incremented or decremented, while the floating part is unchanged, as shown as follows:

```
say 3.14.pred; # 2.14
say 3.14.succ; # 4.14
```

Numeric data type

The Num type is used to store floating-point values. It corresponds to the double precision in C.

Notice that, in Perl 6, the Num value is only created when the numeric literal is spelled in a scientific notation. That is, the E part of the value must be present.

Thus, in the following examples, the numbers with only a decimal point will be of the Rat type:

```
say 3.14;     # Rat
say 123.456;  # Rat
say 0.9;      # Rat
```

The following numbers represent the same values, but are of the Num type, as they use the exponential part in their definition:

```
say 3.14E0;     # Num
say 1.23456E2;  # Num
say 9E-1;       # Num
```

Remember that the Num values use the packed IEEE binary format, so they are limited in precision, while Rat numbers keep their numerator and denominator as two integer numbers.

Among the Num values, there is one outstanding value of NaN, which stands for Not a Number.

Num versus Numeric versus Real

As you saw in the diagram of the type hierarchy, some of the nodes are placed in ovals instead of rectangle boxes. Those are **roles**. Roles provide some interfaces to the classes that are inherited from them. We will talk about roles in more detail in Chapter 8, *Object-Oriented Programming*.

Some of the methods that the Numeric role provides us with are: Real, Int, Rat, Num, and Bool to convert the values to other data types; log, log10, exp, roots, abs, and sqrt for the corresponding mathematical calculations; and the pair prec and succ.

The Real role class gives us, among the rest, the following methods: rand, sign, round, floor, ceiling, and truncate.

If you want to dig deep and see all the connections between the classes, refer to the documentation pages listed at `https://docs.perl6.org/type.html`.

Enumerations

Enumeration is the data type that is used to define, for example, possible values of some concept. For example, traffic light colors take three values:

```
enum TrafficLight <red yellow green>;
```

The names of the values become known to Perl 6 and thus you may use them directly in a program, for example:

```
say red;
```

This code prints the name of the value:

red

In this example, the actual values of the `red`, `yellow`, and `green` names are not important for us but Perl 6 assigns increasing integer values to them.

```
say red + yellow + green; # 6
```

This program is equivalent to `say 0 + 1 + 2`.

When the values are important, then you can specify them explicitly, as we do in the next example:

```
enum Floors (
    garage => -1, ground-floor => 0,
    first  => 1,  second       => 2);
```

We will see one of the examples of the enumeration in the definition of the `Boolean` type in Perl 6 in the next section.

Boolean data type

`Bool` is a Boolean data type and provides two values: `True` and `False`. Technically, this is an enumeration with the two values:

```
enum Bool <True False>
```

The usage of the Boolean type is quite straightforward. We will see more usage of the Boolean datatype in `Chapter 5`, *Control Flow*.

Methods of the Bool type

The `Bool` type has some methods that we have already seen in use with the `Int` and `Rat` data, but their behavior may differ slightly.

Using pred and succ

The two methods, `pred` and `succ`, have a feature caused by the very limited range of the available values. You should not expect the values to be looped. The results of the methods are shown in the comments in the following piece of code:

```
say True.pred;   # False
say True.succ;   # True

say False.pred;  # False
say False.succ;  # True
```

Methods to generate random Boolean values

There are two methods, `pick` and `roll`, both of which can be called with or without the argument. These methods must be called on the class name itself, not on the value of it or a variable.

When either pick or roll is called with no argument, they return a random value, either `True` or `False`. We can see that in the following code snippet:

```
say Bool.pick;
say Bool.roll;
```

When the methods are called with an integer argument, a list of random values is generated. The integer argument defines the number of elements in the list, but on top of that, the `pick` method adds its limitation and returns only unique values, which, in the case of the `Bool` class, is not more than two. Compare the results of the similar calls, as follows:

```
say Bool.pick(4); # (False True) or (True False)
say Bool.roll(4); # e.g. (False True False False)
```

String data type

Strings are represented by the `Str` data type in Perl 6. A string is a sequence of Unicode characters. Considering the following code snippet:

```
my $str = 'Hello, World!';
say $str;
```

Let's go straight to the methods of the `Str` class.

Methods of the Str class

It is important to always keep in mind that all the semantics agree with the rules of Unicode. This means, for example, that converting a string to uppercase will change corresponding characters, even if they need more than one byte of memory.

Converting register

There are many methods to change the register of the letters in a string. The first set contains simple `lc` and `uc`, which converts all characters to lower or upper case. Consider the following code snippet:

```
say 'String'.lc; # string
say 'String'.uc; # STRING
```

The other four methods are more complex.

The `fc` method converts a string to the so-called fold case. It is intended to be used in string comparisons. For example, compare the output of the three methods called on a string with the German letter ß, which is spelled as `SS` in uppercase, but is converted to `ss` in the fold-case. Consider the following code snippet:

```
say 'Hello, Straße!'.lc; # hello, straße!
say 'Hello, Straße!'.uc; # HELLO, STRASSE!
say 'Hello, Straße!'.fc; # hello, strasse!
```

(Keep in mind that, since June 2017, the German language officially has the upper version of ß, we can know about that right here `https://en.wikipedia.org/wiki/Capital_%E1%BA%9E`. The behavior of the methods may change.)

The `tc` method converts a string to the so-called title case, where the first letter of the string is capital.

```
say 'hey, you'.tc; # Hey, you
```

Notice that, if the string already contains uppercase letters, they will remain as is:

```
say 'dear Mr. Johnson'.tc; # Dear Mr. Johnson
```

Use the `tclc` method to convert all the other letters to lowercase:

```
say 'HI THERE!'.tclc; # Hi there!
```

The `wordcase` method capitalizes the first character of each word and makes the rest lowercase:

```
say 'hello WORLD'.wordcase; # Hello World
```

Methods to cut strings

The two methods—`chop` and `chomp`—have similar names but have a different sensitivity to the characters they work with. The `chop` method cuts out the last character of the string. The `chomp` method only cuts the last character if it is a newline character.

```
say "Text\n".chomp; # Text
say "Text\n".chop;  # Text

say "Text".chomp;   # Text
say "Text".chop;    # Tex
```

Another group of methods—`trim`, `trim-leading`, and `trim-trailing`—cuts the spaces at the beginning and/or end of the string. Consider the following code snippet:

```
my $s = ' word '.trim;
say "[$s]"; # [word]

$s = ' word '.trim-leading;
say "[$s]"; # [word ]

$s = ' word '.trim-trailing;
say "[$s]"; # [ word]
```

Methods to check the content of a string

The `Str` class defines a pair of methods—`starts-with` and `ends-with`—that check whether the string contains a given substring at the beginning or end of it, and return a Boolean value. Consider the following example, which displays the behavior of these methods:

```
say 'Hello, World'.starts-with('Hello'); # True
say 'Hello, World'.starts-with('World'); # False

say 'Hello, World'.ends-with('Hello'); # False
say 'Hello, World'.ends-with('World'); # True
```

Regular expressions can be used instead of `starts-with` and `end-with`; refer to Chapter 11, *Regexes*, for the details.

Another set of functions—`index`, `rindex`, and `indices`—find the substring and return its position. The `index` method finds the most left occurrence of the substrings, `rindex` searches from the end of the strings, and `indices` returns a list of indices of all occurrences of the substring.

```
my $town = 'Baden-Baden';

say $town.index('Baden');   # 0
say $town.rindex('Baden');  # 6
say $town.indices('Baden'); # (0 6)
```

It is worth noting that, while the `rindex` method searches from the end of the string, it returns an index of the character that is counted from left to right.

Length of the string

To get the length of the string, call the `chars` method as follows:

```
say 'Düsseldorf'.chars; # 10
```

Reversing a string

The `flip` method returns the string in which all the characters go in a reversed order, as follows:

```
say 'Rose'.flip; # esoR
```

Complex numbers

In Perl 6, there is the `Complex` built-in type to present complex numbers.

Complex numbers have two parts, real and imaginary, and use the following syntax:

```
my $x = 3+4i;
my $y = -5i;
```

It is not necessary to explicitly spell out the real part, but the output always contains it:

```
say $x; # 3+4i
say $y; # -0-5i
say $z; # 0+1i
```

An alternative way to create a `Complex` number is to call a constructor (we will talk about constructors in `Chapter 8`, *Object-Oriented Programming*), as follows:

```
my $n = Complex.new(4, 5);
say $n; # 4+5i
```

Methods of the Complex data type

Some of the methods are already familiar to us. These are `round`, `ceiling`, `floor`, and `truncate`, which change both, the real and imaginary parts of the complex value. Let's take a brief look at the other methods.

Getting real and imaginary parts

The two methods—`re` and `im`—return real and imaginary parts of the complex number, as follows:

```
my $z = 4+5i;

say $z.re; # 4
say $z.im; # 5
```

The imaginary part is returned without the variable `i`.

The `reals` method returns a list containing both values, as shown here:

```
my $z = 4+5i;
say $z.reals; # (4 5)
```

Data types to manipulate date and time

Perl 6 offers built-in support to work with dates and times. This is very handy because date-time calculations are not easy (you need to think about leap years, extra seconds, time zones, calendar corrections, and so on).

We will cover two classes: `Date` and `DateTime`.

Using the Date class

The `Date` class represents the date—a collection of three numbers, year, month, and a day of the month. To create a new date, call a constructor with the three values:

```
my $date = Date.new(2017, 7, 19);
say $date; # 2017-07-19
```

To create a variable based on today's date, use the `today` method, as follows:

```
my $today = Date.today;
say $today; # 2017-07-17
```

To clone a date, call `clone`, as follows:

```
my $date2 = $today.clone;
```

Separate parts of the date are available from the clearly-named methods of the date, as follows:

```
say $date.year;  # 2017
say $date.month; # 7
say $date.day;   # 19
```

Additionally (and this is already a nice bonus), the `Date` class can calculate the day of the week (Monday is 1, Sunday is 7):

```
say $date.day-of-week; # 3 (Wednesday)
```

There are also the `day-of-month` and `day-of-year` methods:

```
say $date.day-of-month; # 19 (same as $date.day)
say $date.day-of-year;  # 20
```

A few methods help with counting weeks:

```
say $date.week;        # (2017 29)
say $date.week-number; # 29
say $date.week-year;   # 2017
```

For the weeks in January, the year returned by the week and week-year methods may either be the previous or the next year, depending on which week the day belongs to. For example, take the last day of 2019 and the first day of 2020. 31st December, 2019 is a Tuesday and 1st January, 2020 is a Wednesday. Both days belong to the same week, so the week-year method returns 2020. Examine the output of the following program to understand how the method works:

```
my $d1 = Date.new(2019, 12, 31);
say $d1.day-of-week; # 3
say $d1.year; # 2019
say $d1.week-year; # 2020

my $d2 = Date.new(2020, 1, 1);
say $d2.day-of-week; # 4
say $d2.year; # 2020
say $d2.week-year; # 2020
```

There's an interesting weekday-of-month method that returns the number of occurrences of this day of the week in this month before the given date. For example, 19 July, 2017 is the third Wednesday in July 2017:

```
say $date.weekday-of-month; # 3
```

Date calculations are very easy with the help of the earlier and later methods:

```
say $today.later(days => 2);   # 2017-07-19
say $today.later(months => 2); # 2017-07-21
```

To get yesterday's and tomorrow's date, use the pred and succ methods, which we have already seen in the numeric data types:

```
say $today.pred; # 2017-07-18
say $today.succ; # 2017-07-20
```

Using the DateTime data type

The usage of the DateTime data type is very similar to working with the Date type. In the DateTime objects, new fields to deal with time appear. We can see that in the following code snippet:

```
my $dt = DateTime.new(
    year   => 2017,
    month  => 7,
    day    => 19,
    hour   => 1,
    minute => 46,
    second => 48);

say $dt;           # 2017-07-19T01:46:48Z

say $dt.year;      # 2017
say $dt.month;     # 7
say $dt.day;       # 19

say $dt.hour;      # 1
say $dt.minute;    # 46
say $dt.second;    # 48
```

To create a new DateTime object and set it to the current moment, use the now constructor, as shown here:

```
my $dt = DateTime.now;
say $dt; # 2017-07-19T01:44:00.301537+02:00
```

The hh-mm-ss and yyyy-mm-dd methods generate formatted strings for time and date:

```
say $dt.yyyy-mm-dd; # 2017-07-19
say $dt.hh-mm-ss;   # 01:45:44
```

Be careful with printing seconds. The second method returns a floating-point number containing fractions of a second. To get an integer value, use the whole-second method:

```
my $now = DateTime.now;
say $now.second;       # 43.3285570144653
say $now.whole-second; # 43
```

Summary

In this chapter, we looked at an overview of the built-in data types in Perl 6 and learned how to work with variables. The most important fact is that variables in Perl 6 are instances of the different built-in data type classes. The details of those classes are located in Chapter 8, *Object-Oriented Programming*, but some elements of the object-oriented programming are needed to successfully create and use variables in Perl 6.

In the first part of the chapter, you learned three structural types of variable containers—scalars, arrays, and hashes—, and examined their main methods. In the second part, we took an in-depth look at different data types, such as integer, rational, floating-point numbers, strings, dates, and times.

In the next chapter, we will continue with observing the flow control in Perl 6 programs.

4

Working with Operators

Operators are the elements of the syntax of the language which perform actions over their operands and return a result. Perl 6 is a language with dozens of operators. Some of them are inherited from Perl 5 (directly or with modifications), some were invented especially for Perl 6. On top of the set of regular operators, Perl 6 defines the so-called meta-operators and hyper-operators, which extend the meaning of regular operators for working on a group of values.

In this chapter, we will cover the following topics:

- Operator classification
- Unary operators
- Binary operators
- Ternary operator
- Bitwise operators
- Miscellaneous operators
- Operator precedence
- Substitution meta-operators
- Assignment meta-operators
- Negation meta-operators
- Reversed meta-operators
- Creating hyper-operators
- Types of hyper-operations
- Reduction hyper-operators
- Cross hyper-operators
- Zip hyper-operator
- Sequential hyper-operators

Operator classification

First, let's remind ourselves of some of the basic terminology that we need when talking about **operators.** Consider a simple example:

```
my $a = 10;
my $b = 20;
my $c = 0;
$c = $a + $b;
say $c; # 30
```

Let's concentrate on the following line of code:

```
$c = $a + $b;
```

Here, we tell the compiler to perform two actions—first, calculate the sum of the $a and $b variables, and second, assign the result to the third variable, that is, $c. There are two operators in this example—+ and =. Operators are presented by their one-character names. In this case, the names are chosen to copy the corresponding operators in mathematics. Later, we will see examples of other operators, which are not just a character. They can be, for example, a sequence of two or three non-alphabetical symbols, such as >= or <= operators. Or, they can be a string identifier, for example—cmp or eq.

Categories of operators

In the previous section, we saw an example of the + operator, which takes two arguments. There are many other operators that are similar to +. For example, * is the operator for multiplication. Like the + operator, the * operator takes two arguments and returns a value.

```
my $c = $a * $b;
```

This kind of operator is called an **infix operator**, or simply **infix.** The operands of such operators are often called the left-hand side and right-hand side operands. As the operators take two arguments, they are also often called **binary operators**.

Another kind of operator needs only one argument. These operators are called **unary operators**. A typical example of a unary operator is unary minus. In the following example, this operator negates the value of its argument:

```
my $a = 10;
my $b = -$a;
say $b; # prints -10
```

Notice that this operator uses the same character as the binary minus operator, but both the programmer and the compiler can distinguish between the two:

```
my $a = 10;
my $b = -$a;      # unary minus, $b becomes -10
my $c = $a - $b; # binary subtraction, $c is 20
```

Different unary operators can be placed either before the argument or after it. For example, the ++ operator has two forms—**prefix** and **postfix**. The following example demonstrates the two alternatives:

```
my $a = 10;
++$a; # prefix operator ++
$a++; # postfix operator ++
```

The position of an operator (it is either placed before or after an argument) changes its meaning.

So far, we've met infix, prefix, and postfix operators. There are two more categories of operators in Perl 6.

Circumfix operators are another kind of unary operators. Unlike operators like unary −, circumfix operators consist of two complementary parts, such as parentheses. The only operand of a circumfix operator is placed between them, for example—the [$a] construction uses the [] circumfix operator that takes $a as an argument.

Finally, there are **postcircumfix operators**. They need two operands, and the syntax is the following—operand1[operand2]. One of the most practical examples of the postcircumfix operator is the function call. We've seen it a few times already—add($a, $b).

Let's summarize the operator categories in the following table using the + operator symbol as an example:

Category	Syntax
infix	operand1 + operand2
prefix	+operand
postfix	operand+
circumfix	(operand)
postcircumfix	operand1[operand2]

Operators as functions

Operators perform some actions over their arguments. Operator's arguments are called **operands.** In the preceding example, the + operator takes two operands, $a and $b. The = operator also takes two operands—on the left side of it, it expects the variable, to which it will assign the value of the operand on the right side.

In any programming language, operators are simply a handy syntactical solution to have more expressive programs and can be replaced with calling a function. For example, in the preceding example, you write $c = $a + $b, but you can also do the same by calling the add function that we saw in Chapter 1, *What is Perl 6?*. Let's rewrite the previous example:

```
my $a = 10;
my $b = 20;
my $c = 0;
$c = add($a, $b);
say $c; # 30

sub add($a, $b) {
    return $a + $b;
}
```

Of course, the add function uses the + operator itself, but we cannot avoid it here because there are no more low-level functions for addition in Perl 6. The purpose of the example was to demonstrate that operators can always be treated as functions that accept a few arguments and return a value, but you do not call them directly; rather via a good-looking operator.

In Perl 6, you may use the functional style when working with operators. For that, use the keyword with the name of the category of the operator followed by the colon and the operator itself in angle brackets. Then, pass the arguments as you do with functions. The following example demonstrates this on the example of the + infix operator:

```
my $a = 10;
my $b = 20;
my $c = infix:<+>($a, $b); # same as $c = $a + $b
say $c; # 40
```

Now, let's discuss the categories of the operators that Perl 6 offers.

And now, it's time to examine the operators one by one.

Operators in Perl 6

There are a few dozen built-in operators in Perl 6. To make the overview more structured, we will group them in groups corresponding to the categories that we described in the previous sections:

- Infix operators
- Postfix operators
- Circumfix operators
- Postcircumfix operators

In the following sections, we will examine operators of Perl 6 grouped into these categories. Within each category, operators are arranged in descending precedence.

Infix operators

Infix operators are probably the most commonly used operators in the language. They are also the most intuitive ones.

Assignment operators

The = operator is an assignment operator. It is used to assign the value of its right-hand side operand to the variable on the left. In the simplest case, the operator is used like this:

```
my $a;
$a = 42;
```

The action is not limited to scalars only. Arrays, hashes, or instances of classes (we will talk about classes in Chapter 8, *Object-Oriented Programming*) work are also processed as expected.

```
my @a = <10 20 30>;
my @b = @a;
```

Here, the assignment operator is used twice, first to initialize the @a array, and then to assign its values to the second array, @b.

Operators for multiplication and division

The * and / operators are the operators for multiplication and division. Their operands are converted to the numeric type if necessary. Consider the following examples:

```
say 10 * 20;
say "10" * "20";
```

Both lines of code print 200. Although, in the first line, the operands of the multiplication operator were both numeric (more precisely, Int). In the second line, we are trying to multiply strings containing numbers. Perl 6 converts the strings for us to make them numbers, and then the * operator does its work.

The * and / operators work well with the floating-point and with complex numbers (because both the Num and Complex types implement the Numeric role):

```
say pi * e;            # 8.53973422267357
say (10+3i) * (2-3.3i); # 29.9-27i
```

Be careful with multiplying complex numbers, as shown in the preceding example. To get the correct result, you should group the parts of the complex numbers in parentheses. If you omit them, the compiler will interpret the expression:

```
say 10 + 3i * 2 - 3.3i; # 10+2.7i
```

As the following:

```
say 10 + (3i * 2) - 3.3i;
```

In arithmetical expressions, * and / have higher precedence than + and –, thus all the calculations are done in the order according to the arithmetic rules. Consider the following code block:

```
say 10 + 3 * 6.3 - 3; # 25.9
```

If you divide two integer values, then the result will be of the Rat type, not the Num type. To get the Num value, at least one of the operands must be Num, as in the following:

```
say (1 / 2).WHAT;        # Rat
say (1 / 2.3).WHAT;      # Rat

say (1e1 / 2.3).WHAT;    # Num
say (1e1 / 2.3e-2).WHAT; # Num
say (1 / 2.3e-2).WHAT;   # Num
```

The * and / operators have equivalent notations in the non-ASCII space; you may use the × and ÷ symbols instead:

```
my $a = 100;
my $b = 25;
say $a × $b; # 2500
say $a ÷ $b; # 4
```

Operators for addition and subtraction

The + and – operators are operators for addition and subtraction. The operands must be of the numeric type.

There is not much to say about the operators; their behavior is self-explanatory, as follows:

```
my $a = 10;
say $a + 3;  # 13

my $b = 20;
say $b - $a; # 10;
```

In combination with, for example, * and /, the + and – operators have lower precedence, thus the standard arithmetical rules apply.

When it is possible to cast the string to a number (either integer or floating-point), that conversion will be performed by the compiler, and the + and – operators will work with two numeric operands. Consider the following example:

```
my $str = "42";
say $str - 2; # 40
```

As the operators expect their arguments to be numeric, you cannot use the + operator to concatenate strings. The naïve attempt to add two strings will be caught by the compiler. Take the following code, for example:

```
my $str1 = "Hello";
my $str2 = "World";
say $str1 + $str2; # Error
```

If you compile that, you get a runtime error:

```
Cannot convert string to number: base-10 number must begin with valid
digits or '.' in '◿Hello' (indicated by ◿)
  in block <unit> at add-str.pl line 3
```

Notice that the string conversion will not happen even if the string starts with a number, for example, the string "10 Hello" leads to another error message:

```
Cannot convert string to number: trailing characters after number in '10◤
Hello' (indicated by ◤)
```

To be correctly converted to a numeric type, the string must contain a number and nothing else. Although, whitespaces are allowed, as shown in the following example:

```
my $str1 = " 10 ";
my $str2 = " 20 ";
say $str1 + $str2; # 30
```

To concatenate strings, use the ~ operator.

It is possible to use the Unicode minus character in place of the – operator. There may not be much visual difference in the terminal, but the codepoints of the characters are different—0x2D for the bare – that you can type from the keyboard and 0x2212 for the Unicode MINUS SIGN:

```
my $a = 20;
my $b = 30;

say $a – $b; # ASCII
say $a – $b; # Unicode
```

Modulo operator

The % is the modulo operator. It returns the remainder of the division of its operands, as shown here:

```
say 100 % 3; # 1
say 10 % 3;  # 1
say 5 % 3;   # 2
```

The result of the modulo operation $a % $b is equivalent to the following wordy expression:

```
$a – $b * floor($a / $b);
```

Here, floor is the function that rounds the value down. Take one of the preceding examples—10 % 3. The result of it means that 3 can be subtracted from 10 a few times until 1 remains, which is less than 3 and thus cannot be decreased by it.

Traditionally, the modulo operator is used with integer operands, but it still works fine with rational and floating-point numbers. The values of these types can be accepted by the % operator without type casts. Let's examine the following examples:

```
say 10 % 3.3;   # 0.1 (Rat numbers)
say 10E1 % 3E0; # 1 (same as 100 % 3 but with Num operands)
```

Divisibility operator

The operator %% is called a divisibility operator. It tells if the left operand can be integer divided by the right operand without a remainder.

For example, the integer division of 10 by 3 gives 1 in the remainder and, thus, the %% operator will return false. If you divide 12 by 3, then there is no remainder, and the result is true, as shown here:

```
say 10 %% 3; # False
say 12 %% 3; # True
```

The result of $a %% $b is the same as the following comparison:

```
($a % $b) == 0
```

It can be used to check the condition in the loop, which we will see loops in more detail in Chapter 5, *Control Flow*. For example, to print the message once per every 1000 iterations, write the following piece of code:

```
for (0 .. 100_000) {
    say $_ if $_ %% 1000;
    # do some work
}
```

It prints 1000, 2000, 3000, and so on, which allows you to see the progress of the program, but does not flood the output with too many numbers.

Integer division and modulo operators

This pair of operators, div and mod, are the integer analogs of the / and % operators. The div and mod operators treat their operands as Int values, and the result is also an integer.

Let's examine a few examples:

```
say 100 div 3;  # 33
say 10 div 3;   # 3
say 10 div 5;   # 2
```

The mod operator returns the remainder of the integer division, as you can see here:

```
say 10 mod 3;  # 1
```

The non-integer operands must be explicitly converted before passing them to the div and mod operators. Otherwise, a compile-time error occurs, as shown here:

```
$ perl6 -e'say 10 div 3.3'
Cannot resolve caller infix:<div>(Int, Rat); none of these signatures
match:
  (Int:D a, Int:D b)
  (int $a, int $b --> int)
   in block <unit> at -e line 1
```

The error message informs us that the compiler sees that the div operator takes an Int and a Rat operand, while it only expects to see Int or int there.

Bitwise operators

The three operators starting with a plus character, that is, +&, +|, and +^, are bitwise operators that perform the AND, OR, and XOR operations over the operands. The operands must be convertible to:

```
say 1024 +| 512;  # 1536
say 512 +| 512;   # 512

say 1024 +& 512;  # 0
say 512 +& 512;   # 512

say 1024 +^ 512;  # 1536
say 512 +^ 512;   # 0
```

The bitwise operations are performed independently over corresponding bits of the operands.

If the operands are not integer values, then they will be converted to integers by calling the `.Numeric.Int` methods on it. Thus, first, the operand that is converted to the `Numeric` value and then to `Int`. From a practical perspective, this means, in particular, that the floating-point values will be truncated. Consider the following examples in comparison to the preceding examples:

```
say 512.67 +| 512;   # 512
say 512.67 +& 512;   # 512
```

Integer shift operators

The `+<` and `+>` operators are the integer shift operators. They shift the bits of its integer operands to the left and right by the distance indicated by the second operand. Consider the following lines of code as an example:

```
say 512 +< 2;  # 2048
say 2048 +> 2; # 512
```

String logical operators

These operators are the logical operators over strings. They start with the `~` character to follow the general idea that string operations use a tilde. The `~&`, `~|`, and `~^` operators do the AND, OR, and XOR operations respectively.

Before the bitwise operation, both operands are converted into the string representation (if necessary). Then, the operation is executed over the corresponding bits.

Let's consider an example of how to make the ASCII alphabetic character lowercase. In ASCII, the difference between the code of the lowercase and uppercase letter is 32 (`0x20` in hexadecimal notation). So, to make the letter lowercase, execute a `~|` operation on it and `0x20`, which is the code of space, to set the fifth bit to `1`:

```
say 'A' ~| ' '; # a
```

With the `~^` operator, you may organize the behavior to change the case, as shown in the following example:

```
say 'a' ~^ ' '; # A
say 'A' ~^ ' '; # a
```

In practice, it is better to avoid the tricks with the bits of the ASCII codes.

Boolean logical operators

These operators are the AND, OR, and XOR operators over Boolean values. The following code examples list the whole table of all the possible combinations of the operands:

```
say True ?| True;    # True
say True ?| False;   # True
say False ?| True;   # True
say False ?| False;  # False

say True ?& True;    # True
say True ?& False;   # False
say False ?& True;   # False
say False ?& False;  # False

say True ?^ True;    # False
say True ?^ False;   # True
say False ?^ True;   # True
say False ?^ False;  # False
```

Great common divisor and least common multiple operators

The gcd and lcm operators calculate the great common divisor and the least common multiple for the given two numbers. These operators are usually not included in the list of operators built into many other languages. In Perl 6, however, you don't need to include any libraries to use them. Consider the following examples of using the gcd and lcm operators:

```
my $a = 20;
my $b = 30;

say $a gcd $b; # Prints 10
say $a lcm $b; # Prints 60
```

Notice that the syntax requires that both gcd and lcm names are used as operators, not as functions. The following code is incorrect:

```
say gcd($a, $b);
say lcm($a, $b);
```

It will generate compiling errors, as you can see here:

```
===SORRY!=== Error while compiling
/Users/ash/Books/Packt/code/operators/gcd.pl
Undeclared routines:
  gcd used at line 4
  lcm used at line 5. Did you mean 'lc'?
```

For the prime numbers, the gcd operators return 1, as there are no other divisors, as shown here:

```
say 17 gcd 31; # 1
```

The lcm operators return a number equal to a product of its operands in the numbers that are prime, as shown here:

```
say 17 lcm 31; # 527
```

Of course, this is not the case for other numbers. Consider the following example:

```
say 20 lcm 40; # 40
```

String repetition operator

The x binary operator is a string repetition operator. It repeats a string the given number of times, as seen in the following example:

```
my $string = 'Developers ';
say $string x 5;
```

This code prints the string containing the initial value of the $string variable five times. The original value is not changed, obviously.

To modify the string and to save the result in the same variable, use the assignment form of the operator:

```
$string x= 2;
say $string;
```

Now, the $string value is twice as long as it was before.

List repetition operator

The operator xx is the list repetition operator. It is visually and ideologically similar to the x operator, but it works with lists. Consider the following example:

```
my @data = (10, 20);
my @big_data = @data xx 100;
say @big_data;
```

Here, the @data array will be repeated 100 times, and the @big_data variable will contain 100 copies of it.

Be careful not to accidentally mix the xx and x operators. If you use x instead of xx, then the compiler will not warn you, but instead, it will treat the argument as a string and perform string concatenation instead of repeating an array.

String concatenation operator

The ~ operator concatenates two strings, as follows.

```
say 'a' ~ 'b'; # ab
```

If the operands are not strings, they are converted to strings before the operation:

```
say 10 ~ 20;
```

This prints the 1020 string.

A form with assignment may also be quite useful in some applications:

```
my $string = 'Hello, ';
$string ~= 'World!';
say $string; # Hello, World!
```

Junction operators

These three operators create junctions. We have already seen junctions in the simplest form of having multiple values in the save variable at the same time:

```
my $odd = 1 | 3 | 5 | 7 | 9;
my $value = 5;
say 'Value is odd' if $value == $odd;
```

The code prints `Value is odd`, as the value in the `$value` variable is one of the values of the `$odd` junction. The `|` operator creates a so-called **any junction**.

The `&` operator creates an **all junction**, where all the values must be non-empty. Consider the following code snippet:

```
my $a = 3;
my $b = 4;

my $both = $a & $b;
say 'ok' if $both; # ok
```

Finally, the `^` operator creates a **one junction**, where only one of the operands must be evaluated as true. Considering the following code snippet:

```
my $c = 'OK';
my $d = '';

my $one = $c ^ $d;
say 'ok' if $one; # ok
```

It is important that the values created with either of the operators are junctions; you can see their type by calling the `WHAT` method, as follows:

```
say $one.WHAT; # (Junction)
```

Do not confuse the `&`, `|`, and `^` operators with the Boolean ones—`&&`, `||`, and `^^`.

The does operator

The `does` operator mixes a role into an object. We will talk about mix-ins in `Chapter 8`, *Object-Oriented Programming*. Anyway, consider a brief example:

```
class Animal {}

role Barking {
    method bark() {
        say "Bow-wow!";
    }
}

my $dog = Animal.new();
$dog does Barking;
$dog.bark();
```

Here, the `$dog` variable is first created as an instance of the `Animal` class. Then, the behavior of the `Barking` role is attached to it. After that, the `$dog` variable can `bark()`.

The but operator

The `but` operator mixes in a role to an object, similar to how the `does` operator is doing that. The `but` operator does not modify an object itself and always returns a new object. In addition, `but` allows us to use already instantiated objects, as shown in the following example:

```
my $value = 0 but True;
say 'It is true' if $value;
```

The `$value` becomes `True` in the Boolean context now, while it still contains pure zero.

In the case of mixing in roles, the same object starts behaving as an object belonging to different types, depending on the situation. Consider the following code snippet:

```
role Barking {
    method bark() {
        say "Bow-wow!";
    }
}

my $dog = 14 but Barking;
say $dog;      # 14
$dog.bark(); # Bow-wow!
```

The `$dog` variable is printed as its numeric value, but it is also possible to call the `bark` method on it.

Introspection shows that the variable is now a combination of both:

```
say $dog.WHAT;
```

This command prints `(Int+{Barking})`.

Universal comparison operator

The `cmp` is a universal comparison operator. Its versatility allows comparing both numeric and string data. Consider the following code snippet:

```
say 10 cmp 2;      # 2 is less than 10
say "10" cmp "2"; # but "2" is more than "10"
```

The return value of one of the three possible values of the Order enumeration is Less, Same, or More. The preceding program prints the following output:

```
More
Less
```

If the operands are of different types, they are converted to the same type, as follows:

```
say 5 cmp "5";  # Same
```

When you compare pairs with cmp, they are compared in such a way that keys are compared first, and values are compared second. Examine the following examples, where we create three pairs with different keys and values and compare them in different combinations:

```
my $a = alpha => '2';
my $b = beta => '1';
my $c = alpha => '1';

say $a cmp $b;  # Less
say $a cmp $c;  # More
```

In the case of $a cmp $b, their keys are sortable alphabetically, and the values are not important. In the case of $a cmp $c, both keys are equal, so the values of each pair are also checked.

String comparison operator leg

The leg operator got its name from the words *less, equal, greater*. It compares two operands as strings. If the values are not strings, they are stringified first.

```
say 10 leg 2;      # Less
say "10" leg "2";  # Less
say 5 leg "5";     # Same
```

The result is one of the values of the Order enumeration (notice that, despite the e in the operator name, the equality of operands returns the value of Same).

Comparison operator for Real numbers

This is a comparison operator that converts its operands to the `Real` type if necessary. The following example demonstrates the results of comparing the same data that we tried with the `cmp` and `leg` operators.

```
say 10 <=> 2;      # More
say "10" <=> "2";  # More
say 5 <=> "5";     # Same
```

Range creating operator

This group of binary operators is used to create ranges. The two operands define the left and right edges of the range. The presence of the ^ character indicates that the corresponding edge is open; thus, it does not include the given number.

Run the following example to see how it works:

```
.say for 1 .. 5;    # Prints the numbers: 1, 2, 3, 4, 5
.say for 1 ..^ 5;   # 1, 2, 3, 4
.say for 1 ^.. 5;   # 2, 3, 4, 5
.say for 1 ^..^ 5;  # 2, 3, 4
```

You may choose your own style regarding the spaces around the operators. So, both `1 ..^5` and `1 ..^ 5` are acceptable. However, it is not possible to insert a space between the characters of the operator, such as `1 .. ^5`.

Equality and non-equality operators

The two operators `==` and `!=` compare the two operands for numeric equality or non-equality. In Perl 6, a number of variations of these operators are defined so that they correctly work with operands of different types, as follows:

```
say 'Equal' if 10 == 10;
say 'Not equal' if 3.14 != pi;
```

If necessary, both operands are converted to `Numeric` values first:

```
say 'Also equal' if "10" == 10;
```

The != operator has a Unicode synonym—≠:

```
say 'Not equal' if e ≠ pi;
```

As a funny example, you may also test the !≠ operator, which is constructed similar to how the != operator is assembled—the exclamation sign negates the next character. This works in Perl 6, but avoid using it in practice; use a conventional == instead.

To compare strings, use the eq and ne operators, which are described later in this chapter.

Numerical comparison operators

The <, <=, ≤, >, >=, and ≥ operators set is used for the numerical comparison of two operands. The operands are converted to Real if they are not numeric. Consider the following code:

```
say 10 < 2;
say "10" < "2";
```

In both cases in this example, the result of the comparison is False.

The two Unicode operators ≤ and ≥ are synonyms of the <= and >= ASCII forms, as follows:

```
say 10 ≤ 10; # True
say 20 ≥ 10; # True
```

String comparison operators eq and ne

The eq and ne operators compare two strings and return a Boolean value.

```
say 'abc' eq 'abc'; # True
say 'abc' ne 'def'; # True
```

The non-string operands are converted to strings before comparison, as follows:

```
say 13 eq '13'; # True
```

To compare numbers, use the == and != operators.

Other string comparison operators

This collection of string comparison operators perform operations *greater* (gt), *greater or equal* (ge), *later* (lt), and *less or equal* (le) respectively. The operators work with strings, so the operands are converted to the Str type if necessary. The return value is a Boolean value.

```
say 'a' lt 'b';
say 'beer' le 'water';

say 'z' gt 'x';
say 'stone' ge 'paper';
```

In all the preceding examples, the result is True.

The before and after operators

The before and after operators return True or False, depending on the order of operands. In Perl 6, these operators are multi-functions that exist for arguments of different types. They work well with both numerical and string data.

Let's consider these examples where comparing strings and numbers gives opposite results:

```
say 10 before 2; # False
say 10 after 2;  # True

say "10" before "2"; # True
say "10" after "2";  # False
```

Unlike the general comparison cmp operators, the ordering operators before and after return a Boolean value.

Equivalency test operator

The eqv operator tests whether its two operands are equivalent. The term assumes that both operands are of the same type and contain the same value. The following examples demonstrate the work of the operator.

Two integer values are equivalent:

```
my $a = 42;
my $b = 42;
say $a eqv $b; # True
```

If one of the values is of another type, say a string, then the result is `False`, even if the value can be converted to the same integer:

```
my $a = 42;
my $c = "42";
say $a eqv $c; # False
```

The `eqv` operator works with arrays, as shown in the following code:

```
my @a = 1, 2, 3;
say @a eqv [1, 2, 3]; # True
```

And, with more complex data structures, say, with nested arrays. Consider the following code snippet:

```
my @b = [[1, 3], [2, 4]];
say @b eqv [[1, 3], [2, 4]]; # True
```

Value identity operator

The `===` operator is the value identity operator. For the scalar values, it gives the same results as the `eqv` operator—it returns true when both the types and the values of the operands are the same, as you can see here:

```
my $a = 42;
my $b = 42;
say $a === $b; # True
```

This is another example with a string and an integer:

```
my $a = 42;
my $c = "42";
say $a === $c; # False
```

For classes, the `===` operator returns True if both operands point to the same object, as shown in this example:

```
class O {
}

my $o1 = O.new();
my $o2 = O.new();
say $o1 === $o2; # False: same class but different objects

my $o3 = $o1;
say $o1 === $o3; # True: the same object
```

More on classes in `Chapter 8`, *Object-Oriented Programming*.

Bound check operator

The bound check operator returns true if both operands are bound to the same variable, or, more precisely, to the same container.

Binding in Perl 6 means that another variable points to the same container and you may change its value using two names. This is demonstrated in the following example:

```
my $a = 42;
my $b := $a;
$b = 30;
say $a; # 30
```

Here, the value that was placed in the $a variable is changed using the $b alias. The =:= operator returns true for such names:

```
say $a =:= $b; # True
```

Smartmatch operator

The ~~ operator is the smartmatch operator. It performs different types of comparison for operands of different types.

```
my $int = 10;
say $int ~~ 10; # True

my $str = 'str';
say $str ~~ 'str'; # True

say $str ~~ /^ str $/; # ⌜str⌟
```

As you can see from the output from this test program, the result of the ~~ operator is not always a Boolean value.

Internally, the $a ~~ $b construction with the smartmatch operator is equivalent to the call of $b.ACCEPTS($a). The ACCEPTS method is a built-in method defined for all types in Perl 6. The preceding three smartmatch operations may be rewritten in the following way:

```
say 10.ACCEPTS($int);
say 'str'.ACCEPTS($str);
say /^str$/.ACCEPTS($str);
```

Approximate-equality operator

This is one of the most unusual operators of programming languages. In Perl 6, the `=~=` operator compares the values for approximate-equality.

The result of an approximate comparison is True if the difference between the operands is less than the value of the `$*TOLERANCE` variable. Its default value is `1E-15`.

Let's check out the two approximations of the value of pi:

```
say pi =~= 3.14159265358979323846;
say pi =~= 3.14;
```

The first one returns `True`, while the second is `False` because it is not accurate enough.

Boolean logical operators

These operators are operators for the Boolean logic that perform the operations AND, OR, and exclusive OR.

With Boolean operands, the result is either `True` or `False`, with the only exception for the `True ^^ True` expression, which returns `Nil`.

The following set of examples demonstrates all possible combinations for the Boolean operands:

```
say False && False; # False
say True  && True;  # True
say True  && False; # False
say False && True;  # False

say False || False; # False
say True  || True;  # True
say True  || False; # True
say False || True;  # True

say False ^^ False; # False
say True  ^^ True;  # Nil
say True  ^^ False; # True
say False ^^ True;  # False
```

With operands of other types, they either return a Boolean value or one of the operands. Let's examine the operators one by one.

The `&&` operator returns the first operand, which in Boolean context can be treated as a `False` value, or the last operand if all the operands are `True` in the Boolean context. For example, the result of the `42 && 14` expression is `14`. Here, both operands are `True`, thus, the second operand is returned after the operation.

Consider these examples:

```
say 42 && 14;           # 14
say 0 && 14;            # 0
say 'Karl' && 'Marta'; # Marta

my $text;
say $text && 'default text'; # (Any)
say 'default text' && $text; # (Any)
```

In the `0 && 14` expression, the first operand is `False`, so the `&&` operator returns it immediately without evaluating the second one. The second expression has two operands that are `True`; thus, `Marta` is the result. Finally, the undefined string is returned in the last two expressions.

Similarly, the `||` operator returns the first `True` operand. If all operands happen to be `False`, then the last one is returned. Let's examine the following examples, which use the same operands as we used in the earlier tests of the `&&` operator:

```
say 42 || 14;           # 42
say 0 || 14;            # 14
say 'Karl' || 'Marta'; # Karl

my $text;
say $text || 'default text'; # default text
say 'default text' || $text; # default text
```

The logic of the `^^` operators for non-Boolean operands is a bit more tricky. If there is only one `True` operand, then that operand is returned. If there is none, then the last operand is returned. If there is more than one `True` operands, the value of Nil is returned.

```
say 42 ^^ 14;           # Nil
say 0 ^^ 14;            # 14
say 'Karl' ^^ 'Marta'; # Nil

my $text;
say $text ^^ 'default text'; # default text
say 'default text' ^^ $text; # default text
```

All the tree operators may be chained, for example, to select the first acceptable value or to take the default one:

```
my $name = '';
my $first_name = '';
say $name || $first_name || 'No name'; # No name
```

These operators has short-circuit sematics and should stop evaluating operands when the value is determined.

Defined-or operator

The `//` operator is called the **defined-or** operator. It returns the first of the defined operands. The most obvious use case for `//` is to supply default values for input data, as shown in the following example:

```
my $planet;

# Some code that may change the value of $planet.
# $planet = 'Mars';

say $planet // 'Earth';
```

The `//` operator is also a short-circuit operator.

Operators for minimum and maximum

The `min` and `max` operators return, respectively, either a minimum or maximum operand. To compare the values, the operators use the same semantics as defined for the `cmp` operator. Consider the following code snippet:

```
say 10 min 2; # 2
say "10" min "2"; # 10

say 10 max 2; # 10
say "10" max "2"; # 2
```

Notice that in Perl 6, there are min and max functions that do the same, but use the function call syntax:

```
say min(2, 10); # 2
say max(2, 10); # 10

say min("2", "10"); # 10
say max("2", "10"); # 2
```

Both operator and function can be used to find a minimum and maximum of more than two values:

```
say 10 min 20 min 30; # 10
say max(10, 20, 30);   # 30
```

Pair creation operator

The => operator creates pairs. It takes the left operand as the key and the right operand as the value.

```
my $pair = 'key' => 'value';
```

The type of the created object is `Pair`.

With the => operator, the key may not be quoted if it passes the restrictions for identifiers in Perl 6. Consider the following example:

```
my $pair1 = alpha => 1;
my $pair2 = beta => 2;
```

Comma operator

Comma creates a list of the operands provided. In the following example, the list is saved in the array variable:

```
my $a = 10;
my $b = 20;
my $c = 30;

my @a = $a, $b, $c;
```

Invocant separator

The : operator does not look like an ordinary infix operator. It is used to separate the invocant argument in method calls. The method call in this call looks like a call to a regular function. Let's see this in a simple example.

First, we will call the index method on the $string.

```
my $string = 'Hello, World!';
my $pos = $string.index('W');
say $pos; # 7
```

The same effect can be achieved by the following lines of code:

```
my $pos = index($string: 'W');
say $pos; # 7
```

As you can see, the $string variable is passed as the first argument of the index routine and is separated from the second argument with a colon.

Zip operator

The Z operator works like a zipper and creates a new array out of the given two arrays. The elements in the new array are picked up from the elements of the operands as the zipper connects its item.

The behavior of the Z operator can be clearly seen in the following example:

```
my @odd = 1, 3, 5, 7, 9;
my @even = 2, 4, 6, 8, 10;
my @all = @odd Z @even;
say @all;
```

This program prints the following list which contains nested lists based on the elements from both the @odd and @even arrays:

```
[(1 2) (3 4) (5 6) (7 8) (9 10)]
```

If one of the array operands is of a different length, the result of the Z operator will contain as many elements as the shortest one contains.

Cross operator

The cross operator X creates all possible combinations of the elements of its operands. Compare the work of this operator on the same data that we used in the example for the Z operator.

```
my @odd = 1, 3, 5, 7, 9;
my @even = 2, 4, 6, 8, 10;
my @all = @odd X @even;
say @all;
```

This time, the resulting array is much bigger, as shown here:

```
[(1 2) (1 4) (1 6) (1 8) (1 10) (3 2) (3 4) (3 6) (3 8) (3 10) (5 2) (5 4)
(5 6) (5 8) (5 10) (7 2) (7 4) (7 6) (7 8) (7 10) (9 2) (9 4) (9 6) (9 8)
(9 10)]
```

Sequence operator

As an infix operator, the three dots are the sequence operator. Perl 6 contains some amount of built-in magic that does what you mean. Let's consider a few examples with the . . . operator:

```
say 5 ... 10;
say 'a' ... 'f';
```

The preceding two lines print the following sequences:

```
(5 6 7 8 9 10)
(a b c d e f)
```

The result of the . . . operation is a sequence. Do not mix this operator with the . . operator which creates ranges.

If you assign the result to a list, then the operators may be interchangeable:

```
my @a = 5...10;
my @b = 5..10;
say @a; # [5 6 7 8 9 10]
say @b; # [5 6 7 8 9 10]
```

The sequence operator can demonstrate a more complicated behavior:

```
my @squares = 1, 2, 4 ... 64;
say @squares;
```

In this example, using the pattern, the . . . operator creates the sequence of squares:

[1 2 4 8 16 32 64]

The sequence operator understands arithmetic and geometric sequences, such as in the following examples:

```
say 1, 2 ... 10;    # Arithmetic
                    # (1 2 3 4 5 6 7 8 9 10)

say 1, 2, 4 ... 32; # Geometric
                    # (1 2 4 8 16 32)
```

Another interesting example of using the . . . operator is the way to generate Fibonacci numbers by presenting the formula with the Whatever (*) character, as you can see here:

```
my @fib = 0, 1, * + * ... *;
say @fib[0..10];
```

The preceding code creates a lazy list @fib, whose elements will be calculated on demand. The first ten numbers are printed, as shown here:

(0 1 1 2 3 5 8 13 21 34 55)

Binding operators

These two operators create bindings. Bindings are synonyms that can be used instead of the original variable names to access their values.

We saw an example of using the := operator in the section about the =:= operator.

The second form, ::=, creates a read-only binding. Currently, it is not yet implemented in Rakudo.

Logical operator with lower precedence

The two operators and and or are semantically equivalent to the logical && and || infix operators, but are of looser precedence.

These low-precedence operators are a perfect match for exceptional situations and false assertions, for example:

```
my $value = prompt('Enter a small value> ');
$value < 10 or die 'Too big';
say 'OK, thanks';
```

Here, the right-hand side of or is only executed if the assertion $value < 10 fails.

Data pipe operators

The ==> and <== operators pass the values similarly to how the | pipe operator passes data in the Unix command-line shells.

Consider the following example:

```
my @a = (10...0 ==> grep {$_ > 5} ==> sort);
say @a;
```

Here, the @a array is created in three steps. , the sequence from 10 to 0 is generated with the ... operator, then the values are passed to the grep function that selects numbers of more than five. After that, the values go to the sort method.

The result of this program is a sorted list of integers between 6 and 10:

```
[6 7 8 9 10]
```

The <== operator organizes data flow in the opposite direction:

```
my @b = (sort() <== grep {$_ > 5} <== 10...0);
say @b; # [6 7 8 9 10]
```

Notice that, in this case, parentheses after the sort call are required, as, otherwise, the Perl 6 compiler will try to interpret the beginning of the <== operator as the opening quote of the < ... > list.

Ternary operator ?? !!

The `??` `!!` operator is the only ternary operator in Perl 6. It is also called the conditional operator. It takes three operands—a condition and two values. If the condition is evaluated as `True`, the second operand is returned as a result of the operation. Otherwise, the third operand is returned.

```
say pi < 3 ?? 'Less than 3' !! 'More than 3';
```

In this example, the `pi < 3` condition is False, so the second string `More than 3` is printed.

The ternary operator can (with care) be used to test more than one condition. Consider the following example:

```
my $value = rand;
say $value;
say $value < 0.3 ?? '0.0 to 0.3'
 !! $value < 0.5 ?? '0.3 to 0.5'
 !! $value < 0.7 ?? '0.5 to 0.7'
 !!                 '0.7 to 1.0';
```

In such cases, the formatting of the code should help you understand the idea of the developer.

Prefix operators

The next set of operators in Perl 6 is the collection of prefix operators. Prefix operators only need one operand and are placed in the code before them.

Increment and decrement operators ++ and --

These are the prefix operators to increment and decrement the value.

Prefix forms of these operators first change the value of the variable and then return the result.

```
my $n = 42;
++$n;
say $n;   # 43
say --$n; # 42
```

In Perl 6, both ++ and -- operators have the form of postfix operators (see examples in the *Postfix operators* section later in this chapter).

Boolean coercion operator

The ? prefix operator is the Boolean coercion operator. It converts its operand to a Boolean value.

The behavior of the operator is quite straightforward. Let's examine the following examples to get an idea of its usage:

```
say ?4; # True
say ?0; # False

say ?'abc'; # True
say ?'';    # False

my $var = 'Hello, World!';
say ?$var; # True

my $undefined_var;
say ?$undefined_var; # False

my $empty_str = '';
say ?$empty_str; # False
```

Boolean negation operator

The ! prefix is the Boolean negation operator. It inverts the Boolean value of its operand.

```
say !True; # False
say !'';   # True
say !0;    # True
say !42;   # False
```

Numeric coercion operator

The + prefix operator coerces the operand to a numeric value.

```
say +True;  # 1
say +42;    # 42
say +'42';  # 42

my $var = '42';
say +$var;  # 42
```

Notice that you cannot use the + prefix operator to parse the number from a string that contains extra characters:

```
# my $text = '12 volts';
# say +$text;
```

The preceding code will generate the following error:

Cannot convert string to number: trailing characters after number

Numeric negation operator

The – prefix operator negates its numeric operand. If the operand is not numeric, it is converted to it first.

```
my $var = 42;
say -$var;  # -42

say -"42";  # -42
```

String coercion operator

The ~ operator, used as a prefix operator, casts its operand to a string.

For simple data types, the action of the operator is quite predictable:

```
my $var = 42;
my $str = ~$var;
say $str.WHAT;  # (Str)
```

With complex data, the string conversion may return the address of the object:

```
class X {
}

my $x = X.new;
say ~$x; # X<140372183360608>
```

To change this default behavior, you may need to define your own converters (we will talk about the gist method in Chapter 8, *Object-Oriented Programming*).

Two-complement binary negation operator

The +^ operator does the two-complement binary negation of the operand, which is converted to an integer value first, as shown in the following code:

```
say +^42; # -43

my $neg = -42;
say +^$neg; # 41

say +^0;  # -1
say +^-1; # 0
```

Boolean coercion and negation operator

The ?^ operator converts its operand to a Boolean value and negates it. The result is the same as the result of the simple ! prefix operator.

```
say ?^True; # False
say ?^'';   # True
say ?^0;    # True
say ?^42;   # False
```

The upto operator

The ^ operator is called the **upto** operator. It creates a range from 0 to the integer value of the operand:

```
say ^5;

my $right = 5;
say ^$right;
```

In the preceding code, Perl 6 prints the range in the form of ^5.

Let's use the range in a loop:

```
say $_ for ^3;
```

This one-line program prints 0, 1, and 2. Thus, the range does not include its upper boundary.

The temp operator

The temp operator temporary replaces a variable with a new value.

Consider the following example:

```
my $var = 1;

f(); # 1

{
    f(); # 1
    temp $var = 2;
    f(); # 2
}

f(); # 1

sub f() {
    say $var;
}
```

The f subroutine prints the value of the global variable $var. Initially, the value of the variable is 1. Thus, the first call of f prints 1.

 Then, we have a block of code between a pair of curly braces. The second call of f is using the save value of $var as before. Then, the value of it is temporarily set to 2. So, the third call of f prints 2.

After exiting from the code block, the scope of the temporary value ends and the original value of $var is restored. So, the fourth call of f prints 1 again. The temp keyword is different from the my keyword, as it does not create a local variable. If you change the code to using my, then the f subroutine will still use the global variable $var, which is unchanged:

```
. . .
{
    f(); # 1
    my $var = 2;
    f(); # 1
}
. . .
```

The let operator

The let operator sets a new value for the variable. The key feature of it is the ability to restore the original value if the code block fails.

Consider the following example. The $var variable is set to a new value inside the code block between the pair of curly braces. The variable is printed after the end of the block. As there are no exceptions, the program prints the new value—2, as shown here:

```
my $var = 1;

{
    let $var = 2;
}

say $var; # 2
```

If the block, for some reason, dies, then the variable will keep the original value. The exception caused by die is caught by the CATCH block. The new value, 2 is then lost, and the program prints 1, as you can see here:

```
my $var = 1;

try {
    let $var = 2;
    die;
}
CATCH {
}

say $var; # 2
```

The `let` operator is very handy if you need to organize some kind of transaction to be sure that all the changes only take place if there are no exceptions.

The not operator

The `not` operator converts its operand to Boolean if needed and negates the value.

```
say not 42;    # False
say not False; # True
```

This operator has a lower precedence than the ! operator.

The so operator

The `so` operator converts the operand to a Boolean value and returns it, as shown in the following example:

```
say so 0;    # False
say so 42;    # True
say so True; # True
```

The ? operator has a higher precedence than the `so` operator.

The `so` routine also exists as a method of the `Mu` class and can be called like `$var.so` on a variable. (Classes are discussed in `Chapter 8`, *Object-Oriented Programming*; `Mu` is one of the classes on the top of Perl 6 class hierarchy.) So, the following code can be read as an English phrase 'If something is so, then do the following':

```
my $smth = True;
if $smth.so {
    say 'True';
}
```

Postfix operators

The set of postfix operators contain a few operators that you put immediately after the operand.

Object-oriented postfix operators

In Perl 6, there is a set of postfix operators that are used with objects. For example, we have used the . operator to call methods on objects, say, on integers or strings:

```
say 42.Str; # 42
say 'Hello'.WHAT # (Str)

say 'UP'.lc; # up
```

We will examine other OOP-related postfix operators in Chapter 8, *Object-Oriented Programming*. These are the following operators—.&, .=, .^, .?, .+, .*, .:, and .::.

Increment and decrement operators

The postfix forms of the increment and decrement operators first return the value of the variable and then change their values. We can see that in the following code:

```
my $n = 42;
$n++;
say $n;    # 43
say $n--; # 43
```

Compare the output of the following example with the program that is shown in the *Prefix operators* section earlier in this chapter.

Circumfix operators

Circumfix operators do not look like regular operators, say +. Circumfix operators contain two parts that surround the operand. The four operators, presented in this section, are built using the pair of two braces of different kinds.

Quote-word operator

The quote-word operator < > creates a list using the whitespace-separated data place between the angle brackets.

The following example prints a list containing three elements:

```
say <a b c>; # (a b c)
```

There is no need to quote elements inside the < > operator. Now, let's save the created array in a variable and see its contents:

```
my @a = < 1-3 two 3+6 four 5/7 >;
say @a.elems;
say @a.join('|');
```

In this program, five elements are put into the @a array, as shown here:

```
5
1-3|two|3+6|four|5/7
```

The elements are separated by whitespaces, so constructions like 1-3 or 5/7 are treated as strings.

Group operator

The group operator is a pair of parentheses—( ). For example, it groups elements in mathematical expressions.

The empty pair of parentheses creates an empty list:

```
say ().WHAT; # (List)
```

Hash or block creation operator

The pair of curly braces ({ }) create either an empty hash or a code block. Perl 6 decides what to do based on the code it sees between the braces.

In the following examples, you may see that Perl 6 does what you mean.

Empty braces or a list of key value pairs create a hash, as shown in the following code:

```
say {}.WHAT;              # (Hash)
say {a => 1, b => 2}.WHAT; # (Hash)
```

While some executable code, referring to placeholder, or default variables creates a code block:

```
say {say 1}.WHAT;       # (Block)
say {$^x * $^y}.WHAT;   # (Block)
say {$_}.WHAT;          # (Block)
say {$_ => 1}.WHAT;     # (Block)
```

Notice that because Perl 6 uses the same curly braces in both hash and block syntax, some confusion may take place, compare the following two examples:

```
say {$_ => 1}.WHAT;  # (Block)
say {a => 1}.WHAT;   # (Hash)
```

Perl 6 will make a block if this is obvious that the code between the braces is executable, such as when it contains a semicolon that separate statements:

```
say {;a => 2}.WHAT;  # (Block)
```

Also, if there are references to implicit or explicit arguments, then this is a block:

```
say {$^a => 2}.WHAT;  # (Block)
```

Both the placeholder $^a and the default variable $_ shows that this is part of the block signature.

Alternatively, the %() syntax can be used to create a hash:

```
say %('a', 2).WHAT;  # (Hash)
```

Attempting to use the $_ variable may lead to an error depending on the content. For example, the following line generates an error Use of uninitialized value $_ of type Any in string context if the code is isolated:

```
say %($_, 2).WHAT;
```

In the case when $_ is defined, a hash will be created without errors:

```
for 1..5 {
    say %($_ => 2 * $_).WHAT; # (Hash)
}
```

Postcircumfix operators

Postcircumfix operators in Perl 6 are postfix operators that use pairs of characters to embrace the rest of the operands.

Positional access operator

The pair of square brackets [ ] organizes access to positional elements of the operand. The simplest case is indexing an array as follows:

```
my @a = <1 3 5 7 9>;
say @a[2]; # 5
```

It is possible to pass a list of indices to request more than one element:

```
say @a[1, 2, 3]; # (3 5 7)
```

A range is another good candidate to select elements:

```
say @a[2..4]; # (5 7 9)
say @a[^4];   # (1 3 5 7)
```

Element access operators

The next group of operators include { }, < >, << >>, and « ».

The main operator { } is used to access values of a hash.

```
my %h = alpha => 'a',
        beta  => 'b',
        gamma => 'c';
say %h{'beta'}; # b
```

Similar to the [ ] operator, multiple keys are accepted by { }:

```
say %h{'alpha', 'beta'}; # (a b)
```

In previous examples, keys of the %h were quoted. The postcircumfix operator, < >, allows us to avoid quoting in the manner the < > circumfix does:

```
say %h<beta>;        # b
say %h<alpha beta>; # (a b)
```

The << >> operator and its Unicode synonym, « », interpolate the operands as if they are strings in double quotes, as you can see here:

```
my $name = 'gamma';
say %h«$name»;    # (c)
say %h<<$name>>; # (c)
```

Invoke operator

The ( ) is an operator that invokes a function or method call on its first operand. The operands, which are placed between parenthesis, are passed as arguments:

```
say 'Hello'.substr(1, 3); # ell
```

Here, the ( ) postcircumfix operator receives three operands—the name of the `substr` method and two integers, 1 and 3.

While the code does not look as if it is using an operator, Perl 6 still treats the pair of parenthesis as a special type of operator, namely, a postcircumfix operator.

Meta-operators in Perl 6

So far, we have covered many of the operators that operate on regular operands—values, variables, objects, and so on. In Perl 6, there are operators of another kind—operators that operate over operators. These operators are called meta-operators. We will examine them in the following sections. With some exceptions, every meta-operator can take any regular operator to create a new operation that follows certain rules. Meta-operators also work with user-defined operators, which we will discuss later in this chapter, in the *User-defined operators* section.

Assignment meta-operator

The assignment meta-operator takes the `op=` form, where `op` is one of the operators available in Perl 6.

For example, take the infix + operator. In its default form, it takes two operands and adds them up, returning the result.

```
my $a = 10;
my $b = 20;
my $c = $a + $b;
say $c;  # 30
```

In this example, the `$c` variable receives the sum of `$a` and `$b`, which stays unchanged.

In the meta-operator form, the += operator changes the left operand and stores the result in it, as shown here:

```
my $d = 10;
my $e = 20;
$e += $d;
say $e;  # 30
```

The $a += $b expression is always equivalent to the following $a = $a + $b form.

The assignment meta-operator works with many other infix operators. Consider the

following example:

```
my $x = pi;
$x *= 2/3;
say $x;
```

Negation meta-operator

The negation meta-operator ! is using the exclamation mark in the !op form with Boolean operators. For example, here is the negation meta-operator created in combination with the smart-match operator, ~~:

```
say 'Hello' ~~ /o/;  # ⌈o⌋
say 'World' !~~ /x/; # True
```

There is no x in World, so the !~~ operator returns True.

Reverse meta-operator

The reverse meta-operator R takes an operator and creates a new one, in which the order of the operands is changed.

For example, take the infix – operator. It subtracts the second operand from the first one as follows:

```
say 20 - 10; # 10
```

Now, let's use the meta-operator R– and see what it changes:

```
say 20 R- 10; # -10
```

As we see, the result is as if the operands were swapped. The action of the meta-operator with two operands `$a Rop $b` is equivalent to `$b op $a`.

Reduction meta-operator

The reduction operator `[op]`, when applied to a list, executes the `op` operation for every subsequent pair of elements. In other words, the list is enrolled and the `op` symbol is inserted between them.

Let's examine the meta-operator in the following example:

```
my @a = (1, 2, 3);
say [+] @a; # 6
```

A `[+] @a` expression is equivalent to the following one:

```
say @a[0] + @a[1] + @a[2];
```

Let's take a look at another example—`[*]`. This meta-operator can be used to calculate factorials:

```
say [*] 1..5; # 120
```

Cross meta-operator

The cross meta-operator `Xop` takes two lists and applies the `op` operator to every possible combination of the elements of the lists.

The result of the operation is another list. Take a look at the following example with two lists of three numbers in each:

```
my @x = (1, 2, 3);
my @y = (4, 5, 6);
say @x X+ @y;
```

The code prints a list with six elements, each of which is the sum of two elements of `@x` and `@y`:

(5 6 7 6 7 8 7 8 9)

Let's use the string concatenation (~) and use the same `@x` and `@y` arrays in the `X~` operation:

```
say @x X~ @y;
```

In this case, every pair of numbers is converted to a pair of strings, and then they are concatenated. You can see how the X meta-operator picks the elements of its operands:

```
(14 15 16 24 25 26 34 35 36)
```

Zip meta-operator

The zip meta-operator Zop 'zips' its list operands and applies the op operation to corresponding elements of the operands.

Let's try the zip meta-operator on the same data as we did with the cross meta-operator:

```
my @x = (1, 2, 3);
my @y = (4, 5, 6);
say @x Z+ @y;
say @x Z~ @y;
```

The program prints two lists of three elements each:

```
(5 7 9)
(14 25 36)
```

Hyper-operators

Hyper-operators in Perl 6 apply the operation to each element of the list operand. They work with both unary and binary operators and use the << and >> symbols, and their synonyms, « and ».

Let's explore hyper-operators with examples:

```
my @a = 1..10;
@a = @a <<+>> 3;
say @a; # [4 5 6 7 8 9 10 11 12 13]
```

In this first example, the value of 3 is added to each element of the @a array. On the left side of the <<+>> hyper-operator is an array with ten elements. On the right side, we have a scalar value. This value is added to all elements of the array on the left.

In this example, the same <<+>> operator is used with two arrays of the same length:

```
my @x = (1, 2, 3);
my @y = (4, 5, 6);
say @x <<+>> @y; # [5 7 9]
```

The result is a new array with three elements; each element is a sum of the corresponding elements of the source arrays.

An ASCII form of <<+>> can be rewritten using quotes:

```
say @x «+» @y; # [5 7 9]
```

The direction of angle brackets defines how the operands are cloned if one of them is shorter than another one.

Let's examine different combinations on the following two arrays:

```
my @short = (1, 2);
my @long = (3, 4, 5, 6);
```

First, use the same operator as we used before:

```
say @short <<+>> @long; # [4 6 6 8]
```

The @short array is repeated twice here so that there are enough elements for the whole @long array. The code is equivalent to adding up two arrays of the same length:

```
say (1, 2, 1, 2) <<+>> (3, 4, 5, 6);
```

Now, use the <<+<< operator as follows:

```
say @short <<+<< @long; # [4 6 6 8]
```

Again, the @short array is repeated.

Reverse the arrows like this:

```
say @short >>+>> @long; # [4 6]
```

The array is not repeated anymore, and the result only contains two elements. The rest of the @long array is ignored.

Finally, let's try the >>+<< operator:

```
say @short >>+<< @long;
```

The shape of the hyper-operator tells us that neither of the operands can be cloned. In this case, the following error occurs:

```
Lists on either side of non-dwimmy hyperop of infix:<+> are not of the same
length
```

It is also possible to create a hyper-operator with unary operators. For example, with postfix increment:

```
my @d = 1..5;
@d>>++;
say @d; # [2 3 4 5 6]
```

Every element of the @d array is incremented by one using the >>++ hyper-operator.

With the prefix form of ++, the same example will look like this:

```
my @d = 1..5;
++<<@d;
say @d; # [2 3 4 5 6]
```

User-defined operators

Perl 6 allows creating new operators. Unlike, for example, C++, new operators are not restricted to the predefined list of existing operators. You are free to name the operators as you want and choose a new combination of characters.

A user-defined operator should belong to one of the preceding-mentioned categories, such as infix, prefix, or circumfix, and so on.

Let's start with creating a new infix operator, +%, which calculates the sum of two numeric operands, but the result does not exceed 100:

```
sub infix:<+%>($a, $b) {
    my $sum = $a + $b;
    return $sum < 100 ?? $sum !! 100;
}
```

Defining an operator is similar to creating a subroutine, but the name of it should contain the name of the category and the operator itself.

It is now time to test the just created +% operator:

```
say 10 +% 20; # 30
say 40 +% 70; # 100
```

Another expressive example is an operator for factorial. In mathematics, a factorial is indicated by the exclamation mark after the value. This is also possible to do in Perl 6 with the user-defined postfix operator:

```
sub postfix:<!>($n) {
    [*] 1..$n
}

say 5!; # 120
```

The postfix operator takes only one operand—$n. In the body of the operator, we use the reduction operation to calculate a factorial.

User-defined operators get the same rights as built-in operators in Perl 6. This, in particular, means that after defining a new operator, you may use it in combination with many meta-operators.

For example, the +% operator gets the +%= form and can be used directly, as follows:

```
my $var = 50;

$var +%= 30;
say $var; # 80

$var +%= 30;
say $var; # 100
```

Or, it can be used with a reduction operator, as follows:

```
say [+%] 1..10; # 55
say [+%] 1..50; # 100
```

There is no intention in Perl 6 design to make user-defined operators cryptic. So, you may come up with better names, including some descriptive string identifiers, as follows:

```
sub postfix:<Factorial>($n) {
    [*] 1..$n
}

say 5Factorial; # 120
```

Summary

In this long chapter, we talked about the operators in Perl 6. There are a few categories of operators, such as infix, prefix, postfix, circumfix, and postcircumfix. We discussed the operators from each group. Then, we looked at how meta-operators and hyper-operators create new operators based on the built-in ones. Finally, you learned how to create user-defined operators, which will be naturally embedded in the language of your program.

Up till now, we have covered all the basics of Perl 6 grammar. In the next chapter, we will move on to the next level of organizing code using subroutines.

5
Control Flow

In this chapter, we will be talking about the main elements in controlling the flow of programs in Perl 6. Most programs are not just a list of instructions, but they should rather react to user input, take decisions based on calculated data, and so on.

In this chapter, we will cover the following topics:

- Code blocks and the `do` keyword
- Conditional checks
- Loops
- Breaking the loop body
- Collecting data using `gather` and `take`
- Setting the topic
- Executing code only once

Understanding code blocks and variable scoping

In the previous chapter, we discussed variables, which are named entities that you use in a program. As in many programming languages, in Perl 6, the names are visible inside their scope and not outside of it.

Take, for instance, a simple program, where the `$name` variable is only used once, as follows:

```
my $name = 'Mark';
say "Hello, $name!";
```

The variable can be reused after it is used in printing the greeting:

```
my $name = 'Mark';
say "Hello, $name!";

$name = 'Carl';
say "Hello, $name!";
```

This works because both the printing statements are located in the same scope and the `$name` variable is visible there.

A **block** in Perl 6 is a piece of code that is located inside a pair of curly braces. A block creates its own scope. Thus, a variable declared in a block is only visible inside it.

The following program will not compile:

```
{
    my $name = 'Mark';
    say "Hello, $name!";
}

$name = 'Carl'; # Error here
say "Hello, $name!";
```

The following error message informs us that, at the place where `$name` is assigned to a new value, the variable with that name is not declared:

```
===SORRY!=== Error while compiling /Users/ash/code/control-flow/3.pl
Variable '$name' is not declared
at /Users/ash/code/control-flow/3.pl:6
------> <BOL>█$name = 'Carl';
```

To make the name visible again, declare it in the outer scope as follows:

```
my $name;

{
    $name = 'Mark';
    say "Hello, $name!";
}

$name = 'Carl';
say "Hello, $name!";
```

In this demonstration, there was not much sense in creating separate code blocks. We will see more useful applications of code blocks when we talk, for example, about conditions, later in this chapter, or in Chapter 6, *Subroutines*, where code blocks are used to keep the body of user-defined functions.

The do keyword

The do keyword is used to execute a code block. The example from the previous section can be rewritten in the following way:

```
my $name;

do {
    $name = 'Mark';
    say "Hello, $name!";
}

$name = 'Carl';
say "Hello, $name!";
```

The necessity for the explicit use of the keyword is obvious when the code block cannot be a separate expression, as shown in the next example:

```
my $name;
$name = 'Carl';
$name and do {say "Hello, $name!"};
```

Here, with the help of the and keyword (see Chapter 4, *Working with Operators*), the program checks whether the $name is defined and, if so, the greeting is printed.

Conditional checks

Taking decisions based on conditions is one of the fundamental needs in programming. The `if` keyword changes the flow of the program, depending on the result of a Boolean test. Considering the following code:

```
my $x = 5;
if $x < 10 {
    say "$x < 10"; # 5 < 10
}
```

In this example, you can see the syntax used with the `if` keyword. The keyword is followed by a Boolean condition `$x < 10`, followed by the block of code in the curly braces. Unlike Perl 5, parentheses around the condition are not necessary.

The block of code is only executed if the condition evaluates to `True`.

The `if` statement can be accomplished by the `else` branch, which will take control when the condition is `False`:

```
my $x = 11;
if $x < 10 {
    say "$x < 10";
}
else {
    say "$x >= 10"; # 11 >= 10
}
```

With the given value of `$x`, the program executes the code followed by the `else` block.

When you need more granular branching, `if-else` checks can be chained. Here, the joint `elsif` keyword comes out:

```
my $x = 10;
if $x < 10 {
    say "$x < 10";
}
elsif $x == 10 {
    say "$x == 10"; # 10 == 10
}
else {
    say "$x > 10";
}
```

The `elsif` branch contains another Boolean expression, which will be checked when the condition of the first `if` test is `False`.

The same program can be re-written using different Boolean tests combinations, for examples:

```
my $x = 10;
if $x < 10 {
    say "$x < 10";
}
elsif $x > 10 {
    say "$x > 10";
}
else {
    say "$x == 10";
}
```

You have to be careful not to mistakenly type `if` instead of `elsif`. If you do so, you create two independent if checks, both of which can trigger their , as shown in the following example.

The following piece of code checks if the variable is either less than five or less than ten:

```
my $x = 3;
if $x < 5 {
    say 'x < 5';
}
elsif $x < 10 {
    say 'x < 10';
}
else {
    say 'x >= 10';
}
```

The first condition `$x < 5` is `True`, so only the first codeblock is executed and the program prints `x < 5`.

Now, lets's replace `elsif` with `if`:

```
my $x = 3;
if $x < 5 {
    say 'x < 5';
}
if $x < 10 {
    say 'x < 10';
}
else {
```

```
    say 'x >= 10';
}
```

In this case, there are two `if` blocks. The `else` block only exists for the second `if`. Both conditions, $x < 5$ and $x < 10$, are both `True` now, and, thus, the program prints the following two lines:

```
x < 5
x < 10
```

Also, make sure you don't use two `else if` keywords instead of a single `elsif` in places where you need an `if-elsif-else` chain. Perl 6 will complain because it expects to find the code block after the `else` keyword:

```
my $x = 3;
if $x < 5 {
    say 'x < 5';
}
else if $x < 10 {
    say 'x < 10';
}
else {
    say 'x >= 10';
}
```

Compilation ends with the following error:

```
===SORRY!=== Error while compiling /Users/ash/ifelseif.pl
In Perl 6, please use "elsif" instead of "else if"
```

Of course, the problem can also be solved using the nested `if-else` statements, which may be a bit ugly and introduce another level of nested code that is not necessary, as you can see in the following example:

```
my $x = 3;
if $x < 5 {
    say 'x < 5';
}
else {
    if $x < 10 {
        say 'x < 10';
    }
    else {
        say 'x >= 10';
    }
}
```

Using loops

Loop constructions help organize repeated actions. There are a few different options in Perl 6 for creating a loop. Let's start with the one that is similar to traditional loops in C style.

The loop cycle

The `loop` keyword expects three elements to control the number or repetitions of the loop body. Consider the following code snippet:

```
loop (my $c = 0; $c < 5; $c++) {
    say $c;
}
```

In this example, `$c` is the counter of the loop iterations. This variable is declared and initialized immediately after the loop keyword—my `$c` = 0. The body of the loop is executed if the condition `$c` < 5 is `True`. After the iteration, the `$c++` statement is executed, which increments the counter, and the cycle repeats. As soon as `$c` becomes equal to five, the condition is not `True` anymore, and the loop stops. So, the whole program prints the numbers from 0 up to, and including, 4.

Some, or even all of the parts in the loop header may be omitted. For example, if the counter variable is initialized before the loop, as shown:

```
my $c = 0;
loop (; $c < 5; $c++) {
    say $c;
}
```

If the increment happens inside the body. We can consider the following code:

```
my $c = 0;
loop (; $c < 5; ) {
    say $c;
    $c++;
}
```

Note that, despite the missing parts, semicolons are still needed.

Finally, if no parameters are given, the loop becomes infinite, and it is your responsibility to stop it, as shown:

```
my $c = 0;
loop (;;) {
    say $c;
    $c++;
}
```

With an empty header, no semi-colons are required, as shown:

```
my $c = 0;
loop {
    say $c;
    $c++;
}
```

The parts of the loop header can contain more than one instruction separated by a comma. For example, here is a loop with two variables:

```
loop (my $x = 0, my $y = 10; $x < 5 && $y > 5; $x++, $y--) {
    say "$x $y";
}
```

This program increments the $x variable and decrements $y. The output looks like this:

```
0 10
1 9
2 8
3 7
4 6
```

Now, let's move on to the `for` cycle.

The for loop

The `for` loop can be said to be a more Perlish way of organizing loops. It does not require a counter and iterates over a list of data.

Consider an example. Here, the list is an array of odd integers:

```
my @data = 1, 3, 5, 7, 9, 11;
for @data {
    say $_;
}
```

The $_ variable is the default variable, also called the **topic**. It takes the value of one of the elements in the current iteration. Thus, the `for` loop prints the numbers from the `@data` array.

There are two important modifications that you can perform with the preceding program.

First, if the body of the loop is a single statement, the loop can be rewritten in the postfix form, as shown here:

```
my @data = 1, 3, 5, 7, 9, 11;
say $_ for @data;
```

Here, the built-in function `say` takes $_ as an argument. It is also possible to call a method with the same name on the topic:

```
$_.say for @data;
```

The default variable can be omitted to make the program even shorter, as you can see here:

```
.say for @data;
```

This is an example of the real Perl 6.

The second change introduces the topic variable explicitly. In this case, you give a name to it. The syntax is simple and can be understood from the following example:

```
my @data = 1, 3, 5, 7, 9, 11;
for @data -> $x {
    say $x;
}
```

The variable is declared after the `->` arrow. You don't have to use the `my` keyword here.

This format has an advantage; in that, it can take more than one value from `@data`. For example, to take two values on each iteration, declare two variables as follows:

```
my @data = 1, 3, 5, 7, 9, 11;
for @data -> $x, $y {
    say "$x + $y = ", $x + $y;
}
```

This program prints the three sums, as you can see here:

```
1 + 3 = 4
5 + 7 = 12
9 + 11 = 20
```

In the case of an odd number of elements, an exception will be fired, as follows:

```
Too few positionals passed; expected 2 arguments but got 1
```

The construction with an arrow (in the following code) is called a **pointy block**. It is equivalent to an anonymous function that takes the named arguments, which is why arguments are mentioned in the error message). We will see more on this in Chapter 6, *Subroutines*.

To properly handle the missing data, default values can be used as follows:

```
my @data = 1, 3, 5, 7, 9, 11, 13;
for @data -> $x, $y = -1 {
    say "$x, $y";
}
```

In this case, on the last iteration, the $y value will be set to –1, as you can see here:

```
1, 3
5, 7
9, 11
13, -1
```

Using while, until, and repeat

With the three keywords, while, until, and repeat, you can create loops that will be repeated a number of times defined by certain conditions. Let's start with the simplest case with a bare keywords while and until:

```
my $letter = 'a';
while $letter ne 'd' {
    say $letter;
    $letter++;
}
```

The body of the while loop will be repeated as long as the condition $letter ne 'd' is True. Here, the control over the variable is done in the body of the loop, while its header only controls the condition. If the condition is False before entering the loop, the body will not be executed, as shown in the following example:

```
my $letter = 't';
while $letter le 'd' { # 't' is not less or equal then 'd';
    say $letter;       # body is not executed.
    $letter++;
}
```

The behavior of the `until` keyword is opposite to `while`. The loop body is executed until the condition becomes `True`.

```
my $letter = 'a';
until $letter eq 'd' {
    say $letter;
    $letter++;
}
```

During the first three iterations, the `$letter eq 'd'` condition is `False`, so the body is executed. As soon as the `$letter` becomes d, the loop stops.

As you have seen, there is no guarantee that the body of the loop will be executed even once. If the condition is `False` (in the case of `while`) or `True` (in the case of `until`) initially, then the code of the loop body is skipped.

The `repeat` keyword moves the check of the condition to the end of the body, so it will be executed at least once. This keyword is used with `while` and `until`.

```
my $letter = 'a';
repeat {
    say $letter;
    $letter++;
} while $letter ne 'd';
```

This loop prints the letters a, b, and c. The condition in the `while` clause is `False` three times, after which it becomes `True`.

Now, let's modify both the condition and the initial value of the variable and run the loop again:

```
my $letter = 't';
repeat {
    say $letter;
    $letter++;
} while $letter le 'd';
```

This time, the letter t is printed. Unlike the bare `while` loop, the `repeat while` loop executes its body before checking the condition.

Notice that the `while` clause may be placed before the code block, as shown:

```
my $letter = 't';
repeat while $letter le 'd' {
    say $letter;
    $letter++;
}
```

There is no difference with the postfix `while` clause in this case.

Similarly, the `until` keyword can be used with `repeat`. The `repeat until` loop is executed at least once. If the condition is `False`, it continues running the code block until the condition becomes `True`.

```
my $letter = 'a';
repeat until $letter eq 'd' {
    say $letter;
    $letter++;
}
```

Or, with the postfix form. Consider the following code snippet:

```
my $letter = 'a';
repeat {
    say $letter;
    $letter++;
} until $letter eq 'd';
```

Both programs print a, b, and c. Choose one for the variants of locating the condition and try to stick to it in practice, or at least inside a project.

Breaking the loop

The execution of the loop can be controlled not only with initial conditions but also from the loop body itself. There are three keywords for that—next, last, and redo. They become more useful when used together with condition checks using `if`.

The `last` keyword just breaks the loop. Let's consider an example of a loop that breaks after it prints a value that is bigger than some predefined threshold:

```
my @data = 3, 1, 7, 12, 50, 2, 14;
for @data -> $x {
    last if $x > 42;
    say $x;
}
say 'Done.';
```

Notice that `if` is used in the postfix form here—it behaves the same as the following code:

```
if $x > 42 {
    last;
}
```

The first few iterations are executed as usual, but when the current value of `$x` becomes `50`, which makes the `$x > 42` condition `True`, the loop is stopped and the execution comes to the code (if there is any) after the loop. The program prints the following lines:

```
3
1
7
12
Done.
```

Notice that the code in the code block, which is located after the `last` instruction, is also executed before the if condition becomes `True`. As soon as the `$x` variable gets the value of 50, the loop is broken.

Another keyword, `next`, skips the rest of the loop body and starts another iteration. For example, let's print even numbers between one and ten:

```
for 1..10 -> $x {
    next if $x % 2;
    say $x;
}
```

This loop does not print a number if the condition `$x % 2` is 1, which is casted to `True`. It happens for even numbers, and thus, `say` only receives odd numbers that pass the filter, as you can see in the following output:

```
2
4
6
8
10
```

Finally, the `redo` keyword restarts the loop from the current position. Like `next` and `last`, it skips the rest of the loop body but does not affect the loop counter.

```
for 1..5 -> $n {
    my $r = rand;
    say "Trying $r";
    redo if $r < 0.5;

    say $n + $r;
}
```

This simple program demonstrates the usage of the `redo` keyword. The program generates a random number between 0 and 1 and only uses it if the number is more than 0.5. In all other cases, the loop iteration is restarted.

Using labels

Let's consider an example with nested loops:

```
for 1..5 -> $x {
    for 1..5 -> $y {
        say "$x * $y = ", $x * $y;
    }
}
```

This program prints the product table for the numbers from 1 to 5. What if, at some point, we want to skip the rest of the table for the given $x, and continue with the next value of $x? The direct usage of `next` inside the loop for $y will only affect the inner loop. To make sure that the `next` statement is modifying the execution of the outer loop, use X_LOOP:

```
X_LOOP: for 1..5 -> $x {
    for 1..5 -> $y {
        next X_LOOP if $y == $x;
        say "$x $y = ", $x $y;
    }
}
```

The label here is a capitalized identifier X_LOOP followed by the colon. It is mentioned in the `next` statement, so the compiler understands that the next iteration should start at the loop marked with X_LOOP.

Labels can also be used with the loops of other types, for example, with the `until` and `while` loops.

Executing code once

In Perl 6, interestingly, it is possible to execute part of the body only once. For example, in the next loop, there should be four iterations done, but the first message will be printed only once:

```
for 1, 2, 3, 4 {
    once {
        say 'Looping from 1 to 4';
    }
    say "Current value is $_";
}
```

The preceding code prints the following output:

```
Looping from 1 to 4
Current value is 1
Current value is 2
Current value is 3
Current value is 4
```

The block of code after the once keyword was executed only once.

This also works with loops of other types, for example, with the loop cycle. Considering the following code snippet:

```
loop (my $c = 1; $c != 5; $c++) {
    once say 'Looping from 1 to 4';
    say "Current value is $c";
}
```

Notice that no curly braces are needed if you only have a single instruction to be executed once.

The once keyword is not only applicable to loops. It can be used in any other part of the code, for example, inside subroutines. We will discuss subroutines in detail in the next Chapter 6, *Subroutines*. For now, here is a simple example that prints the squares of integers and greets us during the first call of the function f:

```
sub f($x) {
    once say 'Hi!';
    say $x * $x;
}

f(1);
f(2);
f(3);
```

The program output is as follows:

```
Hi!
1
4
9
```

Collecting data with gather and take

Preparing data lists can be very expressively organized with a pair of keywords in Perl 6—gather and take. The easiest way to understand how that works is by taking a look at the following example:

```
my @data = gather {
    take 'a';
    take 'b';
}

say @data;
```

The block of code after the gather keyword returns a sequence that is saved in the @data array. The elements of the sequence are provided by the take keywords. So, there will be two elements in @data, as you can see here:

[a b]

Let's consider a bigger example. It contains a two-dimensional matrix of integer numbers and a list of instructions. The instructions are the four directions—left, right, up, and down, and a command— take-it. You should start at the center of the matrix, then move the current position according to the instructions, and pick up numbers if the instruction tells you to.

```
my @matrix = (
    [ 8, 10, 3, 16, 11],
    [ 4, 13, 5, 1, 6],
    [20, 9, 0, 15, 19],
    [14, 2, 24, 7, 23],
    [21, 17, 18, 12, 22],
);

my ($x, $y) = 2, 2; # Starting position
my @instructions = <down down take-it
                    left up up take-it
                    right right up up take-it>;
```

```
my @result = gather {
    for @instructions -> $step {
        if    $step eq 'up'      {$y--}
        elsif $step eq 'down'    {$y++}
        elsif $step eq 'right'   {$x++}
        elsif $step eq 'left'    {$x--}
        elsif $step eq 'take-it' {take @matrix[$y][$x]}
    }
}

say @result; # [18 9 16]
```

The main part of the code is a code block of the `gather` keyword. It contains a loop over `@instructions`, and, depending on the current command, it either changes the coordinates of the current position or takes the number using the `take` keyword, as shown:

```
take @matrix[$y][$x]
```

After the code is completed, the `@result` array will contain three numbers selected according to the given `@instructions`.

Setting the topic with given

In the example in the previous section, we used a chained `if`—`elsif` construction. Let's take a look at this once again:

```
if    $step eq 'up'      {$y--}
elsif $step eq 'down'    {$y++}
elsif $step eq 'right'   {$x++}
elsif $step eq 'left'    {$x--}
elsif $step eq 'take-it' {take @matrix[$y][$x]}
```

It is clearly seen that all the branches contain the same code, which compares the current value of the `$step` variable with one of the predefined values. While being simple and straightforward, this is not the most elegant way of doing such comparisons.

In some languages such as C and C++, the `switch` and `case` keywords help reorganize the `if-else` chain. In Perl 6, we use `given` and `when`. The preceding code can be rewritten in the following way:

```
given $step {
    when 'up'       {$y--}
    when 'down'     {$y++}
    when 'right'    {$x++}
    when 'left'     {$x--}
    when 'take-it' {take @matrix[$y][$x] }
}
```

What happens here is that `given` takes the `$step` variable and makes it the current topic. This means that it is now available via the default variable `$_`. You can clearly see it if you print inside the `given` code block, as shown here:

```
given $step {
    say $_;

    when 'up' {$y--}
    . . .
}
```

Inside `when`, the topic variable is smart-matched with the given value, in other words, `when` `'up'` is equivalent to if `$_` `~~` `'up'`.

After the first keyword `when` finds a match, the rest is not tested. For example, try to print something before the final keyword `when`, as shown here:

```
given $step {
    when 'up'       {$y--}
    when 'down'     {$y++}
    when 'right'    {$x++}
    when 'left'     {$x--}
    say "Can only be 'take-it': $step";
    when 'take-it' {take @matrix[$y][$x] }
}
```

The print instruction will be only accessed when none of the directional commands are caught, as you can see here:

```
Can only be 'take-it': take-it
Can only be 'take-it': take-it
Can only be 'take-it': take-it
[18 9 16]
```

As the `when` keyword performs a smart-match operation, there are more ways to create conditions. For example, it is possible to directly test the type of the variable, as shown in the following piece of code:

```
my @data = 1, 'two', 3, 'four', [1, 2];
for @data {
    when Int {
        say "$_ is an integer";
    }
    when Str {
        say "$_ is a string";
    }
    default {
        say "$_ is something else"
    }
}
```

In this program, the `@data` arrays contain elements of different types—integers and strings. The two `when` statements test the topic against the type names and print one of the following two strings:

```
1 is an integer
two is a string
3 is an integer
four is a string
1 2 is something else
```

If none of the `when` blocks was triggered, the optional `default` block is executed.

As you may have noticed, there is no `given` keyword in the last example. This is because the topic was already set by the `for` loop, and there is no need to set it again.

Conversely, the `given` keyword can be used alone to set the default variable, as you can see here:

```
given 'John' {
    .say # prints $_, which is 'John'
}

given 'John' {
    say "Hello, $_"; # prints 'Hello, John'
}
```

Summary

In this chapter, we covered control flow, which Perl 6 offers for traditional procedural programming. We talked about executing code blocks and taking decisions using the keywords if, else, and elsif. We also talked about different loops—the basic loop, for loops, and the repeat, until, and while loops with pre-conditions or post-conditions. Then we looked at using the gather—take pair to collect data and the way Perl 6 works with topics with the help of the given and when keywords.

Perl 6 is not just capable of working with the procedural programming style. You will find more information about other paradigms in Chapter 13, *Concurrent Programming*, Chapter 14, *Functional Programming*, and Chapter 15, *Reactive Programming*.

Meanwhile, in the next chapter, we will discuss another level for organizing code and subroutines.

6
Subroutines

Subroutines are one of the fundamental concepts in programming. They help organize better-structured code, which is also easy to reuse. Perl 6 offers great support for subroutines and many interesting related features. In Perl 6, subroutines are often called **subs**.

We will cover the following topics in this chapter:

- Creating a subroutine
- Calling a subroutine
- Typed arguments
- Signature properties
- Passing arguments by value or by reference
- Operators as subroutines
- Nested subroutines
- References to subroutines
- Overloading subroutines and multiple dispatch
- Anonymous subroutines and lambdas
- Variable placeholders

Creating and calling subroutines

The `sub` keyword creates a subroutine. A typical subroutine has a name, a list of formal parameters, and a body. However, both the name and the parameter list are optional. In `Chapter 1`, *What is Perl 6?*, we already created a subroutine to add two numbers. Let's recall it here:

```
sub add($x, $y) {
    return $x + $y;
}
```

Here, `add` is the name, which will later be used to call a sub. It is followed by a list of the sub's parameters—`($x, $y)`. The body of the subroutine is enclosed inside a pair of curly braces—`{return $x + $y;}`.

To call a subroutine, use the name again and pass the actual parameters in parentheses:

```
my $a = 17;
my $b = 71;
my $sum = add($a, $b);
say "Sum of $a and $b is $sum"; # Sum of 17 and 71 is 88
```

There are two ways a sub can return a value. The first we just saw in the `add` function. It uses an explicit `return` keyword, as you can see here:

```
return $a + $b;
```

After the `return` call, a sub stops its execution. Any extra code after the `return` statement will not be executed.

In many cases, when the return value is calculated in the last line of the subroutine body, the `return` keyword is not necessary. The last calculated value will be the return value of the subroutine. Taking this into account, let's modify the `add` function as follows:

```
sub add($x, $y) {
    $x + $y
}
```

There is no difference in usage of the function. Notice that a semicolon is not required at the end of the block. In simple functions like the preceding one, this is a good thing to do to make the code a little bit lighter.

Not every subroutine must return a value. It may have some side effects, for example, writing to a database or immediate printing from the subroutine body. In Perl 6, there is no distinction between functions and procedures as in, say, Pascal. To create a sub that does not return a result, simply use the `return` statement with no arguments or omit the whole `return` statement itself. For example, let's modify the `add` subroutine so that it prints the result itself. In this case, it would be better to also rename the subroutine so that the name actually reflects what the sub is doing:

```
sub print_sum($x, $y) {
    say "$x + $y = ", $x + $y;
}

print_sum(10, 30); # 10 + 30 = 40
```

When learning Perl 6, pay additional attention to the spaces between a function name and the opening parenthesis. From Chapter 2, *Writing Code*, we know that when calling a function, no space is allowed between a sub name and the left parenthesis. In many cases, though, no parentheses are required at all. An `add 4, 5` call is behaving exactly the same as `add(4, 5)`. You should devise your own strategy for how you use parentheses with function calls.

Another optional part is the list of arguments. If the sub does not need them, you may either use empty parentheses or omit them completely. In the following example, both styles are used, though it is better to stick to one of them within a program:

```
sub width() {
    1.30
}
sub height {
    2.40
}

say width() * height; # Don't follow this practice
```

Default values

Sometimes, a function, especially when it takes many parameters, can assume some values to be default. In this case, the calling code may omit the default value. To specify the default value of an argument, add the value after the = sign in the function signature:

```
sub add($x, $y = 1) {
    return $x + $y;
}
```

With this function, it is possible to call a function with either one or two arguments, as demonstrated in the following example:

```
say add(5, 6);  # 11
say add(5);     # 6
```

Note that you cannot simply omit an argument if it does not have a default value (or is not declared as optional—see the next section, *Optional parameters*):

```
sub add($x, $y) {
    return $x + $y;
}

say add(5, 6);  # OK
say add(5);     # Error
```

The following compile time error occurs:

```
===SORRY!=== Error while compiling add.pl
Calling add(Int) will never work with declared signature ($x, $y)
at add.pl:6
```

A function cannot have other arguments followed by those that which have default values. So, all the parameters with their default values must be at the end of the argument list. Otherwise, the compiler will not be able to understand what positional arguments are passed to the sub.

Optional parameters

Perl 6 subroutines also allow optional parameters. These parameters are indicated by the question mark in the signature. To check if the argument was passed, use the built-in `defined` built-in function, as demonstrated in the following example:

```
sub greet($name, $greeting?) {
    say((defined $greeting) ?? "$greeting, $name!" !! "$name!");
```

```
}

greet('John');                # John!
greet('John', 'Good morning'); # Good morning, John!
```

Named parameters

So far, we have worked with subs that take a few arguments, and their meaning is defined by their position in the argument list; those arguments are called **positional**. In Perl 6, arguments may also be passed by names. The **named parameters** can appear in the function call at different positions.

Consider an example of a function that calculates the total amount based on the number of items bought and their price, and prints the total value. With regular positional arguments, the function can look like this:

```
sub register($item-name, $item-price, $quantity) {
    my $total = $item-price * $quantity;
    my $plural-ending = $quantity > 1 ?? 's' !! '';
    say "$quantity $item-name$plural-ending cost €$total";
}

register('Book', 30, 1); # 1 Book cost €30
register('Book', 30, 5); # 5 Books cost €150
```

The subroutine takes three parameters and, for the end user, it may be problematic to remember in which order they must follow. Let's avoid this problem by giving the names to the arguments:

```
sub register(:$item-name, :$item-price, :$quantity) {
    my $total = $item-price * $quantity;
    my $plural-ending = $quantity > 1 ?? 's' !! '';
    say "$quantity $item-name$plural-ending cost €$total";
}

register(item-name => 'Book', item-price => 30, quantity => 1);
register(item-name => 'Book', item-price => 30, quantity => 5);
```

Named arguments are prefixed with a colon in the function signature. When calling a function, the values are passed as pairs of their names and values. There are two alternative ways to create a pair—either using the => arrow, as shown in the preceding example, or a colon, as shown in the following example:

```
register(:item-name('Book'), :item-price(30), :quantity(1));
register(:item-name('Book'), :item-price(30), :quantity(5));
```

In the case where you have the values of the function arguments in the variables, whose names are the same as the names of the named parameters, you may pass the values using the same syntax that is used in the definition of a sub, as shown in the following code:

```
my $item-name = 'Book';
my $item-price = 30;
my $quantity = 3;

register(:$item-name, :$item-price, :$quantity); # 3 Books cost €90
```

Positional, optional, and named parameters, as well as parameters with default values, can be used in the same sub. The general rule is that positional parameters come first, and the optional and default come last. If it happens that your function needs too many parameters, maybe it's time to reconsider the approach and introduce, for example, classes (we will discuss them in Chapter 8, *Object-Oriented Programming*), or use **multiple dispatch** as explained later in this chapter in the *Multi subs* section.

Parameter traits

A sub taking arguments uses them in its body. By default, the sub's arguments are read-only values; it is not possible to modify the values inside the sub, as shown in the following code:

```
sub f($a) {
    $a = 0;
}

my $x = 10;
f($x);
```

This leads to the following error:

Cannot assign to a readonly variable ($a) or a value

There are a couple of ways of overcoming that, depending on how you intend to use the modified value. If the modified argument is only needed inside the sub, then create a copy of it, as shown here:

```
sub f($a) {
    my $b = $a;
    $b = 0;
    say "b = $b";
}

my $x = 10;
f($x); # b = 0
```

To avoid creating temporary variables, it is better to mark the sub's argument by appending the is copy trait as follows:

```
sub f($a is copy) {
    $a = 0;
    say "a = $a";
}

my $x = 10;
f($x);   # a = 0
say $x; # 10
```

Perl 6 offers another possibility—the is rw trait—if you want to modify the original variable passed as a parameter to a sub. In this case, the variable outside the sub will have a new value after the call:

```
sub f($a is rw) {
    $a = 0;
}

my $x = 10;
f($x);
say $x; # 0
```

With the is rw trait, it is not possible to pass a constant to a subroutine, because the program will not be able to modify the following:

```
sub f($a is rw) {
    $a = 0;
}

f(5); # Error: Parameter '$a' expected a writable container,
      #          but got Int value
```

Finally, examine the less frequently used trait—is raw. Its behavior is somewhat similar to the is rw trait, but differs in that it can be bound to both variables and constants. Consider the following example of the two subs—one with the is rw trait and another with the is raw argument; neither sub modifies its parameter:

```
sub f($a is rw)  {}
sub g($a is raw) {}
```

Both functions work fine when you pass a variable to it, as shown here:

```
my $x = 10;
f($x);
g($x);
```

However, if you pass a constant, that is, a value without a variable container, the is rw trait will prevent it from being accepted by the sub. The f(5) call emits the following error:

Parameter '$a' expected a writable container, but got Int value

Calling the g function with a constant will still work, although you, of course, will not be able to modify the constant inside the sub:

```
sub g($a is raw) {
    $a = 0;
}

g(5); # Error: Cannot assign to an immutable value
```

Instead of appending the is raw trait, you may use an alternative syntax with the backslash in place of a scalar sigil, as shown in the following code:

```
sub q(\a) {
    a++;
}

my $x = 10;
q($x);
say $x; # 11
```

The backslashed parameters can be found in the source code of the Perl 6 compiler. We will see a few examples in the *Creating operators* section later in this chapter.

Slurpy parameters

The great part of Perl 6 is that it allows passing arrays and hashes in function signatures, Meaning that an array is passed as a single value, not as a list of its values. Consider the following simple example of how the add function can be modified to return the sum of all the elements of an array:

```
sub add(@arr) {
    [+] @arr
}

my @a = <10 20 30>;
say add(@a); # 60
```

The [+] construction is a reduced form of the + operator; see the details in Chapter 4, *Working with Operators*. It returns the sum of all the elements of the @arr array, which is the only argument of the sub.

You may safely add more arguments after the array to the sub. Let's create a function to calculate the sum of the first $n elements of an array:

```
sub sum_first(@a, $n) {
    [+] @a[0..$n - 1]
}

my @a = (1..10);
say sum_first(@a, 5); # 1 + 2 + 3 + 4 + 5 = 15
```

The $n parameter does not get mixed with the contents of the @a array.

What if we try using our previously created add function to get the sum of the elements of an array, which consists of two values?

```
sub add($x, $y) {$x + $y}

my @a = (4, 5);
say add(@a);
```

This code does not compile:

```
===SORRY!=== Error while compiling slurpy.pl
Calling add(Positional) will never work with declared signature ($x, $y)
at slurpy.pl:4
------> say ⬜add(@a);
```

The sub expects one array but gets two scalars, which is wrong. To let the add function accept the values of an array, the array should be **flattened**. That is, when passing to a function, an array becomes a list of its values. Flattening arrays is achieved by prefixing them with a vertical bar, as shown here:

```
sub add($x, $y) {$x + $y}

my @a = (4, 5);
say add(|@a); # 9
```

Now consider the opposite situation—you pass a list of scalars to a function that takes an array. In this case, you should declare the array argument as **slurpy**. It will consume the scalars and accumulate them in a single variable. This is demonstrated in the next example. The slurpy argument is prefixed with a star, as shown in the following lines of code:

```
sub add(*@a) {[+] @a}

say add(3, 4, 5, 6); # 18
```

As the slurpy array will consume the rest of the argument list, it should be the last argument in the sub's signature.

Parameter placeholders

Even if the signature of the sub is missing, the sub can still take and use parameters. Perl 6 defines the so-called **placeholders**, which are the variables with the ^ twigil inside a sub . We can see this in the following code:

```
sub greet {
    say "Hello, $^name!";
}

greet('Mark'); # Hello, Mark!
```

In this code, the $^name variable takes the value of the string passed at the function call. The value becomes a read-only parameter of the sub.

If there is more than one parameter, their order corresponds to the alphabetical order of the placeholders:

```
sub subtract {
    $^b - $^a
}
say subtract(10, 8); # -2
```

The values 10 and 8 reside in the `$^a` and `$^b` variables here.

When using placeholders, a function cannot have a signature that conflicts with the number and type of the placeholders. So, in the preceding examples, you cannot define functions such as `greet() {...}` or `subtract() {...}` with empty parentheses.

Type constraints

In Perl 6, you don't have to declare a type of a variable, but you can do so if you want to. The same rules apply to the arguments of a sub and to its return value.

Typed parameters

In the previous sections of this chapter, we did not say anything about the types of the `$a` and `$b` parameters of the `add` function. The code of the sub assumes that the arguments should be numeric because the + operator is used. Calling a function with two strings as arguments, for example, `add('Hello', 'World')`, will generate the following runtime error:

Cannot convert string to number: base-10 number must begin with valid digits or '.' in '⬜Hello' (indicated by ⬜)

This exception happens at runtime. Although the compiler sees that you pass two strings, it does not check if the + operation is defined for the two arguments of that type. It is possible to prevent these kinds of errors at compile time by specifying the types of the sub arguments, as shown:

```
sub add(Int $x, Int $b) {
    return $x + $b;
}
```

Calling the sub with integer numbers is OK. Calling it with strings raises a compile-time error:

```
===SORRY!=== Error while compiling add.pl
Calling add(Str, Str) will never work with declared signature (Int $x, Int
$b)
```

In the declaration of a sub, the list of arguments is called a **signature**. The error message tells us that the signature of the function that we want to call does not agree with the signature of the function that is defined in the program. Namely, it needs to call a function whose name is add and whose signature is (Str, Str). The code contains a subroutine named add, but its signature is different: (Int $x, Int $b). The names of the parameters themselves are not important in the signature check.

Type constraints can be made even stricter. To prevent a subroutine from accepting undefined values, add the :D trait after the type name as follows:

```
sub add(Int:D $x, Int:D $b) {
    return $x + $b;
}
```

Only defined (thus the name :D) values will pass the type check now:

```
my $a;
my $b = 10;

# add($a, $b); # Run time error because $a is not defined.

add($b, 20);   # Fine. Both operands are Int:D
```

Return type

The type of a value returned from a sub can also be attributed with the particular type constraint. There are three ways of doing it in Perl 6.

The first method is an arrow at the end of the signature:

```
sub add(Int $x, Int $y --> Int) {
    return $x + $y;
}
```

This method is the most universal. It allows not only for specifying the type of the return value, but also for giving an explicit constant:

```
sub funky_add(Int, Int --> 100) {}
```

This function will always return 100, regardless of the argument values. In the next section, *Multi subs*, we will see a more useful application of returning a constant.

Another way of specifying a return type is to use the `of` keyword between the signature and the body of a sub, as shown here:

```
sub add(Int $x, Int $y) of Int {
    return $x + $y;
}
```

Finally, the return type can be placed in front of the sub's name, similar to how the type of a variable is defined. Note that you need to declare a sub as `my` in this case:

```
my Int sub add(Int $x, Int $y) {
    return $x + $y;
}
```

The actual value that is returned from a sub must be of the specified type. If it is not, a runtime error occurs. Let's break our `add` function and return the result of division rather than addition:

```
sub add(Int $x, Int $y --> Int) {
    return $x / $y;
}

say add(1, 2);
```

The code will be compiled, but you cannot execute it:

```
Type check failed for return value; expected Int but got Rat (0.5)
  in sub add at return.pl line 1
  in block <unit> at return.pl line 5
```

Note that the same error will also take place even if the result can be converted to an integer value without losing data, as in the `add(10, 2)` call. The result type here is still `Rat`, not `Int`.

Multi subs

The signature is an important property of a sub. It not only helps to check the types of the arguments, but Perl 6 also uses it to control the number of arguments passed. For example, declare a function for summation that takes three parameters, but call it with only two arguments:

```
sub add($x, $y, $z) {
    return $x + $y + $z;
}

say add(1, 2);
```

This program does not work. Again, signature is our friend:

```
===SORRY!=== Error while compiling add.pl
Calling add(Int, Int) will never work with declared signature ($x, $y, $z)
at add.pl:5
```

So, we see that when deciding which function to call, Perl 6 takes into account the number of the arguments as well as their types together with the name of the sub. A programmer can benefit from this feature by creating different versions of the function, which share the same name. The distinction between them will be resolved via their signatures.

Let's now put both variants of the add function together (I will format it differently this time). To inform the compiler that your intention is to create multiple variants, add the multi keyword:

```
multi sub add($x, $y)     {$x + $y}
multi sub add($x, $y, $z) {$x + $y + $z}
```

Now it is possible to call the add function with either two or three arguments, as shown here:

```
say add(1, 2);    # 3
say add(1, 2, 3); # 6
```

No reasons for the compiler to complain now. It barely calls one of the multi subs, depending on the number of arguments used in a call.

Similarly, typed arguments can be used to choose between multi subs. Let's make it possible to use the `add` name to add strings. For this, a concatenation operator (~) can be used. Let's create two functions with the same name and different signatures:

```
multi sub add(Int $x, Int $y) {$x + $y}
multi sub add(Str $x, Str $y) {$x ~ $y}
```

Now it is possible to write the following code:

```
say add(4, 2);       # 6
say add('4', '2');   # 42
```

Different functions will be called in response to these calls. And, despite the fact that the '4' and '2' strings contain only numbers, they are the values of the Str type in the first place.

Typed arguments may be used for finer separation between different variants of the function. For example, let's create three functions for the Int, Rat, and Num values:

```
multi sub f(Int) {say 'f(Int)'}
multi sub f(Rat) {say 'f(Rat)'}
multi sub f(Num) {say 'f(Num)'}

f(10);    # f(Int)
f(20/2);  # f(Rat)
f(1E1);   # f(Num)
```

This example is only to demonstrate how Perl 6 selects the right **candidate** of the multi sub. The functions do not do anything useful with the arguments, and I did not even give a name to the arguments. As you can see from the output (see the comments in the preceding code), the three calls refer to the three different multi subs.

With `multi`, the `sub` keyword can be omitted, as shown in the following code:

```
multi f(Int) {say 'f(Int)'}
multi f(Rat) {say 'f(Rat)'}
multi f(Num) {say 'f(Num)'}
```

Multi subs can do even more. Multiple dispatch can be routed, based not only on different types, but also values. For example, let's create a sub that takes the Num values and a separate sub that should only be triggered for the value of Pi:

```
multi sub f(pi) {say 'The value of Pi is well-known!'}
multi sub f(Num $n) {say "Value is $n"}

f(pi); # The value of Pi is well-known!
f(e);  # Value is 2.71828182845905
```

This approach also works fine with other data of other types; strings, for instance.

Finally, multi subs are ideal for the types that the user creates. We will talk about using classes in Chapter 8, *Object-Oriented Programming*. So, let's create a subtype and split the values into two groups.

We create two subs, one of which takes a single Str argument, and another that takes only strings that are shorter than ten characters:

```
multi sub message(Str $str) {
    '<p>' ~ $str ~ '</b>'
}
multi sub message(Str $str where {$str.chars < 10}) {
    q{<p class="large">} ~ $str ~ q{</p>}
}

say message('Hi!');
say message('The weather is fine today');
```

The program prints the HTML code with a message, but adds a CSS class to make the font bigger for short texts:

```
<p class="large">Hi!</p>
<p>The weather is fine today</p>
```

An example

To summarize our knowledge of multi subs, let's create an example of recursive calculation of the Fibonacci numbers. We will also use type constraints in this code:

```
multi sub fibonacci(0 --> 0) {}
multi sub fibonacci(1 --> 1) {}
multi sub fibonacci(Int $n --> Int) {
    return fibonacci($n - 1) + fibonacci($n - 2);
}
```

```
my @fib;
push @fib, fibonacci($_) for 1..10;
@fib.join(', ').say;
```

The multi subs are used here to bootstrap the recursive `fibonacci($n - 1) +`
`fibonacci($n - 2)` formula for the values of `$n` less than 2. The first two variants of the
`fibonacci` sub respond to the values of 0 and 1. Instead of returning an integer in the sub
body, we will use the arrow syntax to specify the return value in the signature, as shown
here:

```
multi sub fibonacci(0 --> 0) {}
multi sub fibonacci(1 --> 1) {}
```

Nested subroutines

Subroutines can be nested. In other words, you may define a sub inside another sub. Let's
see it in the next example, which lists the present tense forms of regular English verbs:

```
sub list_verb_forms($verb) {
    sub make_form($base, $pronoun) {
        my $form = $base;
        # Adds the 's' ending for he, she, and it.
        # The check uses a regular expression.
        # We cover regular expressions in Chapter 11, Regexes.
        $form ~= 's' if $pronoun ~~ /^ [ he | she | it ] $/;

        return "$pronoun $form";
    }

    my @pronouns = <I we you he she it they>;

    for @pronouns -> $pronoun {
        say make_form($verb, $pronoun);
    }
}

list_verb_forms('read');
```

The result of this program is exactly what we wanted, as you can see here:

```
I read
we read
you read
he reads
she reads
it reads
they read
```

The `list_verb_forms` function iterates over a list of pronouns in the `@pronouns` array and calls the `make_form` subroutine for each of them. Because we don't need the second sub anywhere in the code, it is logical to limit the scope of it to the body of the first sub.

Nesting a sub inside another sub makes it invisible for the rest of the code. You cannot call the `make_form` sub anywhere outside of the body of `list_verb_forms`:

```
===SORRY!=== Error while compiling /Users/ash/code/nested.pl
Undeclared routine:
    make_form used at line 20
```

Creating operators

Operators in Perl 6 are subroutines. In most cases, operator subs are multisubs. Consider, for example, the + operator. Its semantic is to add two values, which, in turn, can be of different types. You may ask Perl 6 to add two integers, floating points, or complex numbers. Or, the operands may be of different types in the same call, say, when adding a complex number and an integer. The same + operator also works fine with the types representing dates. To achieve all of this flexibility, Perl 6 uses multi subs.

Let's briefly lurk into the source code of Rakudo and search for a few definitions of the + operator:

```
multi sub infix:<+>(Int:D \a, Int:D \b)
multi sub infix:<+>(Num:D \a, Num:D \b)

multi sub infix:<+>(Complex:D \a, Complex:D \b)
multi sub infix:<+>(Complex:D \a, Num(Real) \b)
multi sub infix:<+>(Num(Real) \a, Complex:D \b)

multi sub infix:<+>(Date:D $d, Int:D $x)
multi sub infix:<+>(Int:D $x, Date:D $d)
```

The Rakudo compiler is partially written in Perl 6 itself, so you can easily understand the function headers in these excerpts.

In Perl 6, it is also possible to create a custom operator that can be used in your code. Also, it is possible to extend the behavior of operators for the types created in the program.

For example, if you want the + operator to concatenate strings, simply define its behavior for the string operands, as shown here:

```
multi sub infix:<+>(Str $a, Str $b) {
    $a ~ $b
}

say 'Hello, ' + 'World!';
```

It is very likely that you will also need to think about other possible combinations of operand types. Imagine that we are creating the code to print an error message and want to use a + operator to append a number, as shown:

```
say 'Error at line ' + 5;
```

This will not work because there is no candidate for the + operator that takes a string and an integer. One of the alternatives is to perform a type cast:

```
say 'Error at line ' + ~5;
```

Now we have two strings and the `infix:<+>(Str, Str)` operator will be chosen by the compiler.

To make the work of the developer easier, it is better to define more variants for the operator so that their use becomes intuitive. So, let's add the `infix:<+>(Str, Int)` to our collection:

```
multi sub infix:<+>(Str $a, Int $b) {
    $a ~ ~$b
    # Or: $a ~ $b.Str
}
```

Now the `'Error at line ' + 5` code becomes valid.

Maybe you will also need to define the operator that takes an integer as the left-hand side operand and the string as the right-hand side one:

```
multi sub infix:<+>(Int $a, Str $b) {
    ~$a ~ $b
}

say 5 + ' errors';
```

As we've seen, creating new operators is a very responsible task. You should think and predict possible use cases and define the corresponding subroutines.

In the preceding examples, we used one of the already existing operator signs in Perl 6. In your program, you may also define a new operator and choose how the operator looks yourself. The following example defines an infix operator called `plus`, which adds up two integer numbers similar to how the + operator does:

```
sub infix:<plus>(Int $x, Int $y --> Int) {$x + $y}

say 10 plus 20; # 30
```

When defining new operators, make sure their semantics is clear to the user of your code. For example, if you define the + operator for string operands, that may be confusing, as demonstrated in the following example.

```
multi sub infix:<+>(Str $a, Str $b) {
    $a ~ $b;
}

say "4" + "9";
```

Without the redefined infix operator, the `"4" + "9"` returns `13`, as both operands are converted to Numeric values. With the `infix:<+>(Str, Str)` defined, the program prints `49`, as the operands are strings, and there is an infix sub that accepts two string arguments.

Passing functions as arguments

Functions in Perl 6 can be passed to other functions as arguments. A typical example is a sort algorithm that needs a function to compare two values. Depending on the data types, it can be different functions that know how to compare the values of that type.

Let's examine the following tiny example:

```
sub less($a, $b) {$a < $b}
sub more($a, $b) {$a > $b}

sub compare($a, $b, $f) {
    $f($a, $b)
}

say compare(10, 20, &less); # True
say compare(10, 20, &more); # False
```

The main code calls the `compare` sub with three arguments—two integer numbers and a reference to one of the functions—`&less` or `&more`. An ampersand before the name tells us that a function should not be called at this point (remember that, in Perl 6, parentheses are not required when calling a function).

Inside the `compare` function, the third argument `$f` is a reference to a function. You can now call the referenced function by appending a list of arguments—`$f($a, $b)`. This will be equivalent to calling either `less($a, $b)` or `more($a, $b)`.

The type of the `$f` argument is `Sub`; we can add a type constraint to the sub signature to force that usage:

```
sub compare($a, $b, Sub:D $f) {
    $f($a, $b)
}
```

Notice that the call of `$f $a, $b` will not be compiled, as `$f` is not a name of a sub. Parentheses here are the shortened form of the `.()` postcircumfix call—`$f.($a, $b)`.

Anonymous subs

A subroutine without a name is called an **anonymous sub**. You cannot call it by name, but it is still possible to run it via a handle, which, for example, is stored in a variable. All the attributes of a regular sub, such as a signature and a body, are defined in the same way as the normal subs.

In the following code, we will create an anonymous sub and save it in the `$add` variable; a space before the signature is required:

```
my $add = sub ($x, $y) {$x + $y}
say $add(10, 20); # 30
```

Perl 6 allows a mixture of regular and anonymous subs. The anon keyword creates an anonymous sub out of the regular one, so its name can still be used to call it. First, look at the sub, which can be used both as an anonymous one and be called by its name:

```
my $add = sub add ($x, $y) {$x + $y}
say $add(1, 2); # using anonymous sub
say add(3, 4);  # using regular sub call by name
```

Now, let us use the anon keyword:

```
my $add = anon sub add($a, $b) {$a + $b}
say $add(3, 4);  # ok
# say add(3, 4); # won't compile
```

Calling the function via the $add variable is fine, while an attempt to call a function by its name cannot even be compiled—Perl 6 does not put the add name in the table of local symbols because anon explicitly forbids that.

Instead of anonymous subs, you may also use anonymous blocks of code. They are called **pointy blocks**, as they use an arrow, as shown in this example:

```
my $add = -> $x, $y {$x + $y};
say $add(7, 8); # 15
```

The difference between an anonymous sub and a pointy block is that they return objects of different types. A sub's type is Sub, while a pointy block creates a Block:

```
my $sub = sub ($x) {$x * 2};
my $block = -> $x {$x * 2};

say $sub.^name;   # Sub
say $block.^name; # Block
```

In the hierarchy of Perl 6 object system, the Sub class is a child of the Routine class, which is a child of Block. The Routine class provides us with additional functionality such as adding traits or making the sub a multi-sub.

Also, notice that the arguments of a pointy block are not listed in parentheses. In case you add them, Perl 6 will think that you want to pass an array when calling a block. This is demonstrated in the following example:

```
my $add = -> ($x, $y) {$x + $y};
my @a = <5 6>;
say $add(@a);
```

Passing two arguments leads to the following exception:

```
my $add = -> ($x, $y) {$x + $y};
say $add(5, 6); # Error: Too few positionals passed;
                # expected 2 arguments but got 0 in sub-signature
```

Summary

Subroutines, or subs, are one of the keystones of Perl 6. In this chapter, you learned how to create and use subroutines. We examined in detail the properties of the sub's parameters, such as passing parameters by copy, allowing read-and-write parameters, defining the default value, or providing parameters that are optional. You looked at the slurpy parameters and flattening arrays, learned how to constrain the type of both the arguments, and then return value.

On top of that, other applications of the subroutines were discussed. Namely, we talked about overloading subs with the `multi` keyword, looked at how new operators can be created and embedded in the language, and how to pass functions to other functions. And, finally, we took a brief look at anonymous functions and pointy code blocks.

In the next chapter, we'll talk about modules, which are the next level of encapsulating code in Perl 6.

7
Modules

In the previous chapter, we talked about subroutines. Subroutines make code more readable and easier to reuse.

The following topics will be covered in this chapter:

- Organizing code in modules
- Loading modules
- Exporting names
- Introspection
- Module location
- Installing and uninstalling modules

Creating a module

Modules in Perl 6 serve the purpose of keeping code in separate files. It may be a simple library consisting of a couple of functions developed by you, or it may be a big collection of classes that is developed by an external company. In any case, if you use a module, you get the power of the previous work and have an interface to reach that functionality.

In this chapter, we will talk about organizing code in modules and using them in a program.

Let us create our first module and let's take the simple task of adding numbers that we were exploiting in earlier chapters, for example, in `Chapter 2`, *Writing Code*.

So, we have an add function for adding up two numbers and the code that uses it:

```
sub add($a, $b) {
    return $a + $b;
}

my $a = 10;
my $b = 20;
my $sum = add($a, $b);
say $sum; # 30
```

Our current goal is to put the code of the add function into a separate module and then use that module in the main program.

Perl 6 modules are usually kept in files with the .pm extension (which stands for Perl module). If for some reason you want to emphasize the usage of Perl 6 to distinguish it from Perl 5, for example, you can use the .pm6 extension; in that case it is better to use .p6 as an extension for Perl 6 programs.

Let us create a file for our example and copy the code of the function to it. However, that is not enough. A module must have a name, which is mentioned in the unit module directive, placed in the beginning of the file:

```
unit module Add;

sub add($a, $b) {
    return $a + $b;
}
```

It is better to keep the module's name and the name of the corresponding file consistent. In our case, the Add module is located in the file Add.pm. In the *How Rakudo stores modules* section later in this chapter, you will see how Rakudo manages more complex relations between the names of the files and the names of the modules.

Now, let us try using the module and rewrite the main program so that it calls a function from it:

```
use Add;

my $a = 10;
my $b = 20;
my $sum = add($a, $b);
say $sum;
```

Notice the directive `use Add;` in the beginning of this file. To satisfy that, Perl 6 will find and load the corresponding module file.

Our code is not working yet though. Let us try executing it and then try locating the errors:

```
$ perl6 main.pl

===SORRY!===
Could not find Add at line 1 in:
    /Users/ash/.perl6
    /Applications/Rakudo/share/perl6/site
    /Applications/Rakudo/share/perl6/vendor
    /Applications/Rakudo/share/perl6
    CompUnit::Repository::AbsolutePath<140518513192432>
    CompUnit::Repository::NQP<140518512012576>
    CompUnit::Repository::Perl5<140518512012616>
```

As you see, the compiler was not able to locate the `Add.pm` file. It tried to search in a few directories, which are considered default, but failed. As the file is kept in the same directory where the `main.pl` file is located, we can help the compiler and give it the location using the `-I` command-line option:

```
$ perl6 -I . main.pl
```

Now, the module file is found but we still get an error:

```
===SORRY!=== Error while compiling /Users/ash/code/modules/main.pl
Undeclared routine:
    add used at line 5. Did you mean 'dd'?
```

The problem now is that the name `add` is not known to the compiler. We have a function with that name in the module but it is not visible to the code that uses the module. To solve this, we have to inform the compiler that the name is exported and may be used outside of the module. Append the `is export` trait to the function:

```
unit module Add;

sub add($a, $b) is export {
    return $a + $b;
}
```

With that, we can finally run the program and get the desired result:

```
$ perl6 -I . main.pl
30
```

Without the `is export` trait, any function of the module is hidden from the outside world and can be used inside the module as its internal mechanism, which is not exposed to your code. This helps solve name clashes between the functions in different parts of the program and also allows better interface to the module—it only exports the functions that really need to be exported.

Alternatively, instead of an explicit `use Add;` directive in the main code, you may request loading a module via the command line using the `-M` option:

```
$ perl6 -M Add -I . main.pl
30
```

To simplify the command and avoid repeated instructions, the path to the modules may be passed via the `PERL6LIB` environment variable:

```
$ export PERL6LIB=.
$ perl6 main.pl
```

Multiple directories must be separated by a comma:

```
$ export PERL6LIB=/Users/ash/lib,/Users/ash/code/modules
$ perl6 main.pl
```

Using modules

In the previous section, we created a simple module with a single function in it, and used the module in a program. In this section, we will examine other methods of how Perl 6 can load the module and its functions.

There are four keywords that we are going to explore— `use`, `need`, `require` and `import`. They all are used in the context of loading modules but behave a bit differently.

Using a module assumes at least two things—first, the module file has to be found and compiled; second, the names from the module (such as subroutines or variables) should become visible to the program.

The need keyword

The `need` keyword loads a module at compile time but does not import the names from it. Loading a module also means that all the instructions within it will be executed. Also, the `BEGIN` block will be run. Let us add a couple of printing instructions to the module and see how it changes the output.

Here is the new module:

```
unit module Add;

say 'Start';

sub add($a, $b) is export {
    return $a + $b;
}

BEGIN {
    say 'This is Add.pm';
}
```

In the main program, we use `need` instead of `use` this time, as shown:

```
need Add;

my $a = 10;
my $b = 20;
my $sum = add($a, $b);
say $sum;
```

Because the functions from the module are not imported to the program, it will not work, although, the output from the module itself will appear (the `BEGIN` module is triggered first, as it is in regular programs):

```
$ perl6 -I . main.pl
This is Add.pm
Start
===SORRY!=== Error while compiling /Users/ash/code/modules/main.pl
Undeclared routine:
    add used at line 5. Did you mean 'dd'?
```

The import keyword

The `import` keyword imports the names from the module, which have the `export` trait.

In combination with `need`, `import` completes the process of getting functionality from a module. Let's update the program and run it:

```
need Add;
import Add;

say add(10, 20);
```

This time, everything works and the program prints the result returned by the `add` function. Consider the following code:

```
$ perl6 -I . main.pl
This is Add.pm
Start
30
```

Notice that bare `import` is not sufficient for loading a module. It should follow the `need` instruction.

Both `need` and `import` happen at compile time. This means that after a program is compiled, these instructions are executed before the main program. From a practical point of view that means that you should not reckon on the position of these instructions in your program. For example, the following program still works, while the `need` and `import` pair is located at the end of the code:

```
say add(10, 20); # 30

need Add;
import Add;
```

The use keyword

The `use` keyword actually works as a combination of `need` and `import`. Similarly, it works at compile time, so the actual position of the `use` directive is not important (but see the *Scoping* section later in this chapter).

This keyword is the easiest and the most straightforward way to load a module.

```
use Add;

say add(10, 20); # 30
```

As soon as the module is loaded, use automatically imports the names from it and they become available in the rest of the program.

The require keyword

The last keyword, require, loads a module at runtime. Therefore, order is important. To access the functions from the module, we need fully qualified names now. In turn, to allow a module to use its functions, they must be scoped differently, with the help of our keyword.

The following code is the new version of the file Add.pm:

```
unit module Add;

our sub add($a, $b) {
    return $a + $b;
}
```

And here is a program that requires the module and references the add function using its full name:

```
require Add;

say Add::add(10, 20); # 30
```

Notice that the fully qualified named is constructed with the help of ::. In the next example, we will use the module name that is stored in a variable and may be changed somehow in the rest of the program, before the module is required.

```
my $module = 'Add.pm';
# ...
require $module '&add';
say add(10, 20); # 30
```

Here, the add routine is imported from the Add.pm module. It should be marked as is export there:

```
unit module Add;

our sub add($a, $b) is export {
    return $a + $b;
}
```

Scoping

The above listed four directives for loading modules and how importing names can be scoped, for example, inside functions in the main code. In this case, their action is limited to the given scope.

For example, if the add function is only required inside some function, there is no need to load a module globally, as shown in the following example:

```
say do_calc();

sub do_calc {
    use Add;
    return add(10, 20);
}
```

It is important to realize that although the scope of the exported name is restricted to the do_calc function only, the module is still loaded at compile time. Let us modify both the program and the module so that we see what happens when.

Add a simple say instruction to the program:

```
say 'Starting a program';
say do_calc();

sub do_calc {
    use Add;
    return add(10, 20);
}
```

In the same manner, add it to the module:

```
unit module Add;

say 'Starting a module';

sub add($a, $b) is export {
    return $a + $b;
}
```

Now, run the program and confirm that the module is loaded before the program starts execution:

```
$ perl6 -I . main.pl
Starting a module
Starting a program
30
```

If you want to load a module conditionally so that it only happens under a certain condition or in a particular branch of the code, use the require keyword. In that case, you may easily load the required modules depending on the flow of the program. Consider a variant of the previous program:

```
say 'Starting a program';
say do_calc();

sub do_calc {
    require Add;
    return Add::add(10, 20);
}
```

In this case, the output will be different (don't forget to put our before the function in the module):

```
$ perl6 -I . main.pl
Starting a program
Starting a module
30
```

More on is export

The use of the is export trait, which we saw in the previous sections, is not limited to exporting subs only.

Exporting variables

It is possible to export a variable from a module:

```
unit module Credentials;

our $username is export = 'alpha'
```

Using this variable is as simple as using a regular variable:

```
use Credentials;

say "User = $username";
```

Selective import

Sometimes a module can offer vast functionality and only a portion of it is used by a program. In this case, you may organize a module in such a way that only a limited collection of the names is exported. Perl 6 provides a mechanism for tagging the names, as shown in the following example of a module:

```
unit module Math;

sub add($a, $b) is export(:plusminus) {
    return $a + $b;
}

sub subtract($a, $b) is export(:plusminus) {
    return $a - $b;
}

sub mul($a, $b) is export(:muldiv) {
    return $a * $b;
}

sub div($a, $b) is export(:muldiv) {
    return $a / $b;
}
```

In this module, there are two collections of the functions: two with the `:plusminus` tag and two with the `:muldiv` tag.

While importing a module, use the tag to select the names to import. For example, let us only import the two functions `add` and `subtract`:

```
use Math :plusminus;

say add(10, 20);
say subtract(20, 10);
```

The other two functions, `mul` and `div`, will not be available with that import. To allow them, import the module again with a different tag or list all the required tags as shown in the following example:

```
use Math :plusminus, :muldiv;

say add(10, 20);
say subtract(20, 10);

say mul(1, 2);
say div(5, 2);
```

There are three predefined tags—:ALL, :DEFAULT, and :MANDATORY.

The :ALL tag imports all the names with any is export trait. That includes a bare trait with no tags, a trait with a named tag or a trait with the :ALL tag. For example, instead of two use lines from the previous example, you may use a single line with the same effect:

```
use Math :ALL;
```

The use directive with the :DEFAULT tag loads those names, which are created with the is export trait without any tags.

Finally, to force the import of a name regardless of the importing method, mark it as is export(:MANDATORY) in the module.

Introspection

Perl 6 modules contain a mechanism that allows you to get information about the content of the module. Obtaining this meta-information is called **introspection**.

Take the Math.pm modules from the previous section, *More on* is export, as an example. This is how we can list all the methods that are exported by that module:

```
use Math;

say Math::EXPORT::.keys;
```

This refers to the default EXPORT sub, which the compiler generated for us. The sub returns an object of the EXPORT type that implements the Perl6::Metamodel::PackageHOW interface. We'll not go deep into that theory and will limit ourselves to calling a useful method keys that gives us a list of the tags available in the module:

(plusminus muldiv ALL)

Having the list of tags, we can iterate over them to get the list of subroutines that belong to them:

```
use Math;

say Math::EXPORT::plusminus::.keys;
say Math::EXPORT::muldiv::.keys;
say Math::EXPORT::ALL::.keys;
```

This program prints the following three lines, one per each tag:

```
(&add &subtract)
(&mul &div)
(&mul &div &add &subtract)
```

So, you clearly see that the :plusminus tag corresponds to the functions add and subtract, the :muldiv tag—to mul and div, and the :ALL tag gives the list of all the exported functions. Similarly, if we had subs marked as is export :DEFAULT or is export :MANDATORY, we could request the list of them using the same approach.

Now, let us continue with automation of the process of managing modules in Perl 6.

Using zef

Please note that this section describes a tool that is specific to the Rakudo Star distribution. At the time of writing, Rakudo is the only production-ready Perl 6 compiler available on the market. If you happen to use other compilers, please check their documentation on how to install modules.

The Rakudo Star distribution comes with a handy module management tool called zef. Notice that it has been part of the distribution since Rakudo Star version 2017.01. Earlier releases include another tool, panda, which has now become obsolete.

zef is a command-line tool written in Perl 6. After installing Rakudo Star, its executable file will be in the Rakudo/share/perl6/site/bin directory. The Rakudo installer also fixes the PATH environment variable so that it contains a correct path to the directories with executable files of the distribution.

This tool uses the ecosystem of Perl 6 modules, which is still under active development. To learn more about it, visit the modules.perl6.org page, which contains a list of hundreds of modules available for Perl 6 and zef.

To get zef's help, run it with the -h command-line option:

```
$ zef -h
```

Let us explore the most useful commands.

Installing a module

To install a module, use the `install` command and give the module name, for example:

```
$ zef install XML
```

Before installing a module, you can quickly check whether you already have it installed by asking Perl 6 to load a module with the -M command-line option:

```
$ perl6 -M XML -e1
```

If there's no such module, you'll get an error message listing the folders that Perl 6 scanned in its attempts to find the module:

```
===SORRY!===
Could not find XML at line 1 in:
    /Users/ash/.perl6
    /Applications/Rakudo/share/perl6/site
    /Applications/Rakudo/share/perl6/vendor
    /Applications/Rakudo/share/perl6
```

So, let's install it. If everything goes well, the module will be installed and you can immediately start using it. The output of the installation process may look like the following:

```
$ zef install XML
===> Searching for: XML
===> Fetching: XML
===> Testing: XML:ver('0.0.2'):auth('Timothy Totten')
t/comments.t .......... ok
t/emitter.t .......... ok
t/example.t .......... ok
t/make.t ............. ok
t/namespaces.t ........ ok
t/open-xml.t .......... ok
t/parser.t ........... ok
t/preamble.t .......... ok
t/proxies.t .......... ok
t/query-methods.t ..... ok
t/query-positional.t .. ok
All tests successful.
Files=11, Tests=127, 9 wallclock secs
Result: PASS
===> Testing [OK] for XML:ver('0.0.2'):auth('Timothy Totten')
===> Installing: XML:ver('0.0.2'):auth('Timothy Totten')
```

In this example, we installed the XML module, which required no dependencies. The output displays different stages of the installation process—first, zef looked for the location of the distributive, then it downloaded it, then tested it and finally installed it to the correct location.

It is zef's task to find the location of the distributive files in the internet, download and unpack it. The utility understands a few formats, which is well demonstrated by the following extracts from the documentation.

First, the module can be searched by its name, alternatively with the specification of the author or version number:

```
$ zef install CSV::Parser
$ zef install "CSV::Parser:auth<tony-o>:ver<0.1.2>"
$ zef install "CSV::Parser:ver('0.1.2')"
```

Then, it is possible to install a module by passing the local path:

```
$ zef install ./Perl6-Net--HTTP
```

If zef cannot deduct the URL of the module (which may happen, for example, if the module is not listed on modules.perl6.org), then the URL can be specified explicitly.

```
$ zef -v install git://github.com/ugexe/zef.git
$ zef -v install https://github.com/ugexe/zef/archive/master.tar.gz
$ zef -v install https://github.com/ugexe/zef.git@v0.1.22
```

Notice that zef displays full details of the module it is installing together with its version and the author:

```
===> Installing: XML:ver('0.0.2'):auth('Timothy Totten')
```

Other modules may require dependencies, and zef will try to satisfy them. For example, installing XML::XPath will lead to installing a number of other modules:

```
$ zef install XML::XPath
===> Searching for: XML::XPath
===> Searching for missing dependencies: Test::META
===> Searching for missing dependencies: META6
===> Searching for missing dependencies: JSON::Class
===> Searching for missing dependencies: JSON::Marshal, JSON::Unmarshal
===> Searching for missing dependencies: JSON::Name
===> Fetching: XML::XPath
===> Fetching: Test::META
===> Fetching: META6
===> Fetching: JSON::Class
===> Fetching: JSON::Unmarshal
```

```
===> Fetching: JSON::Marshal
===> Fetching: JSON::Name
```

. . .

The `install` command also accepts fully specified module names, so if you need to install a particular version, say it clearly:

```
$ zef install "XML:ver('0.0.2'):auth('Timothy Totten')"
```

`zef` also supports installing from a given URL or a file.

Searching for a module

Before installing a module, it may be a good idea to see what other modules exist or what other versions of the desired module appear. Use the `search` command:

```
$ zef search Time
===> Found 14 results
```

This is followed by a table displaying all found modules together with their versions and brief descriptions.

Uninstalling modules

To uninstall a module, use the `uninstall` command:

```
$ zef uninstall XML
===> Uninstalled from /Applications/Rakudo/share/perl6/site
XML:ver('0.0.2'):auth('Timothy Totten')
```

If a module was installed together with its dependencies, they will not be removed. For example, let us try uninstalling the `XML::XPath` module, which we installed in the *Installing a module* section earlier in this chapter:

```
$ zef uninstall XML::XPath
===> Uninstalled from /Applications/Rakudo/share/perl6/site
XML::XPath:ver('0.9.0')
```

That's all. Other dependent modules, for example, `JSON::Class`, are still there:

```
$ perl6 -MJSON::Class -e'say 1'
1
```

zef command summary

`zef` is the default module manager for Rakudo Perl 6. The following table summarizes the commands that it provides.

Command	Desciption
`install`	Install specific modules by name or path
`uninstall`	Uninstall specified distributions
`test`	Run tests on a given module's path
`fetch`	Fetch and extract a module's source
`build`	Run `Build.pm` in a given module's path
`look`	Fetch followed by shelling into the module's path
`update`	Update package indexes for repositories
`search`	Show a list of possible distribution candidates for the given terms
`info`	Show detailed distribution information
`list`	List known available distributions
`list --installed`	List installed distributions
`rdepends`	List all distributions directly depending on a given module
`locate`	Lookup installed module information
`smoke`	Run smoke testing on available modules

More information about how to use `zef` can be found on the project page at `github.com/ugexe/zef`.

How Rakudo stores modules

Perl 6 modules are referenced by three parameters: module name, author name and module version. Traditionally, in Perl 5, module names were mapped directly into the file system, but in Perl 6 we have to deal with three dimensions. In this section, we will take a look at the directory in which Rakudo and `zef` store modules and track information about their parameters.

Let us see how Rakudo keeps modules in the filesystem for the example of the XML::XPath module.

In the installation directory of Rakudo (on macOS, this is /Applications/Rakudo), you will find the following four directories:

```
bin
include
lib
share
```

Modules are located inside the tree of the share directory. Every module may have at least three files. First, there is a JSON file in the share/perl6/site/dist directory containing the description of the modules and other modules installed together from the same distribution. The names of the files are some hash-based identifiers. For the version of XML::XPath on my computer, this is 1DB52FD58FC401775EFFF9619F334A566BAA495F.

Let's look inside. The file is quite big, thus we will not copy it here completely, limiting ourselves to the most distinct lines only:

```
{
  "id" : "1DB52FD58FC401775EFFF9619F334A566BAA495F",
  "name" : "XML::XPath",
  "files" : { },
  "api" : null,
  "support" : { },
  "source-url" : "git://github.com/ufobat/p6-XML-XPath.git",
  "resources" : [ ],
  "build-depends" : [ ],
  "auth" : null,
  "provides" : {
    "XML::XPath::ExprOperator::UnaryMinus" : {
      "lib/XML/XPath/ExprOperator/UnaryMinus.pm6" : {
        "cver" : "2017.01",
        "file" : "669A66B0DACE378D3507F21305B3A5AE0030D1E8",
        "time" : null
      }
    },
    "XML::XPath::ExprOperator::Div" : {
      "lib/XML/XPath/ExprOperator/Div.pm6" : {
        "cver" : "2017.01",
        "file" : "3D8EAACC880CA211F6E2D99C3AC0F2B0F64BA267",
        "time" : null
      }
    },

    . . .
```

```
    "Str" : "XML::XPath:ver<0.9.0>:auth<>:api<>",
    "depends" : [
      "XML",
      "Test::META"
    ],
    "license" : null,
    "ver" : "0.9.0",
    "description" : "XPath perl6 library",
    "test-depends" : [ ],
    "identity" : "XML::XPath:ver('0.9.0')"
  }
```

As you can see, it contains some basic meta-information about the module such as name and source address. At the end of the file we see the list of dependencies—XML and Test::META. The provides block lists other modules connected with it. For example, we see that the XML::XPath::ExprOperator::UnaryMinus module is located in the file named 669A66B0DACE378D3507F21305B3A5AE0030D1E8. Similarly, we can find data about the XML::XPath file itself:

```
  "XML::XPath" : {
    "lib/XML/XPath.pm6" : {
      "cver" : "2017.01",
      "file" : "E7C0BBCF69DD5CBC21DBD7027015325F83FADE11",
      "time" : null
    }
  }
```

Indeed, at the location share/perl6/site/sources/E7C0BBCF69DD5CBC21DBD7027015325F83FADE11, we see the source code of XML::XPath:

```
use XML;
use XML::XPath::Actions;
use XML::XPath::Grammar;
use XML::XPath::Utils;

class XML::XPath {
    has $.document;
    has %.registered-namespaces is rw;

    submethod BUILD(:$file, :$xml, :$document) {
        my $doc;
        if $document {
            $doc = $document;
        }

    . . .
```

But this is not all. Together with the source file, Rakudo keeps a precompiled version of the module. It is stored in the file with the same name in one of the subdirectories inside the `share/perl6/site/precomp` directory.

For the developer, it is not necessary to understand the above structure in detail. If you use Perl 6's package manager, it will take care of all the internal details.

Summary

In this chapter, we went through the main steps of working with modules. First, we saw how to create a module and how to tell the compiler where to find it. Then, we examined different ways of loading modules and importing names from them. Finally, we went to a Rakudo-specific module management tool, `zef`, and used it to install and uninstall modules and looked at the internal storage that Rakudo uses for saving the modules on disk.

In the next chapter, `Chapter 8`, *Object-Oriented Programming,* we will talk about classes, which share some common elements with modules in how the code is located in separate files.

8
Object-Oriented Programming

Object-oriented programming (**OOP**) is one of the most required features in modern programming languages. In Perl 6, the approach of how previous versions of Perl worked with OOP was completely redesigned. In this chapter, we will learn about creating classes and working with objects in Perl 6. The following will be covered:

- Creating a class
- Class (read and write, public, private, state attributes)
- Class methods (public and private methods)
- Inheritance (inheriting from a class, overriding methods, submethods, multiple inheritance)
- Roles
- Introspection
- Postfix method operators

Creating a class

In Perl 6, classes are an integral part of the language design. To create a class, use the `class` keyword. The body of the class, containing its definition, is placed between a pair of curly braces.

Let us start creating a program that uses classes. We'll start with an empty class for a house:

```
class House {
}
```

It can be a good practice to begin class names with capital letters. This also agrees with the convention used in Perl 6 itself. Its types are called in the same manner, compare

—Int, Str, Array, and so on.

The preceding code declares a class House and defines its body. Currently, the body is empty, but already you can use this definition to create instances of that class (or, using other terms, create objects of that type).

To some extent, the terms **class** and **type** are interchangeable. For example, you can treat strings as instances of the Str class, or just Str objects, or variables of the Str type.

So, creating a new house:

```
my $house = House.new;
```

The new method, called on the House class name, is a class **constructor**. It is created by Perl 6 for you for every new class. If you prefer, you can append a pair of empty parentheses to the call of new:

```
my $house = House.new();
```

The $house variable is a **scalar** variable. It hosts an object of the House type. To confirm it, call the WHAT method on a variable:

```
say $house.WHAT;
```

It prints (House).

Having a class, we can create another instance, say, $house2:

```
my $house2 = House.new;
say $house.WHAT; # (House)
```

Let us create a street of empty houses:

```
my @street;
push @street, House.new for 1..5;
```

Here, the @street arrays gets five objects of the House type. Let's check it by calling the WHAT method on each array element:

```
say $_.WHAT for @street;
```

As we have seen, to host objects, the same kind of variables are used—scalars for single objects and arrays for multiple collections. For Perl 6, $house is a container, which you may populate with data of any kind, whether it be an Int or a House object.

The two house instances that we've just created are different objects. The === operator can be used to check whether the objects are the same object:

```
say $house === $house2; # False
```

On the other hand, the content of both houses is equal. The eqv operator inspects the inner structure of the objects:

```
say $house eqv $house2; # True
```

Our next step is to fill the House class with useful elements.

Working with attributes

In the previous section, we created the House class, which did not contain anything. Real houses do have some parameters, such as address, area in square meters, number of rooms, height, and so on. All that can be expressed using Perl 6.

Let us start adding the details to the class. We start with the most simple element, the number of rooms. This parameter can be described by an integer value that is attached to the object of the House type. In Perl 6, such data elements are called **attributes** and are declared with the has keyword, as shown in the following example:

```
class House {
    has $.rooms;
}
```

What has been done here? The House class got an attribute $.rooms. This is a scalar value that belongs to the class object. Notice the dot after the dollar sigil. It is a twigil that describes the access level to the attribute; we will talk about it later in this section.

Now, try to create a house as we did in the previous section:

```
my $house = House.new;
```

This time, the object is different from what we had in the *Creating a class* section. It contains an attribute—`$.rooms`. This attribute can be read using the dot syntax, like you would do in Java or other languages for accessing object attributes:

```
say $house.rooms;
```

Because we did not set this attribute to any value, the program tells us that the attribute is empty:

(Any)

To set an initial value to an attribute, constructor arguments can be used. Instead of creating an instance as `House.new`, pass the named argument to it:

```
my $house = House.new(rooms => 2);
```

If you print the value of `$.rooms` now, it will return the value of 2:

```
say $house.rooms; # 2
```

Houses may differ in terms of number of rooms. Let us reflect this in the program:

```
my $house = House.new(rooms => 2);
say $house.rooms; # 2

my $house2 = House.new(rooms => 4);
say $house2.rooms; # 4
```

The `$.rooms` attribute of the variables `$house` and `$house2` are initialized with different values, which are kept with the objects.

Now, the two houses are not only different objects but also are not equivalent as they differ by their content:

```
say $house === $house2; # False
say $house eqv $house2; # False
```

We were printing the number of rooms by accessing the `$.rooms` attribute. For the given object `$house`, the syntax for getting the value of its attribute `$.rooms` is `$house.rooms`.

To set the value, we used a named argument passed to the constructor—`House.new(rooms => 2)`.

 Don't forget that Perl 6 does not allow a white space between the name of the method and the opening parenthesis.

Read-and-write attributes

The value of $.rooms attribute is set at the moment of creating the object $house. What if we need to change its value later? Of course, it is a rare case with real houses that the number of rooms changes but it still may happen, after a new owner takes the house and changes its floor plan, for example.

A naïve attempt to set a new value fails:

```
class House {
    has $.rooms;
}

my $house = House.new(rooms => 2);
$house.rooms = 3; # Fails here
say $house.rooms;
```

At the time of assignment, a runtime error occurs and the program is terminated:

Cannot modify an immutable Int in block <unit> at house.pl line 7

The $.rooms attribute is immutable and cannot be changed. This is the default behavior of class attributes.

To make the attribute mutable, in other words, to allow writing to it, the attribute must be declared with the rw trait:

```
class House {
    has $.rooms is rw;
}
```

Now, the modification is allowed and happens with no exceptions:

```
my $house = House.new(rooms => 2);
say $house.rooms; # 2

$house.rooms = 3;
say $house.rooms; # 3
```

A read-and-write attribute can be used as an lvalue with other operators, for example:

```
my $house2 = House.new(rooms => 3);
$house2.rooms++;
say $house2.rooms; # 4
```

Such attributes can be changed by any code that has access to $house. In many cases, access to internal attributes of the objects must be limited. In the next section, we will talk about how to do that in Perl 6.

Before we go further to learning class methods, let us expand the class with more fields:

```
class House {
    has $.rooms   is rw;
    has $.area    is rw;
    has $.height  is rw;
    has $.address is rw;
}
```

Now, the instance contains four data attributes, which can be initialized in the constructor:

```
my $house = House.new(
    rooms   => 2,
    area    => 100,
    height  => 4,
    address => '22, rue du Grenier-Saint-Lazare, 75003, Paris, France',
);
```

It is fine to put a comma after the last pair of arguments. It is not necessary, but as with creating hashes, it makes the process of adding new elements easier.

Now, all the attributes are initialized. If you print the object, the default stringification mechanism lists all the attributes with their values:

```
say $house;
```

House.new(rooms => 2, area => 100, height => 4, address => "22, rue du Grenier-Saint-Lazare, 75003, Paris, France")

In the next section, we will talk about narrowing the data types that can be stored in attributes.

Typed attributes

We continue with the House class and now it is time to think about the values that can be stored in the attributes.

In the previous examples, we set them to some meaningful values, but the language does not resist if you put some nonsensical data; for example, if we accidentally put an address to the $.area attribute:

```
my $house = House.new(
    rooms    => 2,
    area     => 'Calle Velázquez 57, 28001 Madrid, Spain',
    height   => 4.0,
    address  => 100.0,
);
```

Imagine now that you want to calculate the average area of one room:

```
say $house.area / $house.rooms;
```

This cannot be done, as the $.area attribute contains a string, not a number. The compiler reports a runtime error:

Cannot convert string to number: base-10 number must begin with valid digits or '.'

To prevent storing data of the wrong types in class attributes, Perl 6 offers a mechanism of typed attributes. The idea is the same as with typed variables and is demonstrated in the following code snippet:

```
class House {
    has Int $.rooms   is rw;
    has Real $.area   is rw;
    has Real $.height is rw;
    has Str $.address is rw;
}
```

Now, each attribute of the House class is typed. A compiler knows that the number of rooms is an integer number, the area and height are floating-point numbers and the address is a string. An attempt to store wrong data will be prevented by the compiler:

Type check failed in assignment to $!area; expected Rat but got Str ("Calle Velázquez 57, ...)

The exception also happens at runtime, but you cannot do something with the object, because it will not even be created.

That's not all the restrictions you can put on class attributes. Take, for example, the $.rooms attribute. It can be only an integer but it also should be a positive integer. Perl 6 allows you to specify the subset of values using the `where` keyword:

```
class House {
    has Int  $.rooms   is rw where {$_ > 0};
    has Real $.area    is rw where {$_ > 0};
    has Real $.height  is rw where {$_ > 3};
    has Str  $.address is rw where {$_ ne ''};
}
```

All attributes are now using the subsets of the built-in Perl 6 types. The values of both the $.rooms and $.area attributes should be positive, the height of a house must be at least 3 meters, and the address cannot be an empty string.

Now, if the values passed in the constructor do not meet the conditions, a runtime exception occurs. For example, if the address is empty:

Type check failed in assignment to $!address; expected <anon> but got Str ("")

Let us now take a precise look at the $.address attribute.

Using other classes as data types

In the previous code, the address of a house was a free-text string. In more complex applications, it is better to keep addresses as a set of different fields—country, town, zip code, street name, and house number.

One of the possible implementations is adding more attributes to the House class:

```
class House {
    has Int  $.rooms      is rw where {$_ > 0};
    has Real $.area       is rw where {$_ > 0};
    has Real $.height     is rw where {$_ > 3};

    has Int  $.husenumber is rw where {$_ ne ''};
    has Int  $.zipcode    is rw where {$_ > 0};
    has Str  $.country    is rw where {$_ ne ''};
    has Str  $.town       is rw where {$_ ne ''};
    has Str  $.street     is rw where {$_ ne ''};
}
```

It works but is not the best solution. Address details may be kept together in a separate attribute. To define the internal structure of the address, we introduce another class:

```
class Address {
    has Str $.housenumber is rw where {$_ ne ''};
    has Str $.zipcode is rw where {$_ ne ''};
    has Str $.country    is rw where {$_ ne ''};
    has Str $.town       is rw where {$_ ne ''};
    has Str $.street     is rw where {$_ ne ''};
}
```

The type of the attributes is intentionally chosen to be string to allow house numbers such as 3A and postcodes starting with zeros or containing letters or spaces, such as WC2B 4PH in London. Having this, the House class can contain an attribute of the Address type:

```
class House {
    has Int     $.rooms   is rw where {$_ > 0};
    has Real    $.area    is rw where {$_ > 0};
    has Real    $.height  is rw where {$_ > 3};
    has Address $.address is rw;
}
```

Finally, let us create a House object:

```
my $house = House.new(
    rooms   => 2,
    height  => 4,
    area    => 100,
    address => Address.new(
        housenumber => '31A',
        zipcode     => '00194',
        country     => 'Italy',
        town        => 'Rome',
        street      => 'Via Dante',
    ),
);
```

The object representing the address is created with its own constructor Address.new at the point when it is needed for the $.address attribute of the House object.

There are more things to learn about class attributes, but before we continue, we have to introduce class methods. So, the next section is about class methods, after which we will return to attributes in the *More about attributes* section.

Working with methods

In OOP, objects not only keep data, but also do some actions. In Perl 6, data is saved in attributes, and actions are done via **methods**.

Methods are like regular subs but defined inside a class. They can use the data from object attributes for their work.

Continue with the Address class from the previous sections. The details of the address are kept in separate attributes. This is good for creating a clean and structured representation but, in some cases, we need all data to be used together. For example, let's print a formatted address to put on an envelope:

```
class Address {
    has Str $.housenumber;
    has Str $.zipcode;
    has Str $.country;
    has Str $.town;
    has Str $.street;
}

my $address = Address.new(
    housenumber => '10',
    zipcode     => '1020',
    country     => 'Country',
    town        => 'Town',
    street      => 'Street',
);

print qq:to/ADDRESS/;
    {$address.street} {$address.housenumber}
    {$address.zipcode} {$address.town}
    {$address.country}
ADDRESS
```

The Address class contains a few data elements, which are used in the string interpolation to display their values. Notice that you need to use curly braces so that Perl 6 understands that a dot is a part of the name followed by the attribute name. The result of the program is the address printed in three lines:

```
Street 10
1020 Town
Country
```

We did our task, but think about printing another envelope label for another address. To avoid code duplication, we will have to put the formatting string to a subroutine. To make it even better, the formatting of the address must become a part of the `Address` class. Let us add the `full_address` method to the class:

```
class Address {
    has Str $.housenumber;
    has Str $.zipcode;
    has Str $.country;
    has Str $.town;
    has Str $.street;

    method full_address() {
        return qq:to/ADDRESS/;
            $.street $.housenumber
            $.zipcode $.town
            $.country
        ADDRESS
    }
}
```

Inside the method, object attributes are accessible using their names—`$.street`, `$.zipcode`, and so on.

Let us focus on this important aspect. Outside of the class code, access to the attributes requires an object. For example, if we created an object by calling the `new` constructor:

```
class Address {
    has $.street is rw;
}
my $address = Address.new;
```

Then to gain access to the field of the `$address` attribute, we use the dot syntax:

```
$address.street = 'Ramblas';
say $address.street;
```

As we have already seen before, another address will keep its own value of the `$.street` attribute:

```
my $address2 = Address.new;
$address2.street = 'Calle de Alcalá';

say $address2.street; # Calle de Alcalá
say $address.street;  # Ramblas
```

Now, let us work with attributes from the methods. We create two methods, one for setting a new value of $.street, another for reading it:

```
class Address {
    has $.street is rw;

    method get_street() {
        return $.street;
    }

    method set_street($new_street) {
        $.street = $new_street;
    }
}
```

So, the class now provides the methods get_street() and set_street(), which we are going to use immediately:

```
my $address = Address.new;
$address.set_street('Ramblas');

my $address2 = Address.new;
$address2.set_street('Calle de Alcalá');

say $address.get_street();   # Ramblas
say $address2.get_street(); # Calle de Alcalá
```

Inside the methods, the attribute is referred to as $.street. The same code is used for setting and getting the value of the attribute for both $address and $address2 instances.

Inside the class method, we do not see any mention of $address or $address2, but Perl 6 knows which object to work with, because the methods are invoked for those objects. When the compiler sees a construction such as $address.get_street(), the method receives a pointer to an object. We don't see it explicitly, but you can re-write it in the following way, which resembles the call to regular subroutines:

```
set_street($address: 'New value');
say get_street($address:);
```

The object is now passed as the first argument to the set_street and get_street routines. The object, for which we are calling a method, is called an **invocant**. We discussed the : operator in chapter 4, *Working with Operators*. With traditional syntax such as $address.get_street(), the invocant is still passed to the method but not explicitly.

Private methods

To hide an attribute, you need to change the twigil to `!`. Similarly, it is possible to hide methods by making them private with the same exclamation mark. Private methods cannot be called on the object; they only can be used from other methods of the class. Examine the following example:

```
class X {
    method !a() {
        say 'Private method';
    }

    method b() {
        say 'Public method';
        self!a();
    }
}

my $x = X.new;
```

This class has two methods, a and b. The first of them is declared as private so an attempt to call it as `$x.a()` causes a runtime error:

No such method 'a' for invocant of type 'X'

The b method is public and thus can be called:

```
$x.b();
```

Inside, this method is calling the private method a with the help of the `self` keyword—`self!a()`. The `self` is pointing to the object that is currently being processed, thus it is the same as `$x` in the outside program. You also may use `self` to call public methods—`self.b()`, but it is redundant and should only be used to resolve name conflicts.

Now, after we have talked about class methods, let us return to attribute and see what new information we can learn about them in connection with methods.

More about attributes

We started this chapter with the *Class attributes*, section but some of the features of attributes are closely connected with methods, that's why we made a break and now are able to continue talking about attributes.

Public and private attributes

In the previous code examples, the class attribute was declared with the dot sigil—$.rooms or $.street. A dot at that position means that the attribute is public and may be accessed by code that does not belong to the class.

There is another twigil, !, which makes attributes private. This means that the only way to read or change the value of an attribute is to access it from methods.

Let us return to the House class and change all the twigils of its methods to !:

```
class House {
    has $!rooms;
    has $!area;
    has $!height;
}
```

Creating a house can be done in the same way as before:

```
my $house = House.new(
    rooms  => 2,
    area   => 100,
    height => 3,
);
```

However, it is now not possible to read the value of the attributes. An attempt to get the value of $house.rooms fails:

No such method 'rooms' for invocant of type 'House'

Neither does $house!rooms works:

Private method call to rooms must be fully qualified with the package containing the method

This happens because the ! twigil marks an attribute as a private attribute, which cannot be accessed from outside of the class. We can work with them from the code of methods, though. Let us create the methods get_rooms and set_rooms to get and set the number of rooms:

```
class House {
    has $!rooms;
    has $!area;
    has $!height;
    method get_rooms() {
        return $!rooms;
    }
```

```
    method set_rooms($new_value) {
        $!rooms = $new_value;
    }
}
```

Again, create a new house with some initial values:

```
my $house = House.new(
    rooms => 2,
    area => 100,
    height => 3,
);
```

Now, use the new methods to first modify the number of rooms and then to print it:

```
$house.set_rooms(3);
say $house.get_rooms(); # 3
```

In object-oriented programming theory, hiding object attributes is called encapsulation. Perl 6 uses the ! twigil for that. This attribute becomes a **private** attribute.

Automatic getters and setters

In the previous section, we created a pair of getter and setter methods, `get_rooms` and `set_rooms`, for only one of the attributes of the `House` class. We can also do that for other attributes, such as `$!area` and `$!height`, but that requires a lot of copy-and-paste work and is not the best way to spend your time.

Actually, the dot syntax that we were using earlier in this chapter to set and read attributes is a syntactic cheat to use the getter and setter methods that Perl 6 created for us. Let us examine it step by step.

First, create a simple class with a `$.` attribute:

```
class X {
    has $.y;
}

my $x = X.new(y => 1);
say $x.y; # 1
```

The $x object has an attribute named y. This is a **public** attribute (because of the . twigil) and can be accessed from outside. Behind the scenes, Perl 6 creates a method with the same name y, which returns the value of $.y. So, the call of $x.y actually invokes that invisible method.

Compare this example with its modification, where the method y is defined explicitly:

```
class X {
    has $.y;

    method y() {
        return 2;
    }
}

my $x = X.new(y => 1);
say $x.y; # 2
```

The calling code $x.y did not change but the value printed is now different because our method redefined the method with the same name that the compiler created.

Now, let us set the value by assigning it to $x.y. Of course, the attribute has to be declared with the is rw trait:

```
class X {
    has $.y is rw;
}

my $x = X.new(y => 1);
$x.y = 2;
say $x.y; # 2
```

This time, the compiler creates a setter method that is called when we assign a new value to the $.y attribute. We can imitate the whole picture by creating the pair of **multi-methods**. Multi-methods are methods sharing the same name but having different signatures. In other languages this concept is also known under the terms function overloading or method overloading. They are similar to multi-subroutines, which we covered in Chapter 6, *Subroutines*:

```
class X {
    has $.y is rw;

    multi method y() {
        return $!y;
    }
}
```

```
    multi method y($value) {
        $!y = $value;
    }
}

my $x = X.new(y => 1);
$x.y(2);
say $x.y(); # 2
```

In this code, we only change the value of the $.y attribute using the explicit multi-methods y() and y($value).

Notice that inside the methods, the ! twigil is used for the $.y attribute. When you set or get the attribute using the ! twigil, Perl 6 accesses it's attribute directly without using the automatically generated getter and setter methods. So, even if you have a public attribute $.y, declared with a dot, it is better practice to use direct access $!y inside class methods.

Finally, let us once again take a look at the difference between accessing the public variable and the is rw trait. In the next code, the $.x attribute is public but is not declared as is rw:

```
class C {
    has $.x;

    method set() {
        $!x = 4;
    }
}
```

It is not possible to set the new value from the main program but it is still possible to modify the attribute from the method:

```
my $c = C.new;
$c.set();
say $c; # 4
```

The attribute is public, so the compiler generates a getter method for it, but is not a read-and-write attribute, so the setter is not created.

Class attributes

Assume now that we are building a street and would like to give house numbers to any new object. For simplicity, let us temporarily remove all the attributes except the `$.address` in House and `$.housenumber` in Address:

```
class Address {
    has Int $.housenumber is rw;
}

class House {
    has Address $.address is rw;
}
```

The next step is a loop that builds houses and saves them in the `@street` array:

```
my @street;
for 1..10 {
    push @street, House.new(
        address => Address.new(
            housenumber => @street.elems + 1
        )
    )
}
```

To increment the house number, we use the size of the `@street` in the following way:

```
@street.elems + 1
```

This ensures that every new house gets a number, which is greater than the number of all existing houses. To see that, loop over the array to print the numbers:

```
say $_.address.housenumber for @street;
```

Of course, it is not a big deal to keep an external counter to keep track of created houses, but there is an alternate way—the Address class can itself tell how many objects were created.

We will use the so-called **class attributes**, which belong to the class and not to the instances of it. This means that all the objects share the same class attribute. This is in contrast with regular attributes—each object receives its own container. In other programming languages, class attributes are also known as static data members.

So, here is the code, where the `Address` class is equipped with the class attribute `$last_assigned_number`, which is an integer value declared with the `my` keyword inside the class:

```
class Address {
    my Int $last_assigned_number = 0;
    has Int $.housenumber is rw;

    method assign_next() {
        $last_assigned_number++;
        $.housenumber = $last_assigned_number;
    }
}

class House {
    has Address $.address is rw;
}
```

The `assign_next` method is created to make the necessary actions to increment the value of class attribute `$last_assigned_number` and to assign it to the instance attribute `$.housenumber`.

Let us modify the loop for generating an array of houses to use the `assign_next` method:

```
my @street;
for 1..10 {
    my $house = House.new(
        address => Address.new()
    );
    $house.address.assign_next();
    push @street, $house;
}

say $_.address.housenumber for @street;
```

The program prints 10 numbers from 1 to 10. As you see, all we need to do is to call the method on the `Address` object. All the calculations are now done by the method, not by the code using the classes.

Class methods

In the previous example, we were using the class attribute for keeping the data that is shared between all instances of the class. We were using a method that is working with that attribute.

The idea of class attributes can also be projected on methods. In Perl 6, classes can contain **class methods**, which are defined with the `sub` keyword. Such methods have access to all the class attributes, but do not receive an implicit `self` reference to the object. Consider an example with two classes:

```
class Address {
    my Int $last_assigned_number = 0;
    has Int $.housenumber is rw;

    our sub get_next() {
        return ++$last_assigned_number;
    }
}

class House {
    has Address $.address is rw;
}
```

The `get_next` class method is declared also with the `our` keyword. This is needed because we want to access the method from external code. By default, the scope will be limited to the class only.

Now, make the next iteration of the design of the loop for generating a street:

```
my @street;
for 1..10 {
    my $house = House.new(
        address => Address.new()
    );
    $house.address.housenumber = Address::get_next();
    push @street, $house;
}

say $_.address.housenumber for @street;
```

The main difference here is the way we assign the house number. The `get_next` method cannot be called on the instance of the `Address` class, thus the compiler does not accept the expression `$house.address.get_next`. Symmetrically, you cannot have access to the `self` variable inside the method.

The `get_next` method must be called using the class name—`Address::get_next()`. It changes the value of the `$last_assigned_number` counter. The counter is also a variable that does not belong to any particular instance of the `Address` class. Actually, the `Address::get_next()` method can be called even before creating any object:

```
say Address::get_next(); # 1
say Address::get_next(); # 2
```

Now it is time to learn about the object-oriented facilities of Perl 6 in more detail.

Inheritance

The next feature of object-oriented programming is inheritance. In this section, we talk about inheritance and related topics in Perl 6.

Inheriting from a class

Inheriting in OOP means creating a new class, which extends another already existing class. The simplest form of inheritance is a child-parent pair of two classes.

In the previous sections, we created the `House` class. Let us use it as the parent class for another concept. We will create a `ModernHouse` class, which is a `House` with a solar roof panel. A bare `House`, which we created earlier in this chapter, contains four attributes—number of rooms, area, height, and address. The address attribute was an `Address` object in our previous examples but, in this section, we will keep it simple and assume that the address is a string:

```
class House {
    has $.rooms;
    has $.area;
    has $.height;
    has $.address;
}
```

For a `ModernHouse`, another attribute, the power that the solar panel generates, is added:

```
class ModernHouse is House {
    has $.power;
}
```

The ModernHouse class is now a class that has five attributes, four from the House class and one added in the definition of ModernHouse. From the perspective of the user, all the attributes of the ModernHouse class are equal, you initialize and use them as all they were the attributes defined in the ModernHouse class, as is clearly seen in the following example:

```
my $house = ModernHouse.new(
    rooms   => 5,
    area    => 150,
    height  => 5,
    address => '...',
    power   => 200,
);

say $house.area;   # 100
say $house.power;  # 200
```

In different programming languages, different terminology is used to refer to the classes that take part in inheritance. The House class may be called a **base class**, a **parent class**, or a **superclass**. The ModernHouse class is either a **derived class**, a **child class**, or a **subclass**.

In Perl 6's documentation, the terms parent and child classes are used.

Using child class instances as objects of a base class

An object of the ModernHouse type is also a House. Consider a function f that takes the argument and thinks that it is an object of the House type. The signature of the function applies a restriction to the argument:

```
sub f(House $h) {
    say "There are {$h.rooms} rooms in this house.";
}
```

Now, let's create two different houses and call the function with them:

```
my $house = House.new(rooms => 2);
my $modern_house = ModernHouse.new(rooms => 3, power => 100);

f($house);
f($modern_house);
```

This code works perfectly and prints the expected strings:

```
There are 2 rooms in this house.
There are 3 rooms in this house.
```

The function is only using the attribute, which is defined in the parent class, so it can easily handle the object of the child class, because it also contains the required attribute.

What if we reverse the situation—create a function that expects an object of the child class, and pass an object of the base class to it?

```
sub f2(ModernHouse $h) {
    say "This house generates {$h.power} kWh.";
}

f2($modern_house);
```

So far, it works, as there is no difference in the type of the object:

```
This house generates 100 kWh.
```

The f2 function is accessing the $.power attribute, which is absent in the House class. If you call the function and pass the $house variable to it, an error will be raised:

```
Type check failed in binding to parameter '$h'; expected ModernHouse but
got House (House.new(rooms => 2,...)
```

Consider another example using typed variables. In the next example, the @street array is an array of objects of the House type:

```
my House @street;
push @street, ModernHouse.new(rooms => 3, power => 100);
push @street, House.new(rooms => 2);
```

Both houses are successfully added to the @street array, as they are both compatible with the House type. If you loop over an array, you can read the attributes of the House class, which are also presented in the object of the ModernHouse type:

```
f($_) for @street;
```

If the @street array is declared more strictly, namely, if we use the ModernHouse type as the type of array elements, then the compiler will not accept the objects of the House type:

```
my ModernHouse @street;
push @street, ModernHouse.new(rooms => 3, power => 100);
# push @street, House.new(rooms => 2);
```

If the last line is uncommented, the program stops with the type check error:

```
Type check failed in assignment to @street; expected ModernHouse but got
House (House.new(rooms => 2,...)
```

Overriding methods

In many cases, the methods of child classes should react differently from the methods in parent classes. Here we come to an important concept of redefining or overriding methods.

Let us continue an example with `House` and `ModernHouse` and implement the method to calculate the cost of electricity needed to warm the house. To focus on the main topic, we simplify the classes and the method of calculating the cost, assuming that it is proportional to the area of the house.

In both classes, we define the method named `energy_cost`, which does different calculations for each class:

```
class House {
    has $.area;

    method energy_cost() {
        return 0.8 * $!area;
    }
}

class ModernHouse is House {
    has $.power;

    method energy_cost() {
        return 0.3 * $.area;
    }
}
```

Notice the tiny difference in using the area value. In the `House` class, it is possible to refer to it as to a local attribute with the `$!area` syntax. In the `ModernHouse` class, we have to use the generated getter `$.area`.

Now, create two instances and print the costs:

```
my $house = House.new(area => 100);
my $modern_house = ModernHouse.new(area => 100, power => 150);

say $house.energy_cost();        # 80
say $modern_house.energy_cost(); # 30
```

There is no surprise that each object is using its own variant of the `energy_cost` method.

This behavior is even more interesting when we are keeping different types of houses in the same collection. In the next example, we put two different houses into the `@street` array:

```
my House @street;

push @street, House.new(area => 100);
push @street, ModernHouse.new(area => 100, power => 150);
```

Then, we iterate over the array and calling the `energy_cost` method on a loop variable:

```
say $_.energy_cost() for @street;
```

The output that the program prints is exactly the same as from the previous one. This means that we face **polymorphic** behavior—each object knows which class it belongs to and invokes the correct method.

Polymorphism can be even more complex. Let us reorganize the code from the last example and introduce the `tariff_coef` method, which will be used in calculating the costs:

```
class House {
    has $.area;

    method tariff_coef() {
        return 0.8;
    }

    method energy_cost() {
        return self.tariff_coef() * $!area;
    }
}

class ModernHouse is House {
    has $.power;

    method tariff_coef() {
        return 0.3;
    }
}
```

Now, the `energy_cost` method is defined only in the base class. So, an instance of the `ModernHouse` class will be using that method. However, inside the `energy_cost` method is calling the `tarif_coef` method, and Perl 6 will find the correct implementation of it depending on the type of the object. This is demonstrated in the following code:

```
my $house = House.new(area => 100);
my $modern_house = ModernHouse.new(area => 100, power => 150);

say $house.energy_cost();          # 80
say $modern_house.energy_cost();   # 30
```

Again, the behavior of method resolution shows that it works as expected.

Notice, that the method `energy_cost` must be a public method, otherwise it will not be inherited.

Submethods

As we have seen, a child class receives all the public methods that the base class defines. In some cases, this is not desired. Making the method private is also not always a solution, as you may want to call it on the object of the base class.

Perl 6 allows so-called **submethods**. They are not inherited. Let us learn about them in a small example:

```
class Parent {
    method meth() {
        say 'meth()';
    }

    submethod submeth() {
        say 'submeth()';
    }
}

class Child is Parent {
}
```

Now, create two objects:

```
my $o1 = Parent.new;
my $o2 = Child.new;
```

In the `Parent` class, there are two methods that can be called on the object of that type:

```
$o1.meth();     # meth()
$o1.submeth(); # submeth()
```

In the `Child` class, only the `meth` method is available:

```
$o2.meth(); # meth()
```

Calling the `submeth` submethod is forbidden:

```
No such method 'submeth' for invocant of type 'Child'
```

Multiple inheritance

In Perl 6, multiple inheritance is allowed. Multiple inheritance means that a child class is derived from more than one parent. Examine the following skeleton example:

```
class P1 {
    method p1(){
        say 'p1()';
    }
}

class P2 {
    method p2(){
        say 'p2()';
    }
}

class C is P1 is P2 {
    method c() {
        say 'c()';
    }
}
```

The two parent classes, P1 and P2, define the methods p1 and p2. The child class C is derived from both P1 and P2:

```
class C is P1 is P2 { ... }
```

This means that the instance of the C class received all the methods that are available in any of the three classes:

```
my $c = C.new;
$c.p1();
$c.p2();
$c.c();
```

Multiple inheritance is a powerful technique, but it also can give hidden name conflicts. Imagine that in the previous example, there is another class P, which is the base class for both P1 and P2:

```
class P {
    has $!count;
    method get_count() {
        return $!count++;
    }
}

class P1 is P {
    method p1(){
        say 'p1()';
    }
}

class P2 is P {
    method p2(){
        say 'p2()';
    }

    method get_count() {
        return -1;
    }
}

class C is P1 is P2 {
    method c() {
        say 'c()';
    }
}
```

Both the P and P2 classes have their own implementation of the get_count method. In the P class, this method is using an attribute and returns an incrementing number each time it is called, in the P2 class, the return value is always -1.

What happens when the C class object, which is derived from P1 and P2 and indirectly from P, is calling the get_count method?

```
my $c = C.new;
say $c.get_count();
say $c.get_count();
say $c.get_count();
```

On one hand, the get_count method in the C class is derived from the P class via P1. On the other hand, a method with the same name is derived from P2. Perl 6 chooses the method from P2, as it is closer to C. Thus, the program prints -1 three times.

If you want to learn more about the way Perl 6 resolves name conflicts in multiple inheritance, refer to the **C3 linearization** method resolution order at—https://en.wikipedia.org/wiki/C3_linearization.

So far, we went through the main concepts of classical object-oriented programming. Perl 6 also supports the new concept of roles, which we are going to cover next.

Appending objects and classes using roles

Roles are another mechanism in modern OOP. A role is like an external part of the class, which is appended to an existing object or a class, providing some extra attributes and methods. Roles are very close to interfaces in some programming languages.

Let us take a house and make it a floating house. For simplicity, the House class has only one attribute, the area of the house. The Floating role has an attribute that keeps the weight of the floating house and the method that returns a Boolean value if the house is too heavy and is sinking:

```
class House {
    has $.area is rw;
}

role Floating {
    has $.weight is rw;

    method is_sinking() {
        return $!weight > 500 * $.area;
    }
}
```

Syntactically, the only difference in creating a role is the keyword `role` in place of the `class` keyword.

From now on, there are two ways of applying a role. First, let's take an already existing house and apply a role to it. In the example, the house is created using the constructor `House.new`, and a role is appended using the `does` keyword:

```
my $floating_house = House.new does Floating;
$floating_house.area = 100;
$floating_house.weight = 10_000;

say $floating_house.is_sinking(); # False
```

As you see, both the `$.weight` attribute and the `is_sinking` method from the `Floating` role become available for the `$floating_house` object.

The object gets a compound type `House+{Floating}`:

```
say $floating_house.WHAT; # (House+{Floating})
```

In the second approach, a new class is created first. The `FloatingHouse` class is derived from `House` and imports the `Floating` role. To connect a role, the same `does` keyword is used:

```
class FloatingHouse is House does Floating {
}

my $floating_house = FloatingHouse.new;
$floating_house.area = 100;
$floating_house.weight = 100_000;

say $floating_house.is_sinking(); # True
```

The behavior of the program is the same as in the previous example, but the type of the object is different and does not contain any traces of the role:

```
say $floating_house.WHAT; # (FloatingHouse)
```

Using roles is very close to class inheritance in some aspects. Both approaches may work equally well in some cases. Here's the rule of thumb for choosing between inheritance and roles.

You inherit A from B when you can say that *A is B*; you apply a role when you can say that *A does B*.

For example, a dog is an animal, so you inherit `Dog` from `Animal`. But the dog does bark, so you apply a role `Bark`:

```
class Dog is Animal does Bark { ... }
```

Consider another example, when the above-defined `Floating` role can be used. We are creating a floating restaurant. A restaurant is also a house and it also float. So, the hierarchy may be done like this:

```
class House {
    has $.area is rw;
}

class Restaurant is House {
    has $.seats is rw;
}

role Floating {
    has $.weight is rw;
    method is_sinking() {
        return $!weight > 500 * $.area;
    }
}
```

Here, the `Floating` role is exactly the same role that we used in the previous example with a floating house:

```
my $restaurant = Restaurant.new does Floating;
$restaurant.seats = 30;
$restaurant.area = 100;
$restaurant.weight = 10_000;
```

The `$restaurant` variable is now an object of the `Restaurant+{Floating}` type and can use the `is_sinking` method:

```
say $restaurant.is_sinking(); # False
```

Let's stop here with creating class hierarchy and applying roles and see how Perl 6 can help with examining the internal structure of such objects.

Using introspection to learn more

The Perl 6 object system has a built-in mechanism for introspection, with which you can see what this particular object in hand can do, which class it is implementing, which methods can be used, and so on.

In the previous chapters, we already used one of the mechanisms of introspection—the WHAT method. It returns the **type object** with information about the type of the object that is located in the container now. We are talking about introspection in the chapter dedicated to the object-oriented programming, but you should keep in mind that in Perl 6, many other simple variables such as strings or integers are also objects.

For example, this is how you can see the type of a string and an integer. The program prints the stringified version of what the WHAT method returns:

```
say 'string'.WHAT;  # (Str)
say 42.WHAT;        # (Int)
```

With the user-defined class, the WHAT method gives the name of the class:

```
class C {
}
my $c = C.new;
say $c.WHAT; # (C)
```

The HOW method returns an object of the Perl6::Metamodel::ClassHOW class. This is a part of the so-called meta-object model in Perl 6, which is responsible for how Perl 6 handles objects and their properties and their behavior. We will not go into learning the **meta-object protocol (MOP)**, but will take a look at the two useful methods that it provides—name and mro.

The name method returns the name of the class. Notice that the WHAT method returns a type object, which is stringified in the format of (ClassName) when we print it, while the name method of the Perl6::Metamodel::ClassHOW class returns a string. This is how the name method must be called:

```
say $c.HOW.name($c); # C
```

On a given variable, $c, the method HOW is called. It returns an object, on which the name method is called with the variable $c as its argument. This redundancy is done with some future plans that the Perl 6 developers keep in mind. For practical purposes, it is easier to use an alternative and simpler syntax:

```
say $c.^name; # C
```

The `HOW.mro`, or simply `^mro`, method (the name stands for Method Resolution Order) returns a list showing the class hierarchy. It can be used to understand how the name conflicts will be resolved.

For example, here are a few classes with their child—parent relations:

```
class A {}
class B is A {}
class C is A {}
class D {}
class E is D is B is C {}
```

The `^mro` method may be called on both the class name and the object of the class:

```
say E.^mro;

my $e = E.new;
say $e.^mro;
```

In both cases, the following string will be printed:

```
((E) (D) (B) (C) (A) (Any) (Mu))
```

In the event of difficult relations in the complex hierarchy, you may call this method to see how Perl 6 sees it internally.

Method postfix operators

In Chapter 4, *Working with Operators*, we did not cover the set of special postfix operators, which are related to object-oriented programming. Now it is time to fill that gap. The operators described in this section are the syntactic constructions but they may all be considered postfix operators.

To call a method on an object, the dot operator is used. We have been using it many times in this chapter:

```
class A {
    method m() {
        return 42;
    }
}

my $o = A.new; # calling the 'new' method
say $o.m();    # calling the 'm' method
```

If the method does not exist, say, if you call `$o.n()`, then the call fails:

```
No such method 'n' for invocant of type 'A'
```

To prevent the raise of an exception, the `.?` form of the method call operator can help:

```
say $o.?m(); # 42
say $o.?n(); # Nil
```

An existing method is called as usual, while the call of the non-existing method returns `Nil` and the program continues.

The `.+` and `.*` operators are used to call all the methods with the given name. This may be useful when you have a hierarchy of classes. Consider the following program:

```
class A {
    method m() {
        return 'A::m';
    }
}

class B is A {
    method m() {
        return 'B::m';
    }
}

my $o = B.new;
```

The `m` method is defined in both parent and child classes, so the call of `$o.m()` is routed to the method from the class `B`:

```
say $o.m(); # B::m
```

The `.+` method calls all the methods and returns a list of results:

```
my @result = $o.+m();
say @result; # [B::m A::m]
```

As you see, the call `$o.+m()` lead to calling the `m` methods in the `$o.^mro` order (see the previous section, *Introspection*, for details).

If the method name is unknown, an exception happens. For example, it is not possible to call `$o.+n()`:

```
No such method 'n' for invocant of type 'B'
```

The `.*` operator works similar to the `.+` operator but allows attempts to call a non-existing method:

```
say $o.*m(); # (B::m A::m)
say $o.*n(); # ()
```

For the n method, an empty list of results is returned. To remember the operators, you can compare the semantics of the + and * with the corresponding quantifiers used in regular expressions (see `Chapter 11`, *Regexes*). The + means that there should be at least one method with that name, while the * allows any number of them, including zero.

Let us now see how we can call the method from the base class in the same example. There is the `.::` operator, that can be used to fully qualify the name of the calling method:

```
say $o.A::m(); # A::m
```

Here, the `$o` variable is an object of the B class, but with the help of the `.::` operator the method `A::m` from the parent class is called.

Summary

In this chapter, we learnt about object-oriented support in Perl 6. We went through creating a class, adding attributes and methods to it, and making the methods and class data public or private. We then talked about class hierarchy and an alternative approach using roles and also how to use Perl 6 built-in facilities for introspecting the objects. On a set of examples, we examined many techniques of working with complex objects. Finally, the postfix method operators were listed, with which you may create more universal and robust programs.

In the next chapter, exceptions are described. In Perl 6, they are based on classes, so the knowledge from the current chapter will be very useful for better understanding exceptions.

9
Input and Output

This chapter is devoted to input and output, which is mostly based on the `IO::Handle` class in Perl 6. Computer programs in general communicate with the user. It may either be the input and output in a console application, or reading configuration files, or saving results in a file on disk. In this chapter, we will talk about the input and output facilities in Perl 6.

The following topics will be covered in this chapter:

- Standard input and output
- Working with files
- Analyzing the properties of files and directories
- Methods for reading from input streams
- Methods for writing to output streams
- Formatted output

Standard input and output

In the previous chapters, we have created many programs that print to the console and read data from it. Let us refresh some knowledge from Chapter 2, *Writing Code*, and create a program that asks for the user's name and greets them:

```
my $name = prompt 'What is your name? ';
say "Hello, $name!";
note "Greeted $name at " ~ time;
```

Here, the `prompt` function prints the message and waits until the user enters a string. The string is saved in the `$name` variable, which is later interpolated in a string in double quotes. The `note` function prints the debugging message and logs the time of when the person was greeted.

In this program, Perl 6 uses two standard communication channels, the standard input stream (stdin for short) and the standard output stream (stdout). These are the default streams that receive the user's input and accept what the program prints. Another channel, which we already mentioned in `Chapter 2`, *Writing Code*, is the stream for printing error messages and warnings, the standard error output (stderr).

On Linux systems, the POSIX standard determines that the file descriptors with the numbers 0, 1, and 2 are stdout, stdin, and stderr, respectively. In Perl 6, there are three special variables with dynamic scope, `$*OUT`, `$*IN`, and `$*ERR` that are attached to these channels by default.

The built-in functions such as `print` and `warn` use the values of `$*OUT`, `$*IN`, and `$*ERR`. The following table shows the correspondence between the functions and the channels:

Function	Input/output direction	Input/output stream
print	output	$*OUT
say	output	$*OUT
prompt	output	$*OUT
prompt	input	$*IN
note	output	$*ERR
warn	output	$*ERR

The `$*OUT`, `$*IN`, and `$*ERR` variables are instances of the `IO::Handle` class. Let us explore it.

The `IO::Handle` class represents an open file or an input/output stream. In Perl 6, this class is implementing the `IO` role. In this section we will discuss the most useful methods that the `IO::Handle` class and the `IO` role give to the programmer.

What we will learn is applicable to both standard input/output streams and to working with files.

Working with files and directories

Working with files in Perl 6, as well as in many other languages, is done via file handles. You get the file handle as soon as you open a file; later, you use the handle to write to a file or to read from it. All the other operations, such as flushing a buffer or closing a file, are also performed via the handle.

Opening a file

To open a file, use the `open` function (it is supplied by the `IO` role but can be used as a simple built-in function). It takes the path to the file and a number of optional parameters. The return value is a file handle, as shown:

```
my $fh = open '/etc/passwd';
```

By default, the file is opened in the read-only mode. It is possible to pass the mode name explicitly using the named arguments. The above example is equivalent to the following code:

```
my $fh = open '/etc/passwd', :r;
```

The following table lists the possible modes for opening a file:

Parameter	Description
`:r`	Read-only mode. This is the default mode.
`:w`	Write-only mode. Creates a file if it does not exist and overwrites it otherwise.
`:rw`	Read-write mode. Creates a file if it does not exist and overwrites it otherwise.
`:a`	Append mode. Creates a file if it does not exist. Otherwise, the data will be appended to the end of an existing file.

Depending on the mode in which a file was opened, a set of methods from the IO::Handle class will be available. For example, you cannot write to a file, which is open with the :r option, even if the file handle is still an instance of the universal IO::Handle class. An X::AdHoc exception will be thrown in this case:

```
my $fh = open '/etc/passwd', :r;
try {
    $fh.say('Hello'); # Attempt to write to a read-only file
}
say $!.^name;          # X::AdHoc, see details in Chapter 10, Exceptions
```

The open function also accepts a few configuration parameters, listed in the following table:

Parameter	Description
:bin	Opens a file in binary mode.
:enc('*encoding*')	Associates the given encoding with a file. See an example in the *Writing to a stream* section.
:chomp	If :chomp is set to True, the new line characters will be truncated when reading from file line by line (see the *Reading from a stream* section).

Closing a file

To close a file, call the close method on the file handle:

```
my $fh = open '/etc/passwd';
# .... read from file
$fh.close;
```

Testing file and directory properties

The IO role offers a number of one-letter methods to check different metrics of the files and directories. The return values are Boolean. The methods are listed in the following table:

Method	Description
e	Checks if a path exists
d	Checks if the path is an existing directory
f	Checks if the path is an existing file
l	Checks if the path is a symbolic link

r	Checks if the path is accessible (thus, the read bit is set)
w	Checks if the path is writable (the write bit is set)
x	Checks if the path is executable (the exec bit is set)
rw	Checks if the path is available for both reading and writing
rwx	Checks if all the r, w, and x bits are set for the path
s	Checks if the file is non-empty
z	Checks if the file is of the zero size

Consider these methods as examples. As the methods are defined in the IO role, we have to access them by first calling the IO method on variables, which can represent paths. It can be, for example, a literal string or a variable containing the path to a file or directory. Also, you can call the IO method on file handles.

Let's look at a few examples. Check if the file exits:

```
my $path = '/etc/passwd';
say "File $path exists" if $path.IO.e;
```

Check if a directory exists:

```
if '/Users'.IO.d {
    say '/Users is a directory';
}
```

Notice that the d method only works with directories. If the path exists but it is a file, the method returns `False`:

```
say 'Not a directory' unless '/etc/passwd'.IO.d;
```

To check if the path exists, use the e method. The result does not depend on whether the path is a directory or a file:

```
say 'File or directory exists' if '/'.IO.e;
```

All the preceding methods for testing file and directory properties may be used with a different syntax using the smartmatch operator and adverbial constructions—constructions starting with a colon, such as : e. The following example gives an idea of how to do that; both lines of code do the same:

```
say 'Exists' if 'data.txt'.IO.e;
say 'Exists' if 'data.txt'.IO ~~ :e;
```

Manipulating files

The `path` method, available for the objects of the `IO::Handle` type returns an `IO::Path` object, which is handy for working with physical files on the disk. The `IO::Path` class provides the programmer with a few methods to rename, move, or delete a file. The methods also exist as built-in functions, so you don't need to get or create an `IO::Path` object to manipulate files on disks. On success, they return the `True` value. In case of errors, an exception may be thrown.

In the following table we summarise the most frequently used functions for working with file paths:

Function	Description	Example
copy	Copies a file	`copy 'data.txt', 'data-copy.txt';`
rename	Renames a file	`rename 'old.txt', 'new.txt';`
move	Moves a file (copies a file under a new name and then removes the original)	`move '/old/path/to/file', '/new/path/to/file';`
unlink	Removes a file (unlike moves, it does not copy the file)	`unlink 'secret.txt';`
symlink	Creates a symbolic link	`symlink 'target.txt', 'existing-file.txt';`
chmod	Changes a file's permissions	`chmod 0o755, 'prog.pl';` Notice the octal notation

Having the `IO` object, you may get a number of characteristics of the file. Let's examine them briefly.

The mode methods return the access mode bits of the paths. Consider an example:

```
say '/etc/passwd'.IO.mode;
```

This code prints the value such as `0644`. Notice that this method returns an object of the `IntStr` type, which we did not cover in this book so far. This is a dual value, which in a string context contains the string representation of the octal value `"0644"`, while in an integer context it is an integer value `420`, as demonstrated in the following example:

```
say '/etc/passwd'.IO.mode.Str; # 0644
say '/etc/passwd'.IO.mode.Int; # 420
```

The other three methods, `modified`, `accessed`, and `changed`, return the corresponding time properties of the path. The return value is an object of the `Instant` type. To get the epoch value or the `Date` object, additionally call the `Int` or the `Date` method, as demonstrated in the following example:

```
say '/etc/passwd'.IO.modified;       # Instant:1383139040
say '/etc/passwd'.IO.modified.Int;   # 1383139040
say '/etc/passwd'.IO.modified.Date;  # 2013-10-30
```

Working with directories

The `IO::Path` class has a few methods for working with directories. We will discuss them in this section. Again, the routines are accessible as methods and as standalone subroutines.

The `chdir` function changes the current working directory. The current path can be read from the `$*CWD` variable. The value is of the `IO` type. To get the string, stringify it by either using the `Str` method or by adding a ~ prefix, as shown in the following code:

```
say $*CWD.Str; # /Users/ash/code, for example
chdir '/tmp';
say ~$*CWD;    # /tmp
```

Creating and removing directories is done via the `mkdir` and `rmdir` routines. When creating a directory, an optional parameter may be passed to set permission modes:

```
mkdir 'data';
mkdir 'data/secret', 0o400;
```

The `rmdir` routine only works if the directory is empty:

```
mkdir 'temp';
# ... do something
rmdir 'temp';
```

The dir function returns the content of the directory as a list of the IO objects. This is how you may list the current working directory:

```
my @dir = dir;
say $_.Str for @dir;
```

To specify the path to the directory, either pass it as a parameter, or create an IO object out of a string:

```
my @root_dir = dir('/');
my @temp_dir = '/tmp'.IO.dir;
```

Now, as we know how to work with files and directories, we move on to the methods for reading and writing data.

In the next sections, we will be discussing the methods of the IO::Handle class for reading and writing data. For simplicity, many of the code examples are using the standard input and output. Although, they will work with the $fh file handles returned by the open function.

Reading from a stream

There are many different methods that the IO::Handle class offers us for reading from streams. We already have seen a few in the section *Simple input and output* in Chapter 2, *Writing Code*. Here, we'll discuss them in detail and see other alternatives.

Reading a single line

We start with the get method, which reads a line from the input stream. For example, to read a line from the standard input, call the method on the $*IN instance, as shown in the next example:

```
my $line = $*IN.get;
say $line;
```

The program waits for you to enter some text. After the line is complete and the 'Enter' key is pressed, the get method returns control to the program and then the line is printed to the screen. Alternatively, you may use the facilities of a command-line interpreter to redirect the input streams and passing the contents of the file to a program:

```
$ perl6 get.pl < get.pl
my $line = $*IN.get;
```

This time, the program prints the first line of itself.

The `$*IN.get` construction in the code is equivalent to the bare call of `get`:

```
my $line = get;
say $line;
```

When you work with a file, use the file handle of an open file in the same manner we have just worked with `$*IN`:

```
my $fh = open 'data.txt', :r;
my $line = $fh.get;
say $line;
```

Before running this program, create a new file `data.txt` and put some text in it. If the file does not exist, the `$fh` handle will be set to a `Failure` object, and the following call of the get method will raise an error (more on exceptions and failures in Chapter 10, *Working with Exceptions*):

```
Failed to open file /Users/ash/code/data.txt: no such file or directory
    in block <unit> at open.pl line 1
```

Reading characters

To get a single character, use the `getc` method:

```
my $ch = $*IN.getc;
say $ch;
```

The `getc` method blocks the program execution until a character appears in the stream. If there are no characters left in the stream, an empty value of `Any` is returned. In a Boolean context, it is `False`, so it can be used in a condition of a loop. Let us create a program that reads its input character by character and prints them each on a separate line.

```
while my $ch = $*IN.getc {
    say $ch;
}
```

The `getc` method is quite smart when it deals with the Unicode characters. To demonstrate this behavior, let us create a text file, `text.txt`, and put a single u character in it. Then, pass the file to the program and read the character:

```
$ perl6 getc.pl < text.txt
u
```

This was a single byte with a character from the ASCII subspace. Now, let us use a different character, say, Latvian u with a line above: ū. In Unicode, this character is called LATIN SMALL LETTER U WITH MACRON and has the codepoint number 0x016B. In the UTF-8 encoding, this character consists of two bytes: 0xC5 and 0xAB. So, if you save the character in a file, its size will be two bytes. Now run the program against this file:

```
$ perl6 getc.pl < text.txt
ū
```

As we see, Perl 6 managed to understand that the file starts with the two bytes representing a single UTF-8 character.

Now, a bit more complicated task for getc. This time we will use a decomposed version of the character. In UTF encodings, a character such as ū can be alternatively stored as a sequence of two elements: LATIN SMALL LETTER U with the code 0x0075 (the same as in ASCII) and a COMBINING MACRON (0x0304).

Let us save it in a file. One of the ways to do so is to use Perl 6, print the corresponding bytes, and redirect the output to a file. This is how you do it with a one-liner:

```
$ perl6 -e'print "u"; print 0x0304.chr' > text.txt
```

To print the character rather than an integer value, the chr method is called: 0x0304.chr. The file now contains three bytes: 75 CC 84. Pass it to our program:

```
$ perl6 getc.pl < text.txt
ū
```

There is only one call of getc in the program, and it prints the correct character. Perl 6 did not stop immediately after it saw a valid ASCII character u but tried to verify whether the following bytes are still part of the Unicode representation of a combined character.

Now, let us make the job even more complicated and construct a non-existing character, say u with a double tilde above it and a 'comma' below. There is no codepoint for this character in Unicode but it still can be constructed with three elements—the letter itself and two combining parts—COMBINING ALMOST EQUAL TO ABOVE (0x034C) and COMBINING CEDILLA (0x0327). Prepare the text file:

```
$ perl6 -e'print "u"; print 0x034C.chr; print 0x0327.chr' > text.txt
```

The three elements are now residing in five bytes in the UTF-8 encoding—75 CD 8C CC A7. Still, Perl 6 reads it as a single character, as you can prove by running the program again:

```
$ perl6 getc.pl < text.txt
ũ
```

To read more than one character at a time, use the readchars method. It works similar to the getc method but returns a string with characters. The maximum number of characters to read is passed as the argument:

```
my $str = $*IN.readchars(12); # read 12 characters from standard input
say $str;
```

Note that, to reproduce the examples in this section, you need a terminal that supports Unicode.

Lazy readers

The IO::Handle class defines a few methods for lazy reading. The laziness here means that Perl 6 should perform actual reading when the program really needs another portion of data. So it should not read the whole file immediately.

The lines method returns a list of lines. Here is an example of a short program that copies its input to the output:

```
.say for lines;
```

This can be re-written in a different form with a more traditional syntax:

```
for $*IN.lines -> $line {
    say $line;
}
```

The call of $*IN.lines returns an array of the lines from input. We can directly save it in a variable, for example, and use it for printing:

```
my @lines = $*IN.lines;
.say for @lines;
```

An important thing is that the lines method removes the new line characters from the end of lines. So, if you need to reproduce it, use the say function to print the new line at the end of the output.

The `lines` method accepts an integer argument to indicate the maximum number of lines to read:

```
.say for $*IN.lines(3); # prints the first 3 lines from input
```

Another way to read logical data from an input stream is to use the `words` method. It works similarly to the previously described `lines` method but splits the input to words instead of lines. The separator is a sequence of whitespaces. Consider an example:

```
.say for $*IN.words;
```

This program prints every word from the input on a separate line.

The `split` method generalizes an approach of reading logical elements and allows us to specify a splitter, which will be used for separating the elements. For example, this is how you split the input separated by colon:

```
.say for $*IN.split(':');
```

Now, supply a line from the `/etc/passwd` file, for example, and the program will print separate parts of it:

```
$ cat /etc/passwd | grep nobody | perl6 split.pl
nobody
*
-2
-2
Unprivileged User
/var/empty
/usr/bin/false
```

The `comb` method returns a list of all the matches that it found in the input stream. For matching, a regular expression is used. We will talk about regular expressions in Chapter 11, *Regexes*, but here is a simple example of extracting all numbers from the input:

```
my @numbers = $*IN.comb(/\d+/);
say @numbers.join(', ');
```

The following input demonstrates how this program works. After you enter the text, the program prints a comma-separated list of the integer numbers that it found. The lines in bold are what you enter:

```
$ perl6 comb.pl
There are 3 points in a triangle,
4 points in a square,
and 5 points in a star.
3, 4, 5
```

The eof method

Reading from the file only makes sense when there is data left in it. To check if the file or stream still contains data, use the `eof` method, which returns `False` when the end of file is reached:

```
my $fh = open 'data.txt';
if $fh && !$fh.eof { # Only if file exists and has something to read
    my $line = $fh.get;
    say $line;
}
```

Writing to a stream

In this section, we will examine methods that the `IO::Handle` class offers for writing to a stream.

The print function

We will start with the simple `print` function. Basically, its usage is obvious. It prints the text to the stream. In the case of standard output, use the bare `print` function or the `$*IN.print` method. If you work with a file, use its file handle.

The following program creates a file named `hello.txt` and writes a string to it.:

```
my $fh = open 'hello.txt', :w; # Open a file for writing
$fh.print('Hello, World');     # Print to the file
$fh.close;                     # Close the file so that the data is saved
```

If the file already exists, it will be re-written, and all previous contents will be lost. Use the `:a` append mode if you need to append new output to an existing file:

```
my $fh = open 'hello.txt', :a; # Open in append mode
$fh.print('!');                # Now the file contains 'Hello, World!'
$fh.close;
```

The `close` method closes a file. Actually, this does not need to be done manually as Perl 6 will close the file as soon as the filehandle goes out of its scope.

The :enc named parameter of the open function sets the encoding of a file. Consider the following code. It opens two files and prints the same string to it:

```
my $str = 'ä';

my $fh1 = open 'enc-latin1.txt', :w, enc => 'Latin1';
$fh1.print($str);
$fh1.close;

my $fh2 = open 'enc-utf-8.txt', :w, enc => 'UTF-8';
$fh2.print($str);
$fh2.close;
```

Now, look at the file sizes of the files that this program created:

```
$ ls -la enc-*.txt
-rw-r--r-- 1 ash ash 1 Mar 16 07:59 enc-latin1.txt
-rw-r--r-- 1 ash ash 2 Mar 16 07:59 enc-utf-8.txt
```

As expected, one of the files was written in the Latin-1 encoding. The ä character fits in this encoding fine, so the file contents is a single byte with the code of the character:

```
$ hexdump enc-latin1.txt
0000000 e4
0000001
```

The second file is using the UTF-8 encoding and the same character needs two bytes:

```
$ hexdump enc-utf-8.txt
0000000 c3 a4
0000002
```

In the previous examples, both encoding were able to represent the character that was written to the files. If the chosen encoding cannot support that, a run-time error occurs. In the next program, we are trying to write a Unicode smiley to the file that is open in the Latin-1 encoding:

```
my $fh = open 'smiley.txt', :w, :enc('Latin1');
$fh.print(0x263a.chr); # The WHITE SMILING FACE character
$fh.close;
say 'OK?';
```

The program exits while attempting to write to the file, and the rest of the program is not executed:

```
Error encoding Latin-1 string: could not encode codepoint 9786
  in block <unit> at enc2.pl line 2
```

Notice that in the previous programs the two different syntax options were used to pass the value to the named parameter of a function—enc => 'UTF-8' and :enc('Latin1'). Both forms are equivalent; you may choose the one you like more.

The say method

At first glance, the say method works like the print method and adds a new line character at the end. But this is not the full truth. Internally, say calls the gist method on the object it prints to get the textual representation of it.

For the data types such as strings and integers, their textual forms are straightforward. There will be no difference in the output for print and say in the following example:

```
my $str = 'String';
print $str, "\n";
say $str;

my $int = 42;
print $int, "\n";
say $int;
```

With more complex data structures, the behavior of the two methods is different. The output of the program is shown in the comments:

```
my @array = <10 20 30>;
print @array, "\n"; # 10 20 30
say @array;         # [10 20 30]

my %hash = alpha => 1, beta => 2, gamma => 3;
print %hash, "\n";  # alpha    1
                    # beta     2
                    # gamma    3
say %hash;          # {alpha => 1, beta => 2, gamma => 3}
```

Example of using the gist method

For the user-defined classes, it is possible to create a gist method that prepares the output as desired. Let us try this on the following example.

We create a class for storing chemical formulae. The goal is to allow creating a chemical formula in pure ASCII format and then print it so that numerical indices are displayed as subscripts.

```
class Chemical {
    has $.formula;
    method gist {
        my $output = $!formula;
        $output ~~ s:g/(<[0..9]>)/{(0x2080+$0).chr}/;
        $output;
    }
}
```

The `Chemical` class has a data member `$.formula`, which keeps the original ASCII formula as a string. The `gist` method converts it to a string with subscripts. We make a replacement using regular expressions. Regular expressions are covered in detail in `Chapter 11`, *Regexes*. For now, it is enough to know that the following line of the code replaces all the digits from 0 to 9 with their subscript versions. To get the code value of the subscripted digit, the value of a digit from the formula is added to the codepoint value of the SUBSCRIPT ZERO Unicode character:

```
$output ~~ s:g/(<[0..9]>)/{(0x2080+$0).chr}/;
```

Now, it is time to use the class. In a loop, a few instances are created to test different cases: a simple formula, a formula with parentheses, and a formula with two-digit indices:

```
for < H2O Al2(SO4)3 Al6O13Si2 > {
    my $chem = Chemical.new(formula => $_);
    say $chem;
}
```

The program gives the following output:

```
H₂O
Al₂(SO₄)₃
Al₆O₁₃Si₂
```

If you use the `print` function instead of `say`, then the output will be something like this:

```
Chemical<140226845929544>
Chemical<140226845929664>
Chemical<140226845929704>
```

This output contains the name of the class and an address of the location of the variable in memory. To make the output more useful for the end user, define the `gist` method for the class and use the `say` function to 'print' objects.

The printf method

The `printf` method prints the values in the given format. It is mostly identical to the `printf` function from the C and C++ standard library. The first argument of this method is a string describing the format, and the rest of the arguments are the values that will be substituted instead of the directives, starting with the % character in the format string.

In many cases, formatting can be achieved by string interpolation instead. For example, the following two lines produce the same output:

```
my $temperature = 25.6;
printf("Temperature is %g °C\n", $temperature);
say "Temperature is $temperature °C";
```

In the following tables, the main formatting directives are listed.

Characters and strings

Let us start with printing textual data:

Directive	Description
%%	The % character
%c	A character
%s	A string

Here are some examples of the directives in the preceding table:

```
printf "The percent sign: %%\n";
printf "Character %c\n", 167;
printf "String %s\n", 'Hello, World';
```

This program prints the following lines:

```
The percent sign: %
Character §
String Hello, World
```

Notice that the %c directive treats the corresponding argument as a character, not as an integer.

Integers

There are a few different directives for printing integer numbers in different formats:

Directive	Description
%b	An integer in binary representation
%d or %i	Signed decimal integer
%u	Unsigned decimal integer
%o	An integer in octal format
%x	Unsigned integer in hexadecimal format
%X	Same as %x but in uppercase

Let us print the same number in different formats:

```
printf "Binary: %b, decimal: %d, octal: %o\n", 10, 10, 10;
printf "Hexadecimal: %x, uppercased: %X\n", 10, 10;
```

The output of this program looks like this:

```
Binary: 1010, decimal: 10, octal: 12
Hexadecimal: a, uppercased: A
```

The %u directive expects an unsigned integer, so the compiler raises an error if it sees the negative number:

```
$ perl6 -e'printf "%u", -10'
negative value '-10' for %u in sprintf
Directive u not applicable for type Int
```

Floating-point numbers

For the floating-point numbers, use one of the following formats:

Directive	Description
%e	A floating-point number in scientific notation
%E	Same as %e but with the uppercase E for the exponential part
%f	A floating-point number
%g	Either %e, of %f (whichever is better)

In the following example, the value of pi is printed in different formats:

```
printf "%e, %E\n", pi, pi;
printf "%f, %g\n", pi, pi;
```

This is how the result looks:

```
3.141593e+00, 3.141593E+00
3.141593, 3.14159
```

The `%g` format is the most 'human-oriented'—it displays the floating-point number with limited precision and switches to the scientific notation for very big and very small numbers:

```
printf "%g\n", 0.000001; # 1e-06
printf "%g\n", 0.1;       # 0.1
printf "%g\n", 1;         # 1
printf "%g\n", 10;        # 10
printf "%g\n", 10000000; # 1e+07
```

The number of arguments passed after the formatting string must agree with the number of directives in it. Otherwise an `X::Str::Sprintf::Directives::BadType` exception occurs:

```
$ perl6 -e'printf "%c", 1, 2'
Your printf-style directives specify 1 argument, but 2 arguments were
supplied
```

For a detailed description of the formatting string, please refer to the following documentation page: `docs.perl6.org/type/Str#sub_sprintf`.

Summary

In this chapter, we talked about input and output facilities that are available in Perl 6. The `IO::Handle` class provides the universal way of working with standard input and output streams as well as with files using the same interface. We discussed how to create files and how to test different properties of files and directories and examined various methods of reading and writing.

When working with files, you may sometimes be faced with exceptional situations; we've seen a few examples in this chapter. In the next chapter, we will discuss exceptions in Perl 6 in detail.

10
Working with Exceptions

In the previous two chapters, we talked about object-oriented programming and about input and output, which is implemented using objects. In this chapter, we continue working with objects and will discuss another area in Perl 6, whose implementation extensively uses classes and has a vast hierarchical structure.

Exceptions are situations where the program enters such a state that it cannot run further. Some exceptions are caused by flaws in the design of a program, others happen because of external factors, such as disk failure or broken connection to a database. In this case, an exception is not something extraordinary that has to stop the program but a way to handle the error and continue execution.

In this chapter, we will talk about exceptional situations that a program can be faced with. Moreover, we will also see ways a in which programmer can prevent the consequences of exceptional moments.

The following topics will be covered in this chapter:

- The `try` block
- Catching exceptions with the `CATCH` phase block
- The `Exception` class
- Throwing and rethrowing exceptions
- The `Failure` class and soft failures
- Using typed exceptions
- Creating custom exceptions

The try block

Let us start with one of the simplest exceptions, division by zero. Run the following one-liner:

```
say 1 / 0;
```

The program breaks and prints the following error message:

```
Attempt to divide 1 by zero using div
  in block <unit> at zero-div.pl line 1

Actually thrown at:
  in block <unit> at zero-div.pl line 1
```

We cannot divide by zero. Notice that the error message also contains the stack trace of the program. As we do not use any modules or have any function calls, the stack trace is short.

Now, let's do some other actions before and after the line with the division, which fails:

```
say 'Going to divide 1 by 0';
say 1 / 0;
say 'Division is done';
```

An exception because of division by zero happens at runtime. So, the program executes the first line and prints the first message. Then, an exception occurs and the program terminates. Nothing more will be executed, and the last line will never be reached.

Now let us change the built-in values by entering values from outside. Let the user enter the numbers to divide:

```
my $a = prompt 'Enter dividend > ';
my $b = prompt 'Enter divisor > ';
my $c = $a / $b;
say "The result of $a / $b is $c.";
say 'Done.';
```

If you run this program, it will ask for two numbers and print the result of their division. Try it with some non-zero values:

```
$ perl6 division.pl
Enter dividend > 10
Enter divisor > 2
The result of 10 / 2 is 5.
Done.
```

Now try entering zero as a divisor. Immediately, you get an exception:

```
$ perl6 division.pl
Enter dividend > 10
Enter divisor > 0
Attempt to divide 10 by zero using div
  in block <unit> at division.pl line 4

Actually thrown at:
  in block <unit> at division.pl line 4
```

This behavior may not be the most desired outcome of the program. We should make the program more stable so that it does not depend on wrong numbers from outside.

In Perl 6, the problematic part of the code may be placed into the `try` block. In our example, such a part of the code is the line with the division operation:

```
my $c = $a / $b;
```

Let us put it inside the `try` block together with the line printing the result.

```
my $a = prompt 'Enter dividend > ';
my $b = prompt 'Enter divisor > ';
try {
    my $c = $a / $b;
    say "The result of $a / $b is $c.";
}
say 'Done.';
```

Notice that we have some code after the `try` block in this program.

Run it with the same input values as before. First, with non-zero numbers:

```
$ perl6 division.pl
Enter dividend > 10
Enter divisor > 5
The result of 10 / 5 is 2.
Done.
```

The program behaves exactly as it did prior to introducing the `try` block.

Now, try it with zero:

```
$ perl6 division.pl
Enter dividend > 10
Enter divisor > 0
Done.
```

That's it. There are three things to notice here. First, we do not see the error message about the illegal division. Second, the string The result of ... is not printed. Third, the code following the try block is executed and printed.

What happened here? Inside the try block, an exception happened as before but it did not stop the execution of the program. The try block hid the fact of the exception from us. Of course, we lost the output with the result but we retained the ability to continue with the program.

The $! variable

Now let us see how we can understand if something wrong has happened. In Perl 6, there is a special variable, $!, called the **error variable**. It contains an exception if it happened. Let us use it to check whether everything is OK:

```
my $a = prompt 'Enter dividend > ';
my $b = prompt 'Enter divisor > ';
try {
    my $c = $a / $b;
    say "The result of $a / $b is $c.";
}
if $! {
    say 'Failure!';
}
else {
    say 'All fine.';
}
say 'Done.';
```

We added the test if $!. It treats the $! variable in a Boolean context. Actually, the value of the variable in the presence of an exception is a value of the Exception type. We will see it later in this chapter in the *The Exception object* section. For now, it is enough to know that in a Boolean context an Exception gives a True value. If there were no exceptions, the $! variable would contain the object of the Any type, which is False in a Boolean context.

If you run the updated program and pass zero as the divisor, the program prints the Failure! message:

```
$ perl6 division.pl
Enter dividend > 10
Enter divisor > 0
Failure!
Done.
```

Soft failures

In the previous example, the `try` block contained the instructions for both math calculations and printing the result. In real programs, these actions are often separated. Let us re-write the program so that it divides the numbers in a separate subroutine:

```
my $a = prompt 'Enter dividend > ';
my $b = prompt 'Enter divisor > ';
my $c = calculate($a, $b);
say 'Now ready to print';
say "The result of $a / $b is $c.";
say 'Done.';

sub calculate($a, $b) {
    return $a / $b;
}
```

Now the dangerous action happens inside the `calculate` function and the result is used outside it.

Run the program with values that should cause exception:

```
$ perl6 division.pl
Enter dividend > 10
Enter divisor > 0
Now ready to print
Attempt to divide 10 by zero using div
  in block <unit> at 06.pl line 7

Actually thrown at:
  in block <unit> at 06.pl line 7
```

Examine the output carefully. Before the exception message, the line `Now ready to print` appeared on the screen. At the time when it is printed, calculations are already completed, the illegal division has already taken place but the program is still alive and only fails when the result is about to be printed.

This happens because Perl 6 allows failing softly. A **soft failure** is an unthrown exception. The result of the division is only used in the line where we print the value of `$c`. Before that, nothing stopped the program and it printed the message as if no errors had happened.

Understanding soft failures leads us to the following conclusion. If you use the `try` block to prevent the program from terminating , you should put it around the place where the impossible result is about to be used (such as with the `say` function). The following modification will do the job:

```
try {
    say "The result of $a / $b is $c.";
}
```

Surrounding the division itself is not enough:

```
sub calculate($a, $b) {
    my $result;
    try {
        $result = $a / $b;
    }
    return $result;
}
```

Here, after the `try` block, the `$!` variable contains the `Any` object, as the failure has not happened yet.

The CATCH phaser

Earlier in this chapter, we used the `try` block to catch exceptions. If the exceptions happen inside the `try` block, it sets the `$!` variable, which you can check later.

In Perl 6, this is not the only method to handle exceptions. Let's return to the previous program but this time we'll use the `CATCH` block:

```
my $a = prompt 'Enter dividend > ';
my $b = prompt 'Enter divisor > ';
my $c = $a / $b;
say "The result of $a / $b is $c.";
say 'Done.';

CATCH {
    say 'Exception caught!';
}
```

Run the program:

```
$ perl6 division.pl
Enter dividend > 10
Enter divisor > 0
```

```
Exception caught!
Attempt to divide 10 by zero using div
  in block <unit> at 07.pl line 4

Actually thrown at:
  in block <unit> at 07.pl line 4
```

As soon as the division by zero happens and its result is used, the CATCH block is triggered. A CATCH block is one of the phasers in Perl 6, which we discussed in Chapter 2, *Writing Code*. The compiler passes execution to this block when an exception occurs, and nobody has handled it so far.

Notice again that the exception happens not at the moment of the division by zero but at the moment the result is printed to the console.

If we put the problematic code inside the try block, the CATCH block will not be run, as is seen in the following variant of our program:

```
my $a = prompt 'Enter dividend > ';
my $b = prompt 'Enter divisor > ';
my $c = $a / $b;
try {
    say "The result of $a / $b is $c.";
}
say 'Done.';

CATCH {
    say 'Exception caught!';
}
```

In this program, neither the message from the CATCH block nor the exception message will be printed. The try block hid the exception and set the $! variable. The CATCH block was not initiated because the exception was already handled.

So far, we have covered the basic approaches to handling exceptions. Now it is time to dive a bit deeper and see how Perl 6 actually manipulates exceptions using the Exception class.

The Exception object

Exceptions in Perl 6 are handled via the objects of the classes that are derived from the Exception class. These objects contain all the necessary information regarding the exception, including some text description and stack trace (in Perl 6, it is called **backtrace**).

Perl 6 creates an exception object when an exception arises. We have seen an example of such a situation earlier in this chapter—the error became visible during an attempt to print the result of the illegal mathematical operation. Now, let us produce an exception ourselves using the `die` keyword.

The `die` keyword throws a fatal exception and terminates the program. A typical usage is to stop the program if it cannot open a file or load a resource that is vital for the rest of the program, for example:

```
my $fh = open 'filename.txt' or die 'File not found';
```

If there is no such file, the `$fh` variable in the Boolean context is false and the second branch of the `or` operator will be executed.

The `die` function accepts a text message. Consider an example, where `die` is called unconditionally:

```
say 'Start';
die 'Error message';
say 'Stop';
```

This short program prints the following:

```
Start
Error message
  in block <unit> at die.pl line 2
```

Again, it works fine until an exception occurs and stops working after it. The `die` function takes the text message, which is printed together with the backtrace information. This is an example of how programmers can generate their own error messages. Providing the error with a good description helps to understand the reason behind what went wrong.

To handle this exception, use either the `try` or `CATCH` block. The `try` block suppresses the error message but allows the program to continue:

```
say 'Start';
try {
    die 'Error message';
}
say 'Stop';
```

This program does not quit after the exception:

```
$ perl6 die.pl
Start
Stop
```

With the CATCH block, we catch the exception but the program terminates:

```
say 'Start';
die 'Error message';
say 'Stop';

CATCH {
    say 'Caught';
}
```

The output of the program is the following:

```
$ perl6 die.pl
Start
Caught
Error message
  in block <unit> at die.pl line 2
```

This is what we saw earlier but there are more things involved here, and we are going to examine them.

When entering the CATCH block, Perl 6 puts the exception object into the default variable $_. Use it to analyze the reason and respond accordingly. Let us print some debugging information so that we see what is happening with the $_ and $! variables. In the following code, the ^name method returns the name of the class of the variable:

```
say 'Start';
die 'Error message';
say 'Stop';

CATCH {
    say '== $_.^name ==';
    say $_.^name;
    say '== $_ ==';
    say $_;
    say '== $! ==';
    say $!;
    say 'Caught';
}
```

The result of the program reveals some interesting details:

```
$ perl6 die.pl
Start
== $_.^name ==
(X::AdHoc)
== $_ ==
Error message
```

```
   in block <unit> at 10.pl line 2

== $! ==
Nil
Caught
Error message
   in block <unit> at 10.pl line 2

Actually thrown at:
   in block <unit> at 10.pl line 2
```

The object in `$_` is an instance of the `X::AdHoc` class. An ad hoc exception is an example of the type derived from the `Exception` class. Perl 6 creates such an object in response to the call of `die`. The `X::` namespace is used by convention for the exception classes.

Then, when we print the `$_` variable by passing it to the `say` function, the actual error message is printed:

```
Error message
   in block <unit> at 10.pl line 2
```

Please pay attention to the fact that the `$!` variable is empty—it contains the `Nil` value.

Finally, the compiler prints the message from the `CATCH` block, prints the error message together with the backtrace information, and terminates the program.

Throwing exceptions

Now we can start examining exception objects. The `Exception` base class defines the `throw` method, which you can use to throw an exception. For simplicity, let us start with the `X::AdHoc` exception.

In the following program, an exception is explicitly created with the `new` method and immediately thrown with the `throw` method:

```
say 'Start';
X::AdHoc.new.throw;
say 'Stop';

CATCH {
    say 'Caught';
}
```

The output of the program is familiar to us:

```
Start
Caught
Unexplained error
  in block <unit> at throw.pl line 2
```

We did not provide any error message, and the program printed the default string—Unexplained error.

To use a message, use the payload named argument when creating an exception object:

```
X::AdHoc.new(payload => 'My error message').throw;
```

Resuming from exceptions

As we have seen, the CATCH block stops the execution of the program. This is not always the best strategy. In Perl 6, the exception object (an object whose type is derived from the Exception class) can return control to the place in the code where an error occurred.

To achieve that, call the resume method on the exception object, as shown in the next example:

```
say 'Start';
X::AdHoc.new(payload => 'My error message').throw;
say 'Stop';

CATCH {
    say 'Caught';
    .resume;
}
```

The .resume line calls the method on the default variable $_. It is equivalent to an explicit call $_.resume.

This time, the program does not quit but rather continues working after an exception:

```
Start
Caught
Stop
```

In this case, the error message will not be printed, similar to how it works with the `try` block. For example, resuming reading from a nonexistent file does not make sense. On the other hand, when making a series of calculations, it may be useful to continue even if one of them divides by zero.

Typed exceptions

There are many more classes in the `X::` namespace predefined in Perl 6. To see a full list of built-in exceptions, visit the following page— `docs.perl6.org/type-exceptions.html`. You can create your own class for your specific exceptions. We will first look at how to distinguish between the exceptions of different types in the `CATCH` block.

Let us create a program that tries to change the current working directory to a nonexistent one. In Perl 6, you can use the `chdir` function to change the directory:

```
chdir '/non-existing/directory';
```

The output shows the following error message:

```
Failed to change the working directory to '/non-existing/directory': does
not exist
  in block <unit> at chdir.pl line 1
```

Now, let us see the type of the exception by calling the `^name` method on the `$_` variable inside the `CATCH` block:

```
chdir '/non-existing/directory';
CATCH {
    say $_.^name;
}
```

It will tell us that the `$_` variable contains an object of the `X::IO::Chdir` class.

Now, let's use this knowledge to make different actions in response to different exceptional cases. Let us construct the program, which first changes the directory and then throws an ad hoc exception.

To separate the paths of the different exceptions, we will use the `when` keyword, which matches the `$_` variable against the given type:

```
chdir '/non-existing/directory';
X::AdHoc.new.throw;

CATCH {
```

```
    when X::AdHoc {
        say 'Ad hoc exception';
        .resume;
    }
    when X::IO::Chdir {
        say 'Non-existing directory';
        .resume;
    }
}
```

Run this program and confirm that both exceptions were caught correctly:

```
Non-existing directory
Ad hoc exception
```

In the CATCH block, there are two when branches, one for each exception type, that we want to handle. It is important to realize that, after the when block is found and executed, the CATCH block returns control and ignores all the code after that point. This is why the resume method is put in either when block. If you put it once at the end of the whole CATCH block, that code will only be reached if the exception of other type happened and none of the when blocks were satisfied.

Rethrowing exceptions

Sometimes an exception handler is not capable of processing an exception. In this case, it can throw it again by calling a rethrow method. The exception will be caught by the default exception handler.

Consider the following example:

```
say 1 / 0;
CATCH {
    when X::Numeric::DivideByZero {
        say 'Division by zero caught';
        .rethrow;
    }
}
```

Here, the `X::Numeric::DivideByZero` exception is caught after an attempt to print the result of the division `1 / 0`. Then an exception is re-thrown, and Perl 6 prints the appropriate error message and terminates the program:

```
Division by zero caught
Attempt to divide 1 by zero using div
  in block <unit> at div0.pl line 1

Actually thrown at:
  in block <unit> at div0.pl line 1
```

The Failure object

Let us create a program that tries to open a nonexisting file and read the first line from it:

```
my $f = open 'dummy.txt';
say $f.get;
```

This program will raise an exception:

```
Failed to open file /Users/ash/code/exceptions/dummy.txt: no such file or
directory
  in block <unit> at 14.pl line 1
```

Notice that the exception happens only after an attempt to read from a file happens. Simply opening a file does not create an error, it only sets the `$f` file handler to the `Failure` object.

The failure object is a wrapper around an `Exception` object. The exception itself is reachable via the `exception` method:

```
my $f = open 'dummy.txt';
say $f.exception;
```

It prints the error message:

```
Failed to open file /Users/ash/code/exceptions/dummy.txt: no such file or
directory
```

You can test a failure object in the Boolean context, for example, immediately after opening a file:

```
my $f = open 'dummy.txt';
say 'File not found' unless $f;
```

To see if the failure has been handled, use the `handled` method. In the following example, this method is called twice—before and after the `try` block around the method that raises an exception:

```
my $f = open 'dummy.txt';
say $f.handled; # False
try {
    say $f.get;
}
say $f.handled; # True
```

As soon as the program flow leaves the `try` block, the status of the exception changes to handled.

Creating custom exceptions

In the previous sections, we have seen that exceptions in Perl 6 use the object-oriented approach, which, in particular, helps to distinguish between different exceptions in the CATCH block.

In this section, we will create a custom exception that is integrated into the Perl 6 system as smoothly as any other built-in classes in the X:: namespace. If you do not have any special requirements, create your custom exception classes in the same namespace.

For example, let us create a `Lift` class together with the X::Lift::Overload exception, which will be triggered when too many people enter the lift:

```
class Lift {
    class X::Lift::Overload is Exception {
        method message {
            'Too many people!'
        }
    }

    has $.capacity = 5;
    has $!people;
    method enter(Int $n = 1) {
        $!people += $n;
        X::Lift::Overload.new.throw if $!people > $!capacity;
    }
}
```

We don't need the exception class outside the `Lift` class, so it is better to restrict the scope and define the exception inside the main class.

The X::Lift::Overload class extends the Exception class and must provide at least the message method so that the exception handler can print the error message.

In the List class, there are two data members, $.capacity and $!people, for holding the default capacity and the actual number of people in a lift. The enter method increases that number and checks whether the capacity has been reached. If more people come in, an exception is thrown.

Now, let us create an instance of the Lift class and let a few people enter the lift:

```
my $lift = Lift.new(capacity => 4);
$lift.enter();
$lift.enter(3);
$lift.enter(2);
```

After the third call of enter, there will be five people in a lift with a maximum capacity of four. So, the X::Lift::Overload exception is raised and the program exits with the following error message:

```
Too many people!
  in method enter at lift.pl line 12
  in block <unit> at lift.pl line 20
```

Summary

In this chapter, we learned about working with exceptions in Perl 6. We examined in detail ways to throw, catch, and hide exceptions by using different mechanisms of the language—try blocks and CATCH phasers. We talked about soft failures, which are postponed exceptions that are only thrown when it is really unavoidable. Also, we demonstrated how to use the object-oriented approach to handle exceptions of different types and how to create a custom exception.

11
Regexes

Regular expressions are one of the most valuable features of Perl. In Perl 6, regular expressions were redesigned to make them more regular and powerful. The term also changed—regular expressions are more often called simply **regexes** now. In this chapter, we will go through all the elements of the syntax of regexes.

The following topics will be covered in this chapter:

- Matching against regexes
- Literals
- Character classes
- Quantifiers
- Anchors
- Alternation
- Grouping
- Capturing and named captures
- Named regexes
- The Match object
- Assertions
- Adverbs
- Substitution

Matching against regexes

Regexes describe patterns of text. They provide us with a language, in which we can express the structure of the text.

Consider an example. A phone number is a sequence of digits. The phrase "**sequence of digits**" can be written down as \d+. If we take into account the fact that phone numbers may be written with spaces and dashes, then we have to say that a phone number is a sequence of digits, delimited with spaces or dashes. This is already a more complex regex, which can be written differently, depending on how strict we are, for instance, if we allow two spaces together or if a dash can be followed by a space, or if a group of digits can consist of a single digit.

Let's be least strict and formalize it as (\d || \s || \-)+, that is more than one number of digits (\d) or spaces (\s) or dashes (\-). The double vertical bar stands for "**or**" here, and the + means **more than one**. Finally, an international phone number can be prefixed with a plus character, which is optional. So, our final phone number regex is \+? (\d || \s || \-)+.

This regex is not perfect. Later in this chapter, we will work on making it better and more robust. But let us start with that one and make our first **matching**. Comparing a string with a regex is called matching in Perl. To match against a regex, the double tilde operator is used. The regular expression itself is placed within a pair of slashes:

```
say 'OK' if '+31 645-23-10' ~~ /\+? (\d || \s || \-)+/;
```

This program prints OK , which means that the string with a phone number matched the regex. Let us try some text instead:

```
say 'OK' if 'phone' ~~ /\+? (\d || \s || \-)+/;
```

Inside this string, there are no characters that are required by a regex, and the program prints nothing. The regex did not match.

Both the string and the regex may be placed in variables, which will be matched against each other:

```
my $phone = '+31 645-23-10';
my $re = /\+? (\d || \s || \-)+/;

say 'OK' if $phone ~~ $re;
```

A regex can use other surrounding symbols apart from / ... /. This may be useful if a regex contains many slashes, such as a regex for parsing URLs. You will need the prefixing characters m or rx before the regex in this case. The following examples are all equivalent:

```
/ \d+ /
m/ \d+ /
m{ \d+ }
m| \d+ |
```

To create a regex that will be put in a variable, use rx:

```
my $phone = '+31 65 253-45-93';
my $re = rx/\+? (\d || \s || \-)+/;

say 'OK' if $phone ~~ $re;
```

Delimiters can be different, for example, a pair of braces:

```
my $re = rx{\+? (\d || \s || \-)+};
```

Use m or rx for creating a regex that is used directly in the matching:

```
say 'Not OK' unless 'phone' ~~ m/\+? (\d || \s || \-)+/;
```

To negate the result of matching, Perl 6 offers a different operator, !~~. Choose the one which makes the whole construction easier to understand.

```
say 'Not OK' if 'phone' !~~ rx/\+? (\d || \s || \-)+/;
```

As you can see from the previous two examples, a combination of unless and ~~ is equivalent to if and !~~.

Now, as we know how to match strings against regexes and have made our first regex, let us learn the bits of regexes in detail.

Literals

The syntax of regexes is a small language within Perl 6. As there are many things to express, it uses some characters to convey the meaning. Letters, digits and underscores stand for themselves without any special meaning. These characters can be used as-is, as shown in the following example:

```
my $name = 'John';
say 'OK' if $name ~~ /John/; # OK
```

```
my $id = 534;
say 'OK' if $id ~~ /534/; # OK
```

If the string inside a regex contains other characters, for example, spaces, you should take care of them. One of the possibilities is to quote the whole string:

```
my $name = 'Smith Jr.' ;
say 'Junior' if $last-name ~~ /' Jr'/; # Junior
```

The literal string ' Jr' inside a regex contains a space that will have to be present in the variable $name.

Another alternative is to use a special character, prefixed by a backslash. For matching with a space, use \s:

```
my $name = 'Smith Jr.' ;
say 'Junior' if $name ~~ /\sJr/; # Junior
```

Spaces in Perl 6's regexes are ignored by default. This fact can be exploited to add some **air** to a regex. Compare the regexes that we used earlier, written with no spaces, with their equivalents that use spaces for clarity:

Original regex	Regex with spaces
/John/	/ John /
/' Jr'/	/ ' Jr' /
/\sJr/	/ \s Jr /
/\+?(\d|\s|\-)+/	/ \+? (\d | \s | \-)+ /

Character classes

A character class in regexes is a special sequence that matches characters from some given set. For example, in the previous section, we already used a character class \s, which matches with an ASCII space as well as with some other whitespace characters, such as tabs. Let us explore character classes in regexes of Perl 6.

The . (dot) character

A very simple character, just a single dot, can match with any character in the string. This is often used when you do not care about some character between the two parts. For example, the following code will match with a string that has any two characters between a and d:

```
say 'OK' if 'abcd' ~~ / a . . d /; # OK
say 'OK' if 'aefd' ~~ / a . . d /; # OK
say 'OK' if 'a*^d' ~~ / a . . d /; # OK
```

In the first two examples, each dot matched one of the letters. In the third one, both dots matched with a whitespace.

Backslashed character classes

There is a set of predefined character classes that start with a backslash and have one letter, either lowercase or uppercase. Uppercase versions are opposite to their lowercase and negate the set of the characters, with which a character class matches. The following table contains an overview of the backslashed character classes:

Character class	Negated class	Description
\s	\S	Whitespace
\t	\T	Tabulation
\h	\H	Horizontal space
\v	\V	Vertical space
\n	\N	New line
\d	\D	Digit
\w	\W	Word character

Now we will examine all the character classes in detail.

\s and \S characters

We have already seen an example of such a class—\s for matching a space character. Its uppercase-counterpart, \S, does the opposite—it matches with any character except a space. Let us examine an example:

```
my $str = 'Hello, World!';
say 'OK' if $str ~~ / \s World /; # OK
say 'OK' if $str ~~ / Hello\S /;  # OK
```

Both regexes match. The \s in the first one matches with the space between words. The \S in the second example matches with a comma.

The character class \s is a combination of other whitespace character classes—\h and \v, which are described in the following sections. These classes also include individual characters such as \t (horizontal tabulation, 0x09) or \r (line feed, 0x0A).

\t and \T characters

\t and \T match with tab characters and non-tab characters, respectively. Imagine that you have a line of tab-separated data and you want to put it into an array. The following code will do it for you:

```
my $data = "John\tSmith\t1970";
my @data = $data.split(/\t/);

print qq:to/OUT/
Name          = @data[0]
Last name     = @data[1]
Year of birth = @data[2]
OUT
```

Here, we call the split method on the $data string and pass it a regex containing a single \t character class, which should match with a tab character. Thus, it will split the source line into three parts and put them into the @data array.

The `qq:to/OUT/` construction is the start of the heredoc, which ends at the second occurrence of the label `OUT`. A double `qq` requires variable interpolation inside the heredoc. This approach makes it easier to prepare the template for outputting the data in the desired layout:

```
$ perl6 name-split.pl
Name          = John
Last name     = Smith
Year of birth = 1970
```

\h and \H characters

The lowercase version of these character classes matches with horizontal whitespaces (and, respectively, the uppercase version negates the matching result) .

Among the common space and tabulation characters, there are many other horizontal spaces, for example, the non-breaking space that is marked as ` ` in HTML.

The following table lists all currently defined characters that fall into this character class:

Unicode codepoint	Character name
0x9	CHARACTER TABULATION
0x20	SPACE
0xA0	NO-BREAK SPACE
0x1680	OGHAM SPACE MARK
0x180E	MONGOLIAN VOWEL SEPARATOR
0x2000	EN QUAD
0x2001	EM QUAD
0x2002	EN SPACE
0x2003	EM SPACE
0x2004	THREE-PER-EM SPACE
0x2005	FOUR-PER-EM SPACE
0x2006	SIX-PER-EM SPACE
0x2007	FIGURE SPACE
0x2008	PUNCTUATION SPACE

0x2009	THIN SPACE
0x200A	HAIR SPACE
0x202F	NARROW NO-BREAK SPACE
0x25F	MEDIUM MATHEMATICAL SPACE
0x3000	IDEOGRAPHIC SPACE

There are many characters in this table, which you might never use but looking at the table you can imagine how scrupulous Perl 6 is regarding Unicode and whitespaces.

\v and \V characters

The \v and \V character classes represent the characters for vertical spaces and characters, which are not vertical spaces. Perl 6 knows much less vertical spaces comparing to horizontal spaces set but still, it covers the whole range of different Unicode symbols, as listed in the following table:

Unicode codepoint	Character name
0xA	LINE FEED
0xB	LINE TABULATION
0xC	FORM FEED
0xD	CARRIAGE RETURN
0x85	NEXT LINE
0x2028	LINE SEPARATOR
0x2029	PARAGRAPH SEPARATOR

\n and \N characters

The \n character matches the logical new line. The \N character does the opposite and matches with any character, which is not a new line.

Matching new lines is tricky because there are different conventions on how to separate logical lines in different operating systems. On Unix-like systems, lines are separated by a single \r character (with the code 0x0A). In files created in Windows, the new line separator is a combination of two characters, CARRIAGE RETURN (0x0A) and LINE FEED (0x0D). Perl 6's \n character matches either of them.

Let us demonstrate this in the following example:

```
my $unix-str = "Hello,\rWorld!";
my $windows-str = "Hello,\r\nWorld!";

my @unix-lines = $unix-str.split(/\n/);
my @windows-lines = $windows-str.split(/\n/);

say @unix-lines.join('//');
say @windows-lines.join('//');
```

Here, there are two strings with different new line separators. We then split both lines with the same regex /\n/. The output of the program shows that the lines were split into the same parts:

```
Hello,//World!
Hello,//World!
```

\d and \D characters

The \d character class matches with a digit. A digit here is understood as a Unicode character from the Number category. Among the traditional Arabic numerals 0-9, there are digits from other alphabets and scripts. The whole list of these characters is exhausting but let us give a few examples of other digits:

- Arabic-Indic: ٠ ١ ٢ ٣ ٤ ٥ ٦
- Nko (from the right-to-left alphabets of West Africa): ߿ ߀ ߁ ߂ ߃
- Devanagari (India and Nepal): ० १ २ ३ ४
- Bengali: ০ ১ ২ ৩ ৪
- Mathematical bold: **0 1 2 3 4**
- Mathematical double-struck: 𝟘 𝟙 𝟚 𝟛 𝟜

Any of these digits will match against \d:

```
$ perl6 -e'say "OK" if "৩" ~~ /\d/'
OK
```

\w and \W characters

The \w character class matches with a character that can be part of a word, namely, with letters, digits, and the underscore symbol. The \W matches with all the rest. Letters are understood here in the Unicode sense—these are the characters from the Letter category.

For example, \w will always match with any Greek letter:

```
$ perl6 -e'say "OK" if "λ" ~~ /\w/'
OK
```

As with digits, which we covered in the previous section, you have to be prepared that \w will match with many more characters that you may expect based on the languages you are familiar with.

Character classes

A character class is a mechanism to request a match with a given list of characters. For example, to match hexadecimal numbers, we need to match a character with decimal digits 0 to 9 and with six letters a to f (also including their capital variants A to F).

In Perl 6 regexes, this can be written as a character class <[0..9 a..f A..F]>. Let us apply this regex to the list of uppercase Latin letters:

```
for 'A'..'Z' {
    .print if /<[0..9 a..f A..F]>/;
}
```

This prints the string ABCDEF, containing the letters that match the given regex.

Character classes may also include backslashed sequences. In the phone number regex, we can use a character class that will match with either a digit, a space, or a hyphen:

```
/ \+? <[\d\s\-]>+ /;
```

Let us continue with other character classes that are built-in in the Perl 6 regex engine.

Predefined subrules

Regexes in Perl 6 include some predefined **subrules**, which are also character classes and partially intersect with the backslashed character classes. Syntactically, subrules are the names in angle brackets. The following table summarizes them:

Subrule	Meaning
`<alpha>`	Alphabetical symbols and _
`<alnum>`	Same as `\w`
`<digit>`	Same as `\d`
`<lower>`	Lowercase characters
`<upper>`	Uppercase characters
`<space>`	Whitespace, same as `\s`
`<blank>`	Horizontal space, same as `\h`
`<cntrl>`	Control characters
`<punct>`	Punctuation
`<graph>`	Same as `<alnum>` + `<punct>`
`<print>`	Printable characters, same as `<alnum>` + `<space>` without `<punct>`

Predefined subrules are a valid part of regexes in Perl 6 and can be used in any place of a regex together with other character classes of literals. In the following example, we check whether the string contains a digit followed by a letter:

```
my $regex = / <digit> <alpha> /;

say 'Match'    if '3a' ~~ $regex;    # Match
say 'No match' if 'abcd' !~~ $regex; # No match
say 'No match' if 678 !~~ $regex;    # No match
```

The preceding named subrules are not the only way of selecting characters based on their Unicode properties. In the next section, we will see how to use Unicode categories directly.

Using Unicode properties

Characters in Unicode belong to different categories, such as letters or digits, or punctuation. Categories may have additional levels of detailization, for example letters can be lowercase or uppercase.

Regexes in Perl 6 provide us with a mechanism of character classes based on Unicode categories. To create such a class, use a pair of angle brackets, containing a semicolon followed by a capital first letter of the category name. To specify the subcategory, add a corresponding lowercase letter.

For example, the character class matching letters is <:L>, while the class for the uppercase letters is <:Lu>. In the following example we match a few letters against these character classes:

```
for <A a B b Ω ω 1 2 * ^ > -> $char {
    say "$char ~~ <:L>"  if $char ~~ / <:L> /;
    say "$char ~~ <:Lu>" if $char ~~ / <:Lu> /;
}
```

This code loops over a list of different characters and reports whether they match <:L> or <:Lu>:

```
A ~~ <:L>
A ~~ <:Lu>
a ~~ <:L>
B ~~ <:L>
B ~~ <:Lu>
b ~~ <:L>
Ω ~~ <:L>
Ω ~~ <:Lu>
ω ~~ <:L>
```

As you see from the output, all the letters passed the <:L> filter, uppercase letters matched with the <:Lu> character class, and non-letter characters did not match in either of the tests.

Unicode-related character classes have two names in Perl 6, short and long, which are interchangeable. The same code can be written like this using the long names:

```
for <A a B b Ω ω 1 2 * ^ > -> $char {
    say "$char ~~ <:L>"  if $char ~~ / <:Letter> /;
    say "$char ~~ <:Lu>" if $char ~~ / <:Uppercase_Letter> /;
}
```

The following table lists all the character classes corresponding to the Unicode categories. In the table, a one-letter category is followed by its two-letter subcategories. Notice that some letter combinations are not directly deductible from the full category name; for example, the character class for the `Punctuation, Open` category is called `Ps` in Unicode, thus it is `<:Ps>` in Perl 6:

Short name	Long name	Category	Comment
`<:L>`	`<:Letter>`	Letter	
`<:Ll>`	`<:Lowercase_Letter>`	Letter, lowercase	a, b, and so on.
`<:Lu>`	`<:Uppercase_Letter>`	Letter, uppercase	A, B, and so on.
`<:Lt>`	`<:Titlecase_Letter>`	Letter, titlecase	Ligatures such as Lj
`<:Lm>`	`<:Modifier_Letter>`	Letter, modifier	Some diacritics such as ˜
`<:Lo>`	`<:Other_Letter>`	Letter, other	Letters from alphabets such as Hebrew א or Arabic ک
`<:M>`	`<:Mark>`	Mark	
`<:Mn>`	`<:Nonspacing_Mark>`	Mark, nonspacing	Accents such as grave` or acute´
`<:Mc>`	`<:Spacing_Mark>`	Mark, spacing combining	Some combining characters
`<:Me>`	`<:Enclosing_Mark>`	Mark, enclosing	Symbols, surrounding others, such as the old Cyrillic sign for 1000: ҉
`<:N>`	`<:Number>`	Number	
`<:Nd>`	`<:Decimal_Number>`	Number, decimal digit	0, 1, 2, and so on.
`<:Nl>`	`<:Letter_Number>`	Number, letter	For example, Roman numbers (as separate characters like VIII)
`<:No>`	`<:Other_Number>`	Number, other	Other number-related characters such as ¼
`<:P>`	`<:Punctuation>`	Punctuation	
`<:Pc>`	`<:Connector_Punctuation>`	Punctuation, connector	For example, an arc above letters: ⌒
`<:Pd>`	`<:Dash_Punctuation>`	Punctuation, dash	Symbols such as em dash: —
`<:Ps>`	`<:Open_Punctuation>`	Punctuation, open	Opening pair symbols such as [or (
`<:Pe>`	`<:Close_Punctuation>`	Punctuation, close	Closing pair symbols:),], and so on.
`<:Pi>`	`<:Initial_Punctuation>`	Punctuation, initial quote	Initial quoting characters such as «
`<:Pf>`	`<:Final_Punctuation>`	Punctuation, final quote	Closing quoting characters such as »

`<:Po>`	`<:Other_Punctuation>`	Punctuation, other	Many traditional punctuation characters such as ! or ?
`<:S>`	`<:Symbol>`	Symbol	
`<:Sm>`	`<:Math_Symbol>`	Symbol, math	Mathematical symbols: +, ±, ×, and so on.
`<:Sc>`	`<:Currency_Symbol>`	Symbol, currency	Currency symbols: ¤, €, $, and more.
`<:Sk>`	`<:Modifier_Symbol>`	Symbol, modifier	Diacritics for symbols, for example, cedilla ¸ or diaeresis ¨
`<:So>`	`<:Other_Symbol>`	Symbol, other	Symbols that did not fall into other categories: ©, ®, and so on.
`<:Z>`	`<:Separator>`	Separator	
`<:Zs>`	`<:Space_Separator>`	Separator, space	Various types of spaces
`<:Zl>`	`<:Line_Separator>`	Separator, line	The only symbol LINE SEPARATOR with the code 0x8232
`<:Zp>`	`<:Paragraph_Separator>`	Separator, paragraph	The only symbol PARAGRAPH SEPARATOR with the code 0x2029
`<:C>`	`<:Other>`	Other	
`<:Cc>`	`<:Control>`	Other, control	Control characters such as BELL
`<:Cf>`	`<:Format>`	Other, format	Different formatting characters
`<:Cs>`	`<:Surrogate>`	Surrogate	A few number of surrogate characters

Character class arithmetics

Perl 6 offers great power, allowing you to create new character classes using operations over sets. These are—+ or | for union, – for difference, & for intersection, and ^ for the XOR operation. Additionally, character classes can be negated with either – or !.

Let us look at examples. First, create the joined class that matches with both lowercase letters and digits:

```
for <a A 3> -> $char {
    say "$char is a lowercase letter or a digit"
        if $char ~~ / <:Ll + :Nd> /;
}
```

This program print matches for the characters a and 3. The capital A does not match because it is neither a lowercase letter nor a digit.

In another example, we reinvent uppercase letters by subtracting lowercase letters from the set of all letters:

```
for <a A 3> -> $char {
    say "$char is an uppercase letter" if $char ~~ / <:L - :Ll> /;
}
```

Now, take all the lowercase letters and remove all vowels:

```
for 'a'..'z' -> $char {
    say "$char is consonant" if $char ~~ / <:Ll - [aoeiu]> /;
}
```

(Be careful with this approach if you want to experiment with other languages as <:Ll> includes letters from outside of the English alphabet.)

Subtraction is a useful thing if you need to match with any character except the given ones. For example, this is how you match with anything from the English alphabet, which was not in original Latin language, which did not contain some of the modern English letters:

```
for 'A'..'Z' -> $char {
    say "$char is pure Roman" if $char ~~ / <[A .. Z] - [GJUWY]> /;
}
```

To negate a character class, put a minus before it:

```
say 'OK' if 'x' ~~ / <-[abcdef]>/; # OK
```

The Unicode predefined character classes can be negated with an exclamation mark:

```
say 'OK' if 'x' ~~ / <:!Lu>/; # OK
```

Character classes by themselves match with a single character. To make the regex more powerful, let us examine quantifiers.

Creating repeated patterns with quantifiers

Quantifiers modify the previous atom and request the particular number of repetitions. An **atom** is a character or character class or a string literal or a group (we will talk about groups later in the *Extracting substrings with capturing* section of this chapter).

The + quantifier allows the previous atom to be repeated one or more times. For example, the regex /a+/ matches with a single character a, as well as with a string containing two characters aa, or three, or more—aaaaaa. It will not, however, match with a string that does not contain the a character at all.

The * quantifier allows any number of repetitions, including zero. So, the /a*/ regex matches with strings such as bdef, abc, or baad. Of course, a single /a*/ may not be that useful; the * quantifier's more natural use case is between other substrings, such as /ab*c/. This regex matches with either ac, or abc, or abbc.

The ? quantifier requires an atom to either appear once or to be absent. Consider a regex /colou?r/, which matches with the word in both British and American spelling—colour and color.

It is also possible to request the given number of repetitions using the ** quantifier with a number of repetitions or a range following it. For example, / 'a' 'b' ** 3..4 'c' / matches the strings containing the substrings of bbb or bbbb, for example, abbbc but not abbc and not abbbbbbbbc. With the help of ^, the edges of the range may be excluded—/ 'a' 'b' ** 3..^10 'c' / will match with substrings containing three to nine subsequent letters a. Open intervals such as b ** ^10 (zero to nine bs) or b ** 3..* (three or more times) are also allowed.

There is another pair of quantifiers, % and %%, which are used a bit differently. They work together with the +, ?, *, and ** quantifiers and request the repeated sequence be separated by a separator that is mentioned on the right side of either % or %%. In the case of %%, a separator may also appear after the last repeated element. Consider the following examples:

```
say 1 if 'a,b,c,d' ~~ / \w+ % ',' /;
say 1 if 'a,b,c,d' ~~ / \w ** 2..3 % ',' /;
say 1 if 'a,b,c,d' ~~ / \w ** 2..3 %% ',' /;
```

This code matches with all the four letters in the first case—a, b, c, d and with the first three letters in the second—a, b, c. In the last case, only three letters will be matched but the comma between c and d will also be consumed—a, b, c, .

Greediness

The above described qualifiers behave **greedy** by default. That means that they match as many characters from the source string as they can. For example, in the match 'bbb' ~~ /b*/, all the three characters will always be consumed by the regex. Similarly, the + quantifier tries to consume as many repeated characters as possible.

Sometimes that behavior is not desired. Consider a regex for selecting attributes from HTML tags. From the given string `<a href="index.html" class="menu">`, we want to extract the values of the attributes, which are strings inside the quotes. An attempt to create a regex such as `/ \" .* \" /` will take the whole substring between the first and the last quote—`"index.html" class="menu"`. This is because the `*` quantifier does not want to stop at the end of the first attribute value and continues consuming characters.

It goes further and even passes the last quote and the closing angle bracket. After that, no more characters are left but the regex expects to match with a double quote. So the regex engine performs backtracking, **returning** the consumed characters to the string until the regex is satisfied or failed.

To prevent the greedy nature of the quantifier, add a question mark after it:

    / \" .*? \" /

Now, it will match only with the first attribute value (including quotes)—`"index.html"`.

Notice that, inside a regex, the `"` character should be escaped—`\"`. As we've learned in the *Literals* section, only alphanumeric characters and the underscore symbol match with themselves. Alternatively, we could create a string for the quote by putting the double quote inside a pair of single quotes:

    / '"' .*? '"' /

Anti-greedy behavior can be applied to any quantifier, even to the `?` one. In that case, the modified quantifier `??` will try to match with nothing if that is possible. Thus, if the string `abc` is tested against the `/ab?/` regex, then its substring `ab` will be matched. With a non-greedy `/ab??/` regex, only `a` will match. Of course, if we modify the regex in such a way that `b??` will have to match with something, as in `/ab??c/`, then it will do so.

Extracting substrings with capturing

Matching against regexes is not enough. The real power of regular expressions is not complete without the ability to extract the substrings that agreed with the regex pattern. Saving the parts of the string in special variables is called **capturing**.

Capturing groups

In Perl 6, capturing is achieved by placing the part of a regex in parentheses. Parentheses have as dual meaning in regexes. We already have seen the usage of parentheses for grouping alternatives in the phone number.

Let us continue with the example of extracting values of HTML attributes. We want now to print the values. So, we need to create a regex and mark the borders of the data that we want to extract. Captured data is put into the variables $0, $1, and so on. Numerical indices start with zero and correspond to the order number of capturing parentheses in the regex:

```
my $str = q{<a href="index.html" class="menu">};
$str ~~ / \" (.*?) \" .* \" (.*?) \" /;
say $0;
say $1;
```

Run this code and see what it prints:

```
⌈index.html⌋
⌈menu⌋
```

Indeed, we got the values of HTML attributes that we wanted. They contain those substrings of the $str variable that match the parts of the regex in parentheses—(.*?). As we have two occurrences of them, two variables are populated.

As a side note, at this point we can mention that non-greedy quantifiers are not always the only way to express the meaning. Instead of saying *"take as few characters as possible before the double quote"*, we can demand to *"take as many characters, which are not a quotation sign"* and use the negated characters class:

```
my $str = q{<a href="index.html" class="menu">};
$str ~~ / \" (<-[\"]>+) \" .* \" (<-[\"]>+) \" /;
say $0;
say $1;
```

Again, the quote must be escaped, even inside the character class.

The Match object

You may have noticed, in the output from the previous examples, that the real substring is displayed between the pair of square corner brackets. This is because the content of the $0 and $1 variables is not a bare string but an object of the Match type. While printing using the say or print functions, the Match object is formatted in that manner.

Variables such as $0, $1, and so on, are in fact the shortcut variants of the full form—$/[0], $/[1], and so on. The $/ variable is the **Match object**. It is the default variable, which receives the result of the match with a regex. It contains all the captured strings, as well as the whole substring that matched with the whole regex. To get individual captures, indexes such as $/[1] or $1 are used.

So, let us print the value of $/ from the previous example:

```
my $str = q{<a href="index.html" class="menu">};
$str ~~ / \" (.*?) \" .* \" (.*?) \" /;
say $/;
```

We will get the following:

```
⌈"index.html" class="menu"⌋
 0 => ⌈index.html⌋
 1 => ⌈menu⌋
```

The first part ⌈"index.html" class="menu"⌋ contains the whole substring that the regex matches with. It is followed by a couple of indexed elements that match with the capturing parentheses.

When match objects are interpolated inside strings, they are printed without brackets:

```
'April 2017' ~~ / (\d+) /;
say "Year is $0";
```

Here, $0 will be stringified and the output will be `Year is 2017`.

Named captures

Capturing becomes trickier when a regex has more than one or two capturing groups and if there are alternatives in a regex. For example, consider the following regex:

```
my $re = rx/ (<[a..z]>+) || (<[A..Z]>) (\d) /;
```

It contains two alternatives, but the number of capturing groups is different in each branch. (alternation is described in detail in the next section.)

Now, supply the strings that match with either the `<[a..z]>+` or `<[A..Z]>\d` regex:

```
'letter' ~~ $re;
'A5'     ~~ $re;
```

After the first matching, only $0 will be defined. Printing $1 will give Nil. In the second example, both variables will contain a value. It is also not easy to deduce, which part of the regex matched in each case. The straightforward way of checking how many variables are defined does not work if both alternatives have the same number of captures.

Perl 6 allows you to give names to captures. The following example shows the syntax that is used for named captures:

```
my $re = rx/ $<type>=(<[a..z]>+) ||
             $<letter>=(<[A..Z]>) $<size>=(\d)
           /;

'letter' ~~ $re;
say $/;

'A5' ~~ $re;
say $/;
```

In this example we also see the way of formatting a long regex to make it easier and more logical to read.

Examine the output:

```
⌈letter⌋
 type => ⌈letter⌋
⌈A5⌋
 letter => ⌈A⌋
 size => ⌈5⌋
```

You see that the Match object now has named pairs instead of the numeral indices. The names may also be used as if you treat the $/ variable as a hash:

```
'letter' ~~ $re;
say $<type>;

'A5' ~~ $re;
say $<letter>;
say $<size>;
```

The notation of $<name> is a shortcut for $/<name>.

Using alternations in regexes

Let us look once again to our naïve regex for matching phone numbers:

```
rx/ \+? (\d || \s || \-)+ /
```

Vertical bars separate different variants within the group in parentheses. It can be either \d, or \s, or \-. In the context of regexes, this is call **alternation**. Different variants are, correspondingly, called **alternatives**.

In Perl 6, there are two forms of alternation separator in regexes—single | and double || vertical bars . With a single vertical bar, the longest variant always wins. With the double bar, the first matched alternative wins.

In the phone number example, each alternative is exactly one symbol long. So, there is no difference between | and || there. In other cases, the choice of the operator may drastically change the result.

For example, take the two regexes from the following example and match the forms of an adjective big against them:

```
for <big bigger biggest> -> $form {
    say "Testing '$form'";

    $form ~~ / big | bigger | biggest /;
    say $/;

    $form ~~ / big || bigger || biggest /;
    say $/;
}
```

The output of this program is the following:

```
Testing 'big'
「big」
「big」
Testing 'bigger'
「bigger」
「big」
Testing 'biggest'
「biggest」
「big」
```

Analyzing the output, we can see that with the regex with single vertical bars, the longest alternative is selected each time—big, `bigger`, `biggest`. With another regex, which uses double vertical bars, the first match always wins—`big`, all the other variants are not tried. You may play with the code and change the order of the alternatives in the regexes to see how it changes the behavior of this program.

For instance, if you list the variants in the reverse order of their length, the output will be similar for both regexes:

```
$form ~~ / big | bigger | biggest /;
say $/;

$form ~~ / biggest || bigger || big /;
say $/;
```

Alternatives are often only a part of a regex. In our example, there's a sequence \+? for matching an optional plus in the phone number. This is not part of the list of alternatives. To mark the borders of alternation, parentheses are used.

Parentheses also create an atom, which is later modified by the + quantifier, which is applied to the whole part of the regex inside parentheses.

In the case when parentheses are used only for grouping and no capturing is required, use square brackets:

```
my $phrase = 'Eat an apple, please';

$phrase ~~ / ( apple || pear ) /;
say $0;

say 'Healthy' if $phrase ~~ / [ apple || pear ] /;
```

Here, the first example extracts the fruit that was mentioned in the $phrase, while the second match only checks whether the string contains one of the two desired words and does not save it anywhere. After the second match, the $0 variable will contain Nil.

Positioning regexes with anchors

In many cases, a regex has to be applied to the string in such a way that its beginning coincides with the beginning of the string. For example, if a phone number contains the + character, it can only appear in the first position.

Perl 6 regexes have so-called **anchors**—special characters, that anchor a regex to either the beginning or the end of the string or a logical line.

Matching at the start and at the end of lines or strings

Let us modify the phone number regex so that it forces the regex to match with the whole string containing a potential phone number:

```
/ ^ \+? <[\d\s\-]>+ $ /;
```

Here, ^ is the anchor that matches at the beginning of the string and does not consume any characters. On the other side of the regex, $ requires that the end of the regex matches the end of the string. So, a valid phone number, say +49 20 102-14-25 will pass the filter, while a mathematical expression such as 124 + 35 - 36 will not.

For better visibility, anchors can be written on separate lines in the code:

```
my $rx = /
    ^
        \+?
        <[\d\s\-]>+
    $
/;

say 'OK'     if '+49 20 102-14-25' ~~ $rx; # OK
say 'Not OK' if '124 + 35 - 36'    !~~ $rx; # Not OK
```

Both ^ and $ match with the edge of the string (string as a variable). If you need to match with logical lines (if the string contains a few lines separated by \n), use a different pair of anchors—^^ and $$.

In the next example, we want to select the color of a pineapple:

```
my $fruits = "yellow banana\ngreen pineapple\nred apple";

$fruits ~~ / (\w+) \s pineapple $$ /;
say $0;
```

This code prints green, because (\w+) matches with that word in the pineapple line. The end-of-line anchor $$ matched at the end of that line. The result does not depend on the order of lines in the fruit list. If, instead of $$, a single $ is used, then the regex will only match if the green pineapple is located at the end of the whole string.

Matching word boundaries

To match with the word edges, use one of the following anchors:

Anchor	Description
`<|w>`	Any word border
`<<`	Start of a word
`>>`	End of a word

These anchors match on the edges of words and do not consume characters. For example, `/ <|w> apple /` will match with `apple` but not with `pineapple`.

The `<|w>` anchor has its opposite pair, `<!|w>`, that matches with anything that is not a word border. This anchor also does not consume characters, so `/ o <!|w> p /` matches with `opera`.

To specify the border more precisely, use either `<<` or `>>`:

```
my @words = 'fourty-four' ~~ m:g/ << four /;
say +@words;

@words = 'fourty-four' ~~ m:g/ four >> /;
say +@words;
```

In these examples, the first match will find two words, while in the second attempt, only one word ending with `four` will be found.

Looking forward and backward with assertions

Another topic of manipulating the flow of a regex is **assertions**. During the match process, the pattern consumes characters of the source strings. Assertions help to make some checks at the current position without **eating** characters.

There are two types of assertions in Perl 6 regexes—**lookahead** and **lookbehind**. Each of them can be negated. In the following table, all the possible combinations are listed:

	Positive assertion	Negative assertion
Lookahead	`<?before X>`	`<!before X>`
Lookbehind	`<?after X>`	`<!after X>`

Being placed inside a regex, the lookahead assertion `<?before X>` checks whether at this position the following characters are X. If it is so, then the assertion succeeds and the regex engine continues its work. Other assertions behave following the same logical considerations, for example:

```
'Etiquette' ~~ / (.*?) <?after 'qu'> (e .*) /;
say $/;
```

It prints this result:

```
「Etiquette」
 0 => 「Etiqu」
 1 => 「ette」
```

The word in question was split into two parts. The rule was—split at e, which follows qu. The two characters qu were already consumed by the first .*? capturing block but the look ahead assertion was still able to look at the source string to see whether there is the sequence qu there.

Modifying regexes with adverbs

Adverbs are regex modifiers. They are colon-prefix letters that change the behavior of regexes.

Adverbs exist in two forms—**short** and **long**—and appear in front of a regex, for example:

```
say 'OK' if 'ABCD' ~~ m:i/ abcd /;
```

Notice, that when an adverb is applied to the whole regex as in this example, m or rx is needed. Alternatively, an adverb can be put inside the regex. In this case, it starts its action from the position where it appeared. This is demonstrated in the examples in the next section about the :i adverb.

The following table lists all the adverbs:

Short form	Long form	Description
:i	:ignorecase	Match letters are case-insensitive
:s	:sigspace	Whitespacess are significant
:p(N)	:pos(N)	Start at position N
:g	:global	Match globally
:c	:continue	Continue after the previous match
:r	:ratchet	Disable backtracking
:ov	:overlap	Match with overlapping
:ex	:exhaustive	Find all possible matches

Let us go through the list and examine each of the adverbs.

:i (:ignorecase)

This is the simplest regex adverb. It allows the regex to be case-independent. Thus, each of the two regexes m:i/X/ and m:i/x/ will both successfully match with x and X:

```
my $rx = rx:i/hello/;
say 'Matches' if 'Hello, World!' ~~ $rx;
```

When the :i adverb is located inside the regex, then only the following part is case-insensitive:

```
say 'No match' if 'HeLLO, World!' !~~ /he :i llo/;
say 'Matches'  if 'HeLLO, World!'  ~~ /He :i llo/;
```

To stop the action of the adverb, use the negated version:

```
say 'Matches' if 'HeLLo, World!' ~~ /He :i ll :!i o/;
```

Capturing and non-capturing braces limit the scope of an adverb:

```
say 'Not OK' if $str !~~ / (:i hello)\, \s world /;
say 'OK' if $str ~~ / [:i hello]\, \s World /;
```

In these examples, :i only affects the first word.

:s (:sigspace)

We already have seen many times that additional spaces are ignored in regexes, and they are often used to make a regex more readable. In some cases, however, especially when a regex should match with a string with spaces, it is better to disable this feature and demand that spaces match literary.

In the following example, we extract the three parts from the date—day, month, and year. As there are spaces in the original human-oriented string, we need to take care of them in the regex. By default, spaces are ignored and the regex should include \s in the places where a space is expected:

```
my $date = '19 April 2017';
$date ~~ / (\d+) \s (\w+) \s (\d+) /;

say "Year = $2, month = $1, day = $0";
```

With the :s adverb, literal spaces inside the regex will be matched against the string:

```
my $date = '19 April 2017';
$date ~~ m:s/ (\d+) (\w+) (\d+) /;

say "Year = $2, month = $1, day = $0";
```

The good part of Perl 6 (for some it may be confusing) is that the spaces around the regex are still ignored. In the above example we see that there are spaces immediately after the first slash and before the final slash. Those spaces do not require matches.

:p (:pos)

A regex the with the :p or :pos adverb matches the string from a position that is given in the argument of the adverb. The behavior is clearly seen from the following example.

By default, a regex starts from the beginning of the string:

```
'pineapple' ~~ / (\w+) /;
say $0; # pineapple
```

Due to the greedy nature of \w+, the whole string is consumed and matched. Let us try skipping a few characters and apply the regex to the same string:

```
'pineapple' ~~ m:p(4)/ (\w+) /;
say $0; # apple
```

This time, only the `apple` substring will be matched.

An index of the `:p` adverb also behaves like an anchor. Similar to how `^` ties the regex to the beginning of the string, the `:p(N)` adverb ties it to the given position. Compare the following two matches:

```
'pineapple' ~~ m:p(4)/ (a\w+) /;
'pineapple' ~~ m:p(3)/ (a\w+) /;
```

The first of them succeeds, as it finds `a` at the fourth position in the string. The second one immediately fails when it sees `e` at the third position.

:g (:global)

The :g adverb is used for global matching. The regex will be applied to the string a few times, each time starting from the position where the previous match stopped.

For example, let us split a sentence into separate words:

```
my @words = 'Hello, World!' ~~ m:g/ (\w+) /;
say join ';', @words; # Hello;World
```

Remember the example with of extracting HTML attributes from the *The Match object* section of this chapter. To get two values, the regex contained two copies of the same pattern:

```
my $str = q{<a href="index.html" class="menu">};
$str ~~ / \" (.*?) \" .* \" (.*?) \" /;
```

To avoid that and make the regex more generic, use global matches:

```
my $str = q{<a href="index.html" class="menu">};
$str ~~ m:g/ \" .+? \" /;
say ~$/;
```

This program prints `"index.html"` `"menu"`, which are the two matched elements extracted from the string. The `~$/` syntax stringifies the `Match` object; this action is equivalent to interpolating the object inside a string in double quotes, as we did earlier.

Unlike the `:i` modifier, you cannot put `:g` inside the regex.

:c (:continue)

The :c adverb requests continuation from the last position.

Consider the example from the previous section about the :g adverb. Instead of matching globally, we could match a few times:

```
my $str = q{<a href="index.html" class="menu">};

$str ~~ m/ \" .+? \" /;
say ~$/;

$str ~~ m:c/ \" .+? \" /;
say ~$/;
```

Without the :c, the second match will start from the beginning of the string, and it will return the same result as the first match. With :c, it continues with the same string, so the second attribute will be caught.

This adverb may take an index as an argument. In this case, the corresponding regex matching will start at the given position. This is demonstrated in the following example:

```
my $str = q{<div class="menu"><div class="item">};
$str ~~ m:c(10)/ 'class="' .*? '"' /;
say ~$/;
```

The regex is applied to the string starting at the 10th character. In this case, the first potential match is skipped, and the program finds the second class:

```
class="item"
```

:r (:ratchet)

This adverb disables backtracking in regexes. In the *Greediness* section, we have seen how the regex engine rolls back after a greedy quantifier consumed too many characters to make another attempt with fewer characters. The :r adverb does not let it happen. It explains the name :ratchet—it only goes forward.

For example, in the next example, the regex is created to find all numbers that end with zero:

```
for 1..100 {
    .say if / \d+ 0 /;
}
```

This code prints round numbers 10, 20, and so on. With :r, nothing will be printed because \d+ consumes all the digits from a number and :r did not leave the space for matching with 0.

:ov (:overlap)

The :ov adverb changes the way a regex is applied to the string so that all overlapping matches that are the longest at each position will be found.

Let us illustrate this on the task of finding all digit subsequences inside the value of pi, which start and end with 1:

```
my $pi =
'3.1415926535897932384626433832795028841971693993751058209749445923078164';
my @a = $pi ~~ m:g/1.*?1/;
say ~@a;
```

This code prints the following values:

141 1971 10582097494459230781

You may notice that it found sequences in different parts of the original value, and they are not intersecting.

Now, let's add the :ov adverb. To add another adverb to a regex that already has one, simply append it to the previous one:

```
my $pi =
'3.1415926535897932384626433832795028841971693993751058209749445923078164';
my @a = $pi ~~ m:g:ov/1.*?1/;
say ~@a;
```

This time, the output is different:

141 15926535897932384626433832795028841 1971 1693993751 10582097494459230781

Every next value shares the same character 1 with the previous one. The result contains all the values from the previous example but also includes the values in-between, which also match the pattern 1.*?1.

If we remove the anti-greedy quantifier, the nature of the `:ov` adverb will be even more visible. In this case the regex `m:g:ov/1.*1/` returns the longest match at every position, where it sees `1`. As it goes to the end of the string, submatches become shorter and shorter:

```
14159265358979323846264338327950288419716939937510582097494459230781
159265358979323846264338327950288419716939937510582097494459230781
19716939937510582097494459230781  16939937510582097494459230781
10582097494459230781
```

What if we change the pattern to this one?

```
my @a = $pi ~~ m:g:ov/1.*?2/;
```

After applying it to `$pi`, the program prints the following line:

```
141592  1592  19716939937510582  16939937510582  10582
```

This time, overlapping is even stronger—the string `1592`, for example, is completely included in the first match `141592`.

:ex (:exhaustive)

This adverb finds as many substrings as possible, taking into account every posibility, including overlapping values and substrings of different lengths. This partially resembles the behavior of a regex with the `:ov` adverb but does not select the longest matches.

Let us test this adverb with the same pattern `/1.*1/` on the value of `pi` (but this time, we'll take a shorter string):

```
my $pi = '3.141592653589793238462643383279502884197169';
my @a = $pi ~~ m:g:ex/1.*1/;
say ~@a;
```

We took a shorter version to save a bit of space in the output:

```
1415926535897932384626433832795028841971
1415926535897932384626433832795028841  141
15926535897932384626433832795028841971  15926535897932384626433832795028841
1971
```

As an exercise, try the same value with another regex with a non-greedy quantifier—`m:g:ex/1.*?1/`.

Substitution and altering strings with regexes

Matching strings with a regex often extracts some information from the given data. Another common task is to replace parts of the text with different characters. In Perl 6, the s built-in function does that.

It takes two arguments, a regex and a replacement. When a regex is applied to the source string and the pattern is matched, the part of the string that matches is replaced with the second argument.

Consider a simple example:

```
my $str = 'Its length is 10 mm';
$str ~~ s/<<mm>>/millimeters/;
say $str; # Its length is 10 millimeters
```

The regex here, /<<mm>>/, matches with the word mm. The second part tells to replace it with the full name of the measurement unit. The replacement happens in-place and the original string is modified.

Traditionally, s uses slashes as delimiters but different characters can be used. Look at the examples that do the same replacement as in the preceding code:

```
$str ~~ s|<<mm>>|millimeters|;
$str ~~ s;<<mm>>;millimeters;;
```

In the second example, the last two semicolons mean different things—one of them is a delimiter for the regex and replacement, while the other one is the delimiter of Perl 6 expressions.

In the replacement part, a substitution text may use variable interpolation:

```
my $str = 'Its length is 10 mm';
my $standard-length = 7;
$str ~~ s/\d+/$standard-length/;
say $str; # Its length is 7 mm;
```

Values that were captured in the first part of s/// may also be used for substitution:

```
my $date = '20070419';
$date ~~ s/ (\d ** 4) (\d\d) (\d\d) /$2.$1.$0/;
say $date;
```

A regex in s separates the date into year, month, and day parts and combines them in a different order in the replacement pattern.

Summary

In this chapter, we discussed about regexes in Perl 6. They share many common ideas with regular expressions in Perl 5 but also offer many fascinating new things. We examined the methods of constructing regexes and matching with text, learned how to extend the power of a regex engine by using character classes, written by you or built-in. We also looked at the way Perl 6 stores results in the Match object and how to make substitution and replacement in strings using regexes.

In the next chapter, we will meet an even more powerful tool that tremendously extends regexes, grammars.

12
Grammars

Perl 6 has brought out an extremely useful and powerful mechanism to accomplish regexes—grammars.

Grammars are a mini-language inside Perl 6 that allows you to describe the rules of other languages (including Perl 6 itself). With grammars, it is quite easy to create a parser, a translator, or a compiler of a **domain-specific language** (**DSL**) or a programming language, or even a parser that can work with human languages.

In this chapter, we will be learning Perl 6's grammars by way of creating a compiler for the subset of Perl 6. The following topics will be covered in this chapter:

- Creating a grammar
- Elements of grammars—rules and tokens
- The `TOP` rule
- Whitespace handling
- Parsing texts
- Using actions
- Using an **abstract syntax tree** (**AST**)

This chapter assumes that you are familiar with regexes. If you have not read Chapter 11, *Regexes*, now is the right moment to do so. Also, an understanding of organizing classes in Perl 6 is required, which is covered in Chapter 8, *Object-Oriented Programming*.

Creating a grammar

Like regexes, grammars define some rules to extract information from given text. A typical application for regexes is finding fragments in text chunks and splitting them into meaningful pieces, for example, finding an email or checking if its format is correct. Grammars have a bigger goal—their task is often to read the whole text and understand all its content. For example, if a grammar is applied to a code source written in some programming language, the grammar must check its validity and create the syntax tree of the program. This difference is still a convention—grammars can parse small text sections just as regexes can be used for analyzing big text sections.

The syntax for grammars in Perl 6 is like defining a class. A grammar starts with the `grammar` keyword:

```
grammar G {
}
```

This grammar is empty and cannot be applied to a text. We have to add the starting rule, which will be the entry point in the grammar.

Grammars contain **rules** and **tokens**. We will talk about them in this chapter in more detail but at the moment we need to create the main rule, which is the first rule that the grammar applies to the text:

```
grammar G {
    rule TOP {
        .*
    }
}
```

As you see, rules are similar to the methods of a class. Unlike methods, rules contain regexes in their body blocks. The `TOP` rule in this example matches the pattern `.*`, which actually matches everything. This is enough for now, as first we have to create a minimal grammar to see how to apply it to a text. `TOP` is a predefined name, which you give to the first rule in the grammar.

As mentioned at the beginning of this chapter, we will be creating a parser for the small subset of Perl 6 (we will ignore some edge cases of real Perl 6 grammar for simplicity). Thus, our first text, which the grammar will be parsing, may look like this:

```
my $text = 'my $x;';
```

To parse the `$text` using our grammar, `G`, call the parse method on it:

```
my $result = G.parse($text);
say $result;
```

The result is a complex grammar object that contains the text that was matched. In our simple case, the `TOP` rule consumes the whole text and the stringified value looks like this:

⌈my $x⌋

There are at least three goals in applying a grammar:

1. Check if the source text is grammatically correct.
2. Split the text into syntactical elements.
3. Execute actions according to the language rules.

In this chapter, we will be programming all three parts but our first task is to learn how to check whether the text agrees with the grammar.

Matching a grammar

Our sample program, which will be parsed line by line in the rest of the chapter, looks like this:

```
my $x;
$x = 5;
say $x;  # 5

my $y;
$y = $x;
say $y;  # 5

my $z;
$z = $x + $y;
say $z;  # 10
```

This is a valid Perl 6 program, and we have to create the grammar that parses and executes it.

Let us save the reference program in a separate file, say, `refer.pl`, and use the `parsefile` method instead of the `parse` one:

```
my $result = G.parsefile('refer.pl');
say $result;
```

This program prints the whole content of the file, as the TOP rule still matches with everything it gets. To make sure the grammar is parsing the whole file, let us add anchors to tie the beginning and the end of the text:

```
grammar G {
    rule TOP {
        ^ .* $
    }
}
```

You may feel free to use whitespaces inside the rules to make the regex clearer:

```
rule TOP {
    ^

        .*

    $
}
```

The next subgoal is to parse every line of the code separately. To be precise, the grammar should not parse lines of the source text but rather instructions separated by semicolons. The parser should not depend on how many whitespaces and newlines are added to the code.

Now we have to formalize what was just said using grammars. A source program is a list of statements separated by a semicolon. Let us modify the TOP rule to express that:

```
rule TOP {
    ^

        (.*? ';')*

    $
}
```

We start with the minimal program:

```
my $x;
$x = 5;
say $x;
```

If you look at the output of the program that prints the `$result`, you will see the whole content of the file followed by separate instructions like this:

```
⌈my $x;
$x = 5;
say $x;⌋
  0 => ⌈my $x;⌋
  0 => ⌈
$x = 5;⌋
```

```
0 => ⌈
say $x; ⌋;
```

The output is a little messy but we can see that each statement from the source file was put into a separate element of the $result, similarly to how the Match object contained the parts of the matching string against a regex.

The extracted fragments contain leading whitespaces, which we can easily suppress by allowing them in the grammar:

```
rule TOP {
    ^
            [\s* (.*? ';')]*
    $
}
```

To avoid unneeded capturing, square brackets are used. Now the output looks much clearer:

```
⌈my $x;
$x = 5;
say $x;⌋
  0 => ⌈my $x;⌋
  0 => ⌈$x = 5;⌋
  0 => ⌈say $x;⌋
```

All the statements from the reference program are caught; we only need to teach the grammar to ignore comments:

```
rule TOP {
    ^
            [\s* (.*? ';') ['#' <-[\n]>* ]? ]*
    $
}
```

The additional part of the regex, ['#' <-[\n]>*]?, finds optional substrings that start with the # character and follow until the end of the line (in other words, they contain characters that are not \n).

The regex of the TOP rule becomes more and more complex, so it is time to split it into parts to make the whole grammar more readable and more maintainable.

Using rules and tokens

Grammars in Perl 6 offers a very useful way to split the grammar elements into parts. Let us use it to clarify the grammar elements.

The complex regex \s* (.*? ';') ['#' <-[\n]>*]? contains two parts—the regex to extract a statement and the regex for comments. We are extracting them into separate rules. A single **rule** describes a small piece of the grammar and can refer to other rules. Examine the following example:

```
grammar G {
    rule TOP {
        ^
            [ <statement> \s* <comment>? ]*
        $
    }

    rule statement {
        .*? ';'
    }

    rule comment {
        '#' <-[\n]>*
    }
}
```

Now the TOP rule is much clearer and you immediately see that the program is a sequence of statements with optional comments after them (our grammar does not allow a comment without a statement).

So far, the grammar parses the refer.pl file completely but we can go further. We can extract statements and the next task is to understand them. Let us now parse the file line by line, adding the new lines together with the grammar rules that can parse the statements. You can do it by embedding the source text to our main file:

```
my $prog = q:to/END/;
my $x;
END

my $result = G.parse($prog);
say $result;
```

The first line `my $x` contains a statement that is a variable declaration. As we start with the grammar that can only parse variable declarations, here is the modified `statement` rule:

```
rule statement {
    <variable-declaration> ';'
}
```

A variable declaration is a sequence of `my` keyword and a variable:

```
rule variable-declaration {
    'my' <variable>
}
```

This `variable-declaration` rule contains two parts—a literal string `'my'` and a reference to another rule `<variable>`. We do not explicitly say anything about the spaces between these two parts. Rules in Perl 6 care about those spaces for you. Thus, the rule can parse variable declarations that contain one, or two, or more spaces between `my` and the variable. Even the following string can be properly parsed—`my$x`.

To describe a variable, we create a **token**. Tokens are like rules but do not allow spaces between their elements. So a valid variable name should be a string without spaces:

```
token variable {
    <sigil> <identifier>
}
```

A sigil is either a scalar sigil `$` or an array sigil `@`. Although we did not have any arrays in the sample program at the beginning of the chapter, let's prepare the grammar to work with them in the future:

```
token sigil {
    '$' | '@'
}
```

Finally, describe an identifier:

```
token identifier {
    <alpha> <alnum>*
}
```

In the language that this grammar describes, an identifier is a sequence of alphanumeric characters starting with a letter.

With the previously listed rules and tokens, the grammar parses the first line from our reference program and this is how it sees it:

```
⌈my $x;
⌋
  statement => ⌈my $x;
⌋
    variable-declaration => ⌈my $x⌋
      variable => ⌈$x⌋
        sigil => ⌈$⌋
          identifier => ⌈x⌋
            alpha => ⌈x⌋
```

The output displays the parse tree of the program. Indentation helps to understand the structure better. At the top level, we see that the program my $x consists of a statement my $x, which is a variable declaration. The variable is $x, it includes a sigil $ and an identifier x that starts with an alphabetical character x.

For a longer variable name, say, @array, the parse tree will contain all the letters that match with the `<alnum>*` part of the `identifier` rule:

```
variable-declaration => ⌈my @array⌋
  variable => ⌈@array⌋
    sigil => ⌈@⌋
    identifier => ⌈array⌋
      alpha => ⌈a⌋
      alnum => ⌈r⌋
      alnum => ⌈r⌋
      alnum => ⌈a⌋
      alnum => ⌈y⌋
```

Let us parse the second line of the file, which contains the assignment:

```
my $prog = q:to/END/;
my $x;
$x = 100;
END
```

An `assignment` is also a `statement`, so to parse it, the `statement` rule has to know what an `assignment` is:

```
rule statement {
    [
        | <variable-declaration>
```

```
        | <assignment>
    ]
    ';'
}
```

The new rule contains a list of alternatives separated by the vertical bar; a pair of square brackets groups alternatives without capturing the text. Actually, the first vertical bar is not needed, but you may add it to make the code look more structured.

The first approach to the assignment rule includes assignments to numeric values only:

```
rule assignment {
    <variable> '=' <value>
}

token value {
    <number>
}

token number {
    <digit>+
}
```

At this point, the grammar parses the following program:

```
my $x;
$x = 100;
```

The second statement is parsed according to the grammar and forms the following parse tree:

```
statement => ⌈$x = 100;
⌋
  assignment => ⌈$x = 100⌋
    variable => ⌈$x⌋
      sigil => ⌈$⌋
      identifier => ⌈x⌋
        alpha => ⌈x⌋
    value => ⌈100⌋
      number => ⌈100⌋
        digit => ⌈1⌋
        digit => ⌈0⌋
        digit => ⌈0⌋
```

The third line of the program is `say $x;`. Let's call this kind of statement `say-function` and implement the rule for it:

```
rule say-function {
    'say' <variable>
}
```

As you can see, this is extremely easy because we already have a rule for parsing variables. Finally, the new rule must be added to the list of alternatives in the `statement` rule:

```
rule statement {
    [
        | <variable-declaration>
        | <assignment>
        | <say-function>
    ]
    ';'
}
```

The statement is successfully parsed:

```
statement => ⌜say $x;
⌟
  say-function => ⌜say $x⌟
    variable => ⌜$x⌟
      sigil => ⌜$⌟
      identifier => ⌜x⌟
        alpha => ⌜x⌟
```

Let us now take a break and teach our compiler not only to parse the program but also to execute it. Here, actions come in.

Using actions

Grammars by themselves do not just parse the source text and extract data pieces from it. To make the program execute the code, actions are needed. Actions in grammars are pieces of Perl 6 code that are triggered when the grammar successfully parses a rule or a token.

Let us take a look at the `variable-declaration` rule:

```
rule variable-declaration {
    'my' <variable>
}
```

When the grammar finds the sequence my $x in the source text, the rule is satisfied. At this point, you may add an action:

```
rule variable-declaration {
    'my' <variable> {say 'Declaring a variable'}
}
```

An action can be a simple alert like this but it also may be much more complex code that will be executed as a reaction to the variable declaration.

To make the action act properly, it needs to know the type of the variable (whether it contains the $ or the @ sigil) and its name. Actions have access to Match objects reflecting the current state of the parsed fragment. Named subrules can be found in the Match object by their names; for example, $<variable> returns the string $x.

To dig deeper, take the nested elements of the Match object:

```
rule variable-declaration {
    'my' <variable> {
        say 'Declaring ' ~
            ($<variable><sigil> eq '$'
             ?? 'a scalar variable'
             !! 'an array') ~
            ' "' ~ $<variable><identifier> ~ '"';
    }
}
```

Run the code against the program with two variable declarations:

```
my $prog = q:to/END/;
my $x;
my @array;
END

G.parse($prog);
```

It prints the following:

```
Declaring a scalar variable "x"
Declaring an array "array"
```

This proves that the grammar understood the program and the action got the correct names and types of the variables.

As soon as we can distinguish between scalars and arrays, we can save their values for future use. For that, define two global variables:

```
my %scalar;
my %array;
```

The keys of these hashes correspond to the names of the variables. We will populate the storage inside the grammar actions:

```
rule variable-declaration {
    'my' <variable> {
        given $<variable><sigil> {
            when '$' {
                %scalar{$<variable><identifier>} = 'undefined';
            }
            when '@' {
                %array{$<variable><identifier>} = 'undefined';
            }
        }
    }
}
```

Before the end of the program, let's print the content of the variable storages:

```
say %scalar;
say %array;
```

The output tells us that the variables were successfully found and the slots for them were created in the storage:

```
{x => undefined}
{array => undefined}
```

Think about the next step. Naturally, it would be great to assign the values to the variables. In the above code, we were separating the code for scalars and arrays using the given/when selector. What if we want to add the support for hashes? A new when branch is fine but then we have to make similar branches in all the actions that work with variables.

One of the solutions is to ask the grammar to distinguish between the types of the variables:

```
token variable {
    | <scalar-variable>
    | <array-variable>
}
```

```
token scalar-variable {
    '$' <identifier>
}
token array-variable {
    '@' <identifier>
}
```

Another solution is to make the variable storage a single variable %var and use it as a two-dimensional hash:

```
my %var;

# . . .

rule variable-declaration {
    'my' <variable> {
        %var{$<variable><sigil>}{$<variable><identifier>} =
            'undefined';
    }
}
```

With this, the %var container will get the following content:

```
{$ => {x => undefined}, @ => {array => undefined}}
```

To assign a value to a variable, an action should be written. The grammar already has the assignment rule, so adding an action is an easy task:

```
rule assignment {
    <variable> '=' <value> {
        %var{$<variable><sigil>}{$<variable><identifier>} =
            ~$<value>;
    }
}
```

On the left-hand side of the assignment inside the action, we see the same code that we were already using for accessing variables in the %var storage. The expression on the right-hand side needs extra attention.

The bare $<value> currently contains the object of the G type. To make it a string, the string coercion operator (prefix ~) is used. Thus, it will be stringified and the variable gets the value that we wanted to save there:

```
{$ => {x => 100}}
```

To confirm that all works as expected, let us parse a program that uses two scalar variables:

```
my $prog = q:to/END/;
my $alpha;
$alpha = 50;
say $alpha;

my $beta;
$beta = 60;
say $beta;
END

G.parse($prog);
say %var; # {$ => {alpha => 50, beta => 60}}
```

Now let's shift our attention to implementing the `say` function. It should not be a difficult task, as we already have all the code pieces in other rules and actions. Just combine them together:

```
rule say-function {
    'say' <variable> {
        say %var{$<variable><sigil>}{$<variable><identifier>};
    }
}
```

Now, the compiler understands three syntax constructions—declaring a variable, assigning a value to it, and printing the content of scalar variables. As homework, you can implement error handling for when the program wants to use a variable that is either not declared or still contains the undefined value.

The grammar is already quite sophisticated but it is not very difficult to add more and more features to it. Each new feature normally requires the modification of existing rules and actions or adding the new ones.

Using abstract syntax tree attributes

Currently, the G grammar only parses the constructions when an integer value is assigned to a variable:

```
$x = 100;
```

Let us see how to add support for the following assignments:

```
$x = $y;
```

The rule for parsing constructions like $x = 100 used the following rule:

```
rule assignment {
    <variable> '=' <value> { . . . }
}
```

On the right-hand side of the equals sign, we see a value, which we can replace with a more general item, expression. In the end, the expression may be any expression that a language understands, such as 10, $x, 10 + 3, or $x + $y, and more. Let us approach that point step by step. First, introduce the expression rule. The problem is that we have to return the value of the expression to the action that makes an assignment.

To keep temporary values, Perl 6 grammars offer the attributes of the **abstract syntax tree** (**AST**). To save the value, use the $/.make method. To get it, use the $/.made or $/.ast method (they are synonyms):

```
rule assignment {
    <variable> '=' <expression> {
        %var{$<variable><sigil>}{$<variable><identifier>} =
            $<expression>.made;
    }
}

rule expression {
    | <value> {
        $/.make(~$<value>)
    }
    | <variable> {
        $/.make(%var{$<variable><sigil>}{$<variable><identifier>})
    }
}
```

The values that we pass using the $/.make method are attributes attached to the nodes of the parse tree. These values do not disappear after the action is executed and stay available for the actions of other rules via the $/ variable.

In the preceding code, for example, the stringified value parsed in the first branch of the expression rule is attached to the corresponding node—$/.make(~$<value>). Later, this value is used in the assignment action $<expression>.made. We have seen in Chapter 11, *Regexes*, that $<expression> is the short form of the full expression $/<expression>.

The second branch of the expression rule becomes active when the grammar meets an assignment such as $x = $y. In this case, it gets the value of the variable from the %var storage and puts it in the AST attribute. At this point, our compiler can handle the following program:

```
my $x;
$x = 100;

my $y;
$y = $x;
say $y; # 100
```

Handling expressions

In many grammars that aim to parse source code in different programming languages, one of the central parts is handling expressions. We have already introduced the expression rule, and it can understand simple expressions such as 100 or $x.

Let us continue with expressions and teach the compiler to parse and calculate expressions with the + operator. We will start with a simple case when both operands are integer literals:

```
rule expression {
    | <value> '+' <value> {
        $/.make($<value>[0].ast + $<value>[1].ast)
    }
    | <value> {
        $/.make(~$<value>)
    }
    | <variable> {
        $/.make(%var{$<variable><sigil>}{$<variable><identifier>})
    }
}
```

The rule got a new branch <value> '+' <value>, which uses two rules with the same name. In the action, the two operands are extracted from the ast (or made) attributes of the two elements of the array—$<value>[0] and $<value>[1].

Another change should be made in the `value` token. Until now, we have not saved anything in the AST. If you do not do that, then further parsing will have to deal with complex structures instead of simple values. So just add it to the tree:

```
token value {
    <number> {$/.make(+$<number>)}
}
```

The prefix + is used here to cast the value to a numeric type.

The next step is to allow variables so that we can parse expressions such as `3 + $x`.

As we have seen before, the `expression` rule can represent the value of a variable. So let us use it instead of the second `value` in the `expression` rule:

```
rule expression {
    | <value> '+' <expression> {
        $/.make($<value>.ast + $<expression>.ast)
    }
    | <value> {
        $/.make(~$<value>)
    }
    | <variable> {
        $/.make(%var{$<variable><sigil>}{$<variable><identifier>})
    }
}
```

Also, update the `variable` rule to save the value of the variable in AST:

```
token variable {
    <sigil> <identifier> {
        $/.make(%var{$<sigil>}{$<identifier>})
    }
}
```

This is all that is needed to use variables as the second operand of the + operator. The grammar now parses the program like this:

```
my $x;
my $y;

$x = 3;
$y = 4 + $x;

say $y; # 7
```

Allowing variables on the left-hand side of the + operator is a bit more difficult. The thing is that so far we have used the `expression` rule in places where we may expect a variable:

```
rule expression {
    | <value> '+' <expression>
    ...
}
```

It is not possible just to change the left `value` to an `expression`:

```
rule expression {
    | <expression> '+' <expression>
    ...
}
```

This change leads to an infinite recursion—to understand what an expression is you need to parse an expression, which is an expression plus expression and so on. One possible solution is to implicitly list the options that the first operand can be:

```
rule expression {
    | <value> '+' <expression> {
          $/.make($<value>.ast + $<expression>.ast)
      }
    | <variable> '+' <expression> {
          $/.make($<variable>.ast + $<expression>.ast)
      }
    | <value> {
          $/.make(~$<value>)
      }
    | <variable> {
          $/.make(%var{$<variable><sigil>}{$<variable><identifier>})
      }
}
```

A better approach is to introduce another rule, `term`, that can be either a `value` or a `variable`:

```
rule expression {
    | <term> '+' <expression> {
          $/.make($<term>.ast + $<expression>.ast)
      }
    | <value> {
          $/.make(~$<value>)
      }
    | <variable> {
          $/.make(%var{$<variable><sigil>}{$<variable><identifier>})
      }
```

```
}

rule term {
    | <value> {$/.make($<value>.ast)}
    | <variable> {$/.make($<variable>.ast)}
}
```

What can be done at the moment? The (already quite complicated) program in the tiny subset of the Perl 6 language can be parsed and executed:

```
my $x;
my $y;

$x = 3;
$y = 4 + $x;
say $y; # 7

my $z;
$z = $x + $y;
say $z; # 10

my $a;
$a = $z + 5;
say $a; # 15
```

As a bonus, the program can also parse complex expressions involving the + operator:

```
my $b;
$b = $a + $x + $y + $z + 7;
say $b; # 42
```

We did not do anything special to allow this to work but the grammar splits the expression into simple expressions such as $a + $x, calculates the value, and goes further. With each step, a simple operation with two operands is executed.

Using the actions class

The more complex a grammar becomes, the more complex the actions. Almost every rule or token in our current grammar has an action. Even if most of the actions are just one or two lines of code, the fact that the Perl 6 code is mixed with the grammar language makes reading the code difficult. Formatting the code also becomes a difficult task, as you need to add more spaces to indent the code properly. In this section, we will see what Perl 6 offers to tackle this issue.

All actions may be moved to a separate class. Thus, the complete grammar contains a grammar itself and an actions class. Correspondence between the grammar rules and tokens and the actions is achieved by simply giving the same names to the methods of the action class. Let us convert our grammar to use the split approach.

First of all, create a class for actions and pass it to the parser:

```
grammar G {
    ...
}

class A {
    ...
}

...

G.parse($prog, :actions(A));
```

Now, move the action code from the grammar rules or tokens to separate methods in the actions class.

Take, for example, the `variable` rule:

```
token variable {
    <sigil> <identifier> {
        $/.make(%var{$<sigil>}{$<identifier>})
    }
}
```

This code should be split into the grammar rule and the action:

```
grammar G {
    ...
    token variable {
        <sigil> <identifier>
    }
    ...
}

class A {
    ...
    method variable($/) {
        $/.make(%var{$<sigil>}{$<identifier>})
    }
    ...
}
```

As the code is now placed outside the grammar, we have to pass the $/ variable as an argument of the method. It is possible to use any other name for this argument but the $/ seems to be the most common and conventional choice.

In the same manner, other actions can be extracted and put to the actions class. We will not spend time describing those repeated code changes (you can see the final code at the end of this chapter) but instead we will directly look at the rules with alternatives. There are two such rules in the grammar—expression and term.

Consider the term rule:

```
rule term {
    | <value> {$/.make($<value>.ast)}
    | <variable> {$/.make($<variable>.ast)}
}
```

We have two different actions here but we only can add one method to the actions class.

There are at least three solutions. First, the rule can be split into two rules, and thus two separate actions. Second, we can analyze the contents of the $/ variable and execute one of the branches:

```
method term($/) {
    if $<value> {
        $/.make($<value>.ast)
    }
    elsif $<variable> {
        $/.make($<variable>.ast)
    }
}
```

But Perl 6 gives us an even better choice—using multi-methods and making them sensitive to the data received in the $/ argument:

```
multi method term($/ where $/<value>) {
    $/.make($<value>.ast)
}

multi method term($/ where $/<variable>) {
    $/.make($<variable>.ast)
}
```

In the signatures of the methods, a subtype is created. Each variant of the multi-method is called in response to matches of different branches of the rules. We used this trick in the *Multi subs* section in Chapter 6, *Subroutines*.

After all the actions are moved to a separate class, it is also wise to move the global variable `%var` to the class. Currently, the skeleton of the whole program looks like this:

```
grammar G {
    ...
}

class A {
    my %var;
    ...
}

G.parse($prog, :actions(A));
```

The `%var` storage is now the class attribute—it belongs to the class, not to the instances of it. Actually, we do not create any instances of A—the G.parse method receives the name of the class. This may be fine for some application but, to make sure that the variable storage does not keep the values from the previous runs of the parser, it is better to make `%var` a private attribute:

```
class A {
    has %!var;
    ...
}
```

The class needs to be instantiated first. Otherwise, no memory will be allocated for the `%var` attribute. The parse method also accepts an instance of the action class:

```
G.parse($prog, :actions(A.new));
```

The whole program

We achieved a lot by learning about grammars in Perl 6. Just imagine the program we created can parse another program written in Perl 6!

There is still much room for improvement but you will definitely be able to do that. For example, you can start with implementing support for arrays.

Here is the full code of the compiler that we created in this chapter:

```
grammar G {
    rule TOP {
        ^
            [ <statement> \s* <comment>? ]*
        $
```

```
}

rule statement {
    [
        | <variable-declaration>
        | <assignment>
        | <say-function>
    ]
    ';'
}

rule comment {
    '#' <-[\n]>*
}

rule variable-declaration {
    'my' <variable>
}

token variable {
    <sigil> <identifier>
}

token sigil {
    '$' | '@'
}

token identifier {
    <alpha> <alnum>*
}

rule assignment {
    <variable> '=' <expression>
}

rule expression {
    | <term> '+' <expression>
    | <value>
    | <variable>
}

rule term {
    | <value>
    | <variable>
}

token value {
    <number>
```

```
    }

    token number {
        <digit>+
    }

    rule say-function {
        'say' <variable>
    }
}

class A {
    has %!var;

    method variable-declaration($/) {
        %!var{$<variable><sigil>}{$<variable><identifier>} =
            'undefined';
    }

    method variable($/) {
        $/.make(%!var{$<sigil>}{$<identifier>})
    }

    method assignment($/) {
        %!var{$<variable><sigil>}{$<variable><identifier>} =
            $<expression>.ast;
    }

    method value($/) {
        $/.make(+$<number>)
    }

    method say-function($/) {
        say %!var{$<variable><sigil>}{$<variable><identifier>};
    }

    multi method term($/ where $/<value>) {
        $/.make($<value>.ast)
    }

    multi method term($/ where $/<variable>) {
        $/.make($<variable>.ast)
    }

    multi method expression($/ where $/<term>) {
        $/.make($<term>.ast + $<expression>.ast)
    }
```

```
    multi method expression($/ where $/<value>) {
        $/.make(~$<value>)
    }

    multi method expression($/ where $/<variable>) {
        $/.make(%!var{$<variable><sigil>}{$<variable><identifier>})
    }
}

my $prog = q:to/END/;
my $x;
$x = 5;
say $x;# 5
my $y;
$y = $x;
say $y; # 5
my $z;
$z = $x + $y;
say $z; # 10
my $sum;
$sum = 10 + 12 + $x + $y + $z;
say $sum; # 42
END

G.parse($prog, :actions(A.new));
```

Summary

In this chapter, we discussed grammars, the leading new feature of Perl 6. Grammars allow building parsers for your own domain-specific languages and are already built-in to the language, so no external modules are required to start using them.

Using the example of a compiler of the subset of Perl 6, we created a grammar and looked at its elements—rules and tokens. Later we updated the grammar with actions and finally moved the actions into a separate class to make the code more maintainable and clean.

In the next chapters, we will talk about concurrent, reactive, and functional programming in Perl 6.

13

Concurrent Programming

Perl 6 is a language that was created entirely in the twenty-first century. It is not a surprise that it comes with built-in support of some basic concepts, which makes it easy to create applications that supports parallel and concurrent programming.

In this chapter, we will cover the following topics.

- Junctions
- Threads
- Promises
- Channels

Junctions

Junctions are one of the simplest examples of where Perl 6 can work in parallel. In the version of Rakudo, which is available at the time of writing this book, this feature is not fully implemented.

A junction is a value that keeps many values at the same time. Examine the following code:

```
my $j = 1 | 3 | 5;
say 'OK' if $j == 3;
say 'Not OK' if $j != 2;
```

The variable $j is a junction that keeps three odd numbers, 1, 3, and 5. You may compare $j with an integer and get the Boolean True if the value is one of the values hosted by the junction. In the case of comparing with 3, the result is True , while the second comparison with 2 fails.

Autothreading

Now try passing a junction to a function that takes a scalar:

```
sub f($x) {
    say $x;
    return $x;
}

say 'OK' if f(1 | 3 | 5) == 3;
say 'Not OK' if f(1 | 3 | 5) != 2;
```

The behavior is intuitively understandable—the function is executed for each of the values of the junction separately. The values that the function returns are then used as the values of a junction.

The preceding code works the same as the following code, where the function receives a single scalar value:

```
say 'OK' if f(1) | f(3) | f(5) == 3;
say 'Not OK' if f(1) | f(3) | f(5) != 2;
```

Moving the junction operation outside the function argument is called **autothreading**. In theory, the code from the last example may be executed in parallel.

Now, let us move to the next topic and see how we can create threads explicitly.

Threads

In Perl 6, there is the `Thread` class, which takes care of creating and running threads. To see in which thread you are at the moment, use the `$*THREAD` pseudo constant:

```
say $*THREAD;
```

It returns a value of the `Thread` class, and the default stringified representation of it is a string containing the identifier and the name of the thread:

Thread #1 (Initial thread)

Don't rely on the particular value of the thread identifier as it may be different even for the main thread.

Starting a thread

In this and in the following sections, we will examine the methods of the Thread class. We will start, though, with the start method, which creates a thread and starts its execution.

In the following example, three threads are created. Each of them receives a name and a code block. Code blocks do the same job in each thread and only print the value of the $*THREAD variable, which will be different within different threads:

```
say $*THREAD;

my $t1 = Thread.start(name => 'Test 1', sub {say $*THREAD});
my $t2 = Thread.start(name => 'Test 2', sub {say $*THREAD});
my $t3 = Thread.start(name => 'Test 3', sub {say $*THREAD});

say $t1.WHAT;
say $t2.WHAT;
say $t3.WHAT;
```

Run the program and see what it prints. Your output may differ from the following snippet:

```
Thread #1 (Initial thread)
Thread #3 (Test 1)
(Thread)
Thread #5 (Test 3)
(Thread)
Thread #4 (Test 2)
(Thread)
```

As you see, the program prints from four different threads—the initial thread #1 and the three threads that we created. They get the identifiers 3, 4, and 5. The Rakudo developers told me that the thread #2 was probably used by the virtual machine during startup. Again, the main property of these numbers is that they are unique but do not necessarily go in order.

Also notice that the output of different threads is overlapping. Running the program several times most likely will give different results.

The threads are created at the moment Thread.start is called and then the execution goes back to the main thread. The easiest way to see this is to embed different delays in the sub used as a thread code block.

In the following program, three anonymous (in the sense that they are not saved in a variable) threads are created. Their names are different, as well as the delay and the output they produce in their bodies:

```
say $*THREAD;

Thread.start(
    name => 'Sleep 3 seconds',
    sub {
        say $*THREAD;
        sleep 3;
        say 1;
    });

Thread.start(
    name => 'Sleep 2 seconds',
    sub {
        say $*THREAD;
        sleep 2;
        say 2;
    });

Thread.start(
    name => 'Sleep 1 second',
    sub {
        say $*THREAD;
        sleep 1;
        say 3;
    });
```

Run it and this is what you will get in the console:

```
Thread #1 (Initial thread)
Thread #3 (Sleep 3 seconds)
Thread #4 (Sleep 2 seconds)
Thread #5 (Sleep 1 second)
3
2
1
```

The first four lines are printed immediately after the program start, while the rest is printed with a delay—each number after a delay of 1 second. So, the Thread.start creates a thread and exits, while the thread is being executed in parallel with the main program (and with other threads).

As threads are working in parallel, it is not possible to predict in which order they will produce side-effects (such as printing to the console). Look at the program that creates two threads, each of which prints five numbers. The first thread prints the numbers from 1 to 5, while the second one prints the numbers from 11 to 15:

```
Thread.start(sub {
    .say for 1..5;
});

Thread.start(sub {
    .say for 11..15;
});
```

Both threads are executed in parallel. The actual implementation, whether the code is distributed over different cores of the processor or if the threads are initated by granting them dedicated time atoms, is not defined in the language specification, so you should not count on either implementation when creating threads in Perl 6.

Run the program a few times and see that the results are different:

```
1
11
12
2
3
13
4
5
14
15
```

It may also be that the second thread may start printing before the first one:

```
11
1
2
12
13
3
14
15
4
5
```

Using the `Thread.start` method is easy but in some cases you may want to have finer control over the creation and running of the threads.

Creating and running a new thread

To create a thread object, use the constructor of the `Thread` class. It takes the name of the thread and the code block in the corresponding named parameters `name` and `code`:

```
my $t = Thread.new(
    name => 'My thread',
    code => sub {
        say 'Hi there!';
    }
);
```

The thread is now created but is not activated. To run it, the `run` method must be called:

```
$t.run();
```

Execute the following example and examine the order, in which the lines appear on the screen:

```
my $t = Thread.new(
    name => 'My thread',
    code => sub {
        say 'Start';
        sleep 2;
        say 'End';
    }
);

say 'Before';
$t.run();
say 'After';
```

As soon as the thread is running, it prints its two messages, `Start` and `End`, separated by a delay of 2 seconds:

```
Before
After
Start
End
```

It is possible to postpone the main program until the thread finishes its work. Use the `finish` method:

```
say 'Before';
$t.run();
$t.finish();
say 'After';
```

The program will wait until the thread code block finishes its work, and only then continues from the next instruction:

```
Before
Start
End
After
```

The `finish` method has a synonym `join`—`$t.join()`, which does exactly the same as `$t.finish()`.

The id and name methods

In the *Starting a new thread* section, we have already seen a few examples of how identifiers are assigned to the new threads. In the `Thread` class, there is a method that returns an `id`:

```
say $*THREAD;

my $t1 = Thread.start(sub {});
my $t2 = Thread.start(sub {});
my $t3 = Thread.start(sub {});

say $t1.id();
say $t2.id();
say $t3.id();
```

One of the possible outputs of the program is this:

```
3
4
5
```

Thread identifiers may be used if you want to keep some tracking information in the main thread, for example.

Another way of identifying threads is using names. Names are string labels that you assign to the thread when creating it via the `name` argument:

```
my $t1 = Thread.start(name => 'My thread one', sub {});
my $t2 = Thread.start(name => 'My thread two', sub {});
my $t3 = Thread.start(name => 'My thread three', sub {});

say $*THREAD.name();
say $t1.name();
say $t2.name();
say $t3.name();
```

The name of the main thread is `Initial thread`:

```
Initial thread
My thread one
My thread two
My thread three
```

The names need not be unique, so you are free to choose any names you want.

Printing thread objects as a string

The `Str` method of the `Thread` class defines the behavior when the thread object is being printed, via the `say` function:

```
my $t1 = Thread.start(name => 'My thread one', sub {});
my $t2 = Thread.start(name => 'My thread two', sub {});
my $t3 = Thread.start(name => 'My thread three', sub {});

say $*THREAD;
say $t1;
say $t2;
say $t3;
```

The default string contains the number of the thread and its name (if it is defined).

```
Thread #1 (Initial thread)
Thread #3 (My thread one)
Thread #4 (My thread two)
Thread #5 (My thread three)
```

In this example, all the threads have different IDs (they are always different) and different names (this is defined by the programmer).

Lifetime threads

When creating a new thread, it is possible to set the `app_lifetime` attribute, which requests that the thread lives until the end of the main program. Otherwise it will be terminated after its body is executed. To add this flag, either add it as `:app_lifetime` or by explicitly passing the `True` value to the constructor—`app_lifetime => True`:

```
Thread.new(
    name => 'Long thread',
    code => sub {
        say 'OK';
```

```
    },
    :app_lifetime,
).run().join();

say 'Done';
```

It is important to wait for the thread (using either the `finish` or `join` method). Otherwise the main thread may stop executing before the thread returns.

Using locks in Perl 6

Perl 6 offers a mechanism of ensuring that a particular part of the code is executed by a single thread only. If there are other threads that would like to access the variables from this code, they should wait until it is unlocked.

To enclose the **critical code**, use the `protect` method of the `Lock` class. Examine the following example from the Perl 6 documentation:

```
my $x = 0;
my $l = Lock.new;
await (^10).map: {
    start {
        $l.protect({ $x++ });
    }
}
say $x; # OUTPUT: «10$_L»
```

We will talk about the `await` function in the *Factory methods* section later in this chapter.

The critical code is protected in such a way that only one thread can access the `$x` counter at a time.

Locks are not recommended to be used directly, as they provide too low-level an interface. Instead, use promises, channels, and supplies. We will talk about the first two concepts later in this chapter, while supplies are discussed in `Chapter 15`, *Reactive Programming*.

Promises

In the previous section, we were creating some code blocks that were running in parallel. Promises help to see the status of the completeness of such blocks. In Perl 6, promises are handled by the `Promise` class.

Creating a promise

To create a promise, just call the constructor of the Promise class:

```
my $promise = Promise.new();
```

The created object does nothing yet. In the *Factory methods* section later in this chapter, we will see how to create a promise that executes some code. Meanwhile, let's see the properties that a promise has.

Statuses of a promise

The power of promises is that they can be either kept or broken, and you can keep track of them. A new promise that is created by calling Promise.new is neither kept nor broken. Its status is Planned. To see the status, call the status method:

```
my $promise = Promise.new();
say $promise.status(); # Planned
```

The Promise class also provides us with a pair of methods, keep and break, which change the status of a promise to Kept or Broken. This is demonstrated in the following example, where one of the promises is marked as kept while the second is forced to be broken:

```
my $promise1 = Promise.new();
my $promise2 = Promise.new();

$promise1.keep();
$promise2.break();

say $promise1.status();
say $promise2.status();
```

The output is:

```
Kept
Broken
```

Now, after we know how to change the status and how to read it, we are going to use promises for executing code in parallel.

Factory methods

Let us start with a simple program that creates a promise with a code block that prints something and exits. The `Promise.start` method creates a block and returns a promise. Notice that the returned value is a promise, not a thread. To wait until the code block of the promise is done, use the `await` function:

```
my $promise = Promise.start({
    say 'I am a promise';
});
await $promise;
```

The program waits until the message is printed by the code block and exits:

I am a promise

In the preceding example, the `start` routine is called as a method of the `Promise` class. Alternatively, a promise can be created by a self-standing `start` function:

```
my $promise = start {
    say 'I am a promise';
};

await $promise;
```

Notice that there are no parentheses around the code block.

Let us modify the previous example and create a promise that just sleeps for a second. Immediately after the promise is created, its status is printed for the first time. The delay of a second is important here to make sure that the promise does not finish its work before we check for the status in the next line.

Then, `await` waits until the promise's code is done, and the status is checked for the second time:

```
my $promise = Promise.start({
    sleep 1;
});

say $promise.status;
await $promise;
say $promise.status;
```

This is what the program prints:

```
Planned
Kept
```

For dealing with time, there is another factory method, `Promise.in` that may be used instead of the combination of `start` and `sleep`. It creates a promise, which becomes kept after the given number of seconds:

```
my $promise = Promise.in(2);
await $promise;
say 'Done';
say $promise.status; # Kept
```

This program creates and waits for a promise. After 2 seconds the promise is kept and the program continues. The status of the promise becomes `Kept` after that.

The result of a promise

Another interesting feature of promises is that they can return a result. This result is calculated by the code block, and the last calculated value is what is returned. Consider the following example:

```
my $promise = Promise.start({
    sleep 1;
    'Result'; # no return keyword!
});

await $promise;
say $promise.result;
```

Here, the code block returns a string, `Result`, which is then printed using the `result` method called on the `$promise` variable.

It logically follows that the result is only available after the promise is kept. In the previous example, an explicit `await` was used. Actually, it is redundant, because the call of the `result` method will wait until the code is completed. Thus, the code may be simplified as follows:

```
my $promise = Promise.start({
    sleep 1;
    'Result';
});

say $promise.result; # waits
```

Combining promises

In real programs, more than one promise can be used. Combining different promises can give very expressive ways of coding complex relationships between different parts of the code.

Let us start with a simple example and create three promises using the standalone `start` function:

```
say 'Start';
await
    start {sleep 2; say 2;},
    start {sleep 3; say 3;},
    start {sleep 1; say 1;};
say 'Done';
```

The goal is to pause the program until all the promises are kept. As you can see from this example, the `await` function accepts a list of promises and waits until all of them are completed. The output of the program looks like this:

```
Start
1
2
3
Done
```

Each promise creates a separate thread, which can be clearly seen by printing the `$*THREAD` variable:

```
await
    start {say $*THREAD;},
    start {say $*THREAD;},
    start {say $*THREAD;};
```

Each `start` created its own thread:

```
Thread #3
Thread #5
Thread #4
```

Executing code after the promise is kept or broken

The `Promise` class has the `then` method, which can be used to bind the code that will be executed after the promise is kept or broken. In fact, this method creates and returns a new promise, which will be run after the initial promise status change:

```
my $promise = Promise.in(1);
my $next = $promise.then({
    say 'Done';
});
await $next;
```

This program prints `Done` 1 second after it starts. The first promise, saved in the `$promise` variable, is kept after a given time delay. Then, the `then` creates another promise, which is saved in the `$next` variable. To join to the main program, it is necessary to wait until `$next` prints the output and is thus completed.

The anyof and allof methods

The two methods from the Promise class, `anyof` and `allof`, create a new promise that is kept when either any of the promises are kept or all of them are kept. The methods accept a list of promises.

Let us illustrate the work of the `anyof` method on the following example, that checks if the long-running code is executing too long:

```
my $timeout = Promise.in(2).then({
    say 'Timeout'
});
my $long_code = start {
    sleep 3;
    say 'Work done';
};

await Promise.anyof($timeout, $long_code);
say 'Continuing';
```

Two promises are created. The `$timeout` one is kept in 2 seconds after its creation. The `$long_code` imitates the slow part of the code, which executes longer than the timer can wait. Then, both promises are passed to the `Promise.anyof` method that returns another promise, which is kept when either timeout happens or the long-running code is executed.

Play with different combinations of the delays and see the different results of the outcome of this program.

Channels

Channels are the communication mean that can be used for passing data from one piece of code to another. The great thing about channels is that they are thread-compatible, thus it is possible for different threads to talk to each other. In this section, we will learn how to use channels in Perl 6.

Basic use cases

Channels are defined by the `Channel` class. To create a new channel variable, call the constructor:

```
my $channel = Channel.new;
```

Now, we can send data to the channel using the `send` method and receive it with the `receive` method:

```
my $channel = Channel.new;
$channel.send(42);

my $value = $channel.receive();
say $value;
```

This program does a trivial thing—it sends the value to the channel and reads it immediately. The program prints the value of 42, which went through the channel.

Now, let us modify the program and introduce a second thread in it so that the channel is populated in that thread and the result is read in the main program:

```
my $channel = Channel.new();
start {
    $channel.send(42);
};

my $value = $channel.receive;
say $value;
```

The result of the execution is the same as before, 42 is printed, while the logistics of passing this value are completely different.

The `receive` method waits until the channel has enough data to read. If we add a delay to the threaded code, then the program will be paused until the thread sends data to the channel:

```
my $channel = Channel.new();
start {
    sleep 1;
    $channel.send(42);
};

my $value = $channel.receive;
say $value;
```

The only difference between the last two examples is the delay before calling the `$channel.send` method.

To wait or not to wait?

As we have seen in the previous section, the `receive` method of the `Channel` class stalls if there is no data in the channel.

The `poll` method also reads from the channel but does not block the execution of the program. If there is nothing to read, then it returns an empty value immediately. Let us modify the last example a little bit more and read from the channel five times with a 1-second delay between the `poll` calls:

```
my $channel = Channel.new();

start {
    sleep 3;
    $channel.send(42);
};

for 1..5 {
    my $value = $channel.poll;
    say $value;
    sleep 1;
}
```

This programs prints the following output:

(Any)
(Any)
(Any)
42
(Any)

The first three attempts could not get any values because nothing is sent to the $channel, as there is a 3-second delay before it. On the fourth iteration, the value is available and can be read. After being read, the value is removed from the channel and thus the next call of poll returns an empty value again.

Closing channels

The close method closes a channel. This means that no more data will be added to it. To check if the channel is closed, call the closed method:

```
my $channel = Channel.new();
say 'Open' unless $channel.closed(); # Open

$channel.close();
say 'Closed' if $channel.closed();    # Closed
```

The return value of the closed method is not a Boolean value. Instead, the method returns a promise, which becomes kept after the channel closes:

```
my $channel = Channel.new();
say $channel.closed().status(); # Planned

$channel.close();
say $channel.closed().status(); # Kept
```

The promise can be used, for example, to run some code in response to closing a channel, as shown in the following example:

```
my $channel = Channel.new();

my $promise = $channel.closed();
$promise.then({
    say 'Channel is closed';
});

say 'Before calling close()';
$channel.close();
say 'After calling close()';
```

The output of running this program may look like this:

```
Before calling close()
After calling close()
Channel is closed
```

Because the promise is executed in a separate thread, the lines may be unpredictably printed in a different order. We can see it if we add a small delay before printing the strings in the main thread:

```
say 'Before calling close()';
$channel.close();
sleep 1;
say 'After calling close()';
```

In this case, the code of the $promise will be finished before the second say instruction:

```
Before calling close()
Channel is closed
After calling close()
```

Channels as queues

When more then one value is sent to the channel, they in fact become queues. So the first value added will be the first value received from the channel.

As the channels are thread-safe, nobody restricts us about the number of threads, in which we are going to write to a channel or read from it. The following example demonstrates how one channel is shared between a few threads.

This program prints the squares of the numbers from 0 to 10. The numbers are first sent to the channel:

```
my $channel = Channel.new();
$channel.send($_) for 0..10;
$channel.close;
```

The channel is closed after all the number are sent. In the next phase, three threads are created by calling the start function (don't forget that this function creates a thread indirectly by creating a promise). In each thread, an infinite loop tries receiving values from the same channel:

```
my @readers;
for 1..3 {
    push @readers, start {
```

```
while 1 {
    my $value = $channel.poll;
    last if $value === Any;
    say "$value² = " ~ $value * $value;
}
};
}
```

The non-blocking poll method is used here to read from the channel. If the queue is consumed and the returned value is empty, the loop is broken and the thread is done.

Before quitting the main program, we have to wait until all the promises are kept:

```
await @readers;
```

Each thread calculates the square of the value that it can read from the channel:

```
0²  = 0
2²  = 4
1²  = 1
3²  = 9
5²  = 25
4²  = 16
6²  = 36
7²  = 49
8²  = 64
10² = 100
9²  = 81
```

Run the program a few times and to see that it produces different outputs. Of course, the same values are calculated in each run but the order of the output lines may vary. The channel returns numbers in the same order, in which we sent them to it. Threads are concurrent, so some of them print their results and pick the next value before others. Despite the order in which threads work, the channel gives any number only once.

Summary

In this chapter, we briefly talked about the parallel nature of junctions, and spent the rest of the time deeply examining threads, promises, and channels—the mechanism that implement parallel and concurrent features in Perl 6. Using them is quite easy for the developer and does not require any manual manipulation of underlying mechanisms for ensuring that threads are executing without collisions.

14
Functional Programming

Perl 6 is a multi-paradigm programming language. In the previous chapters, we mostly used traditional imperative programming. In this chapter, we will talk about the ways you can use a functional programming style with Perl 6.

These topics will be covered in this chapter:

- Principles of functional programming
- Re-writing traditional programs using recursion
- Reduction operations
- Higher-order functions, lambdas, and the whatever code blocks
- Piping data with feed operators
- Closures, currying, and dynamic scoping
- Lazy and infinite lists and sequence generators

Before we go into any detail of the previously-listed topics, let us talk about what functional programming is.

What is functional programming?

Functional programming is the way of computing using a series of functions. Functions are understood here in the mathematical sense, not in the sense of subroutines in Perl 6. A very important principle of functional programming is that functions must have no side effects. In particular, that means that variables must be immutable—assigning a new value is forbidden.

All the topics that we will discuss in this chapter are the consequences of the preceding restrictions. It is important to realize that, for example, lambda functions are not the core essence of functional programming but are just one of the ways of following the main principle of having no side effects, such is changing some global variables that affect the result of the function.

Let us take a function f ($x) and call it twice with the same argument. Will the second call return the same result as the first one? In functional programming, it is required that a function always returns the same result if it is called with the same argument(s).

Here is an example of such a function that returns $x + 1:

```
sub f($x) {
    return $x + 1;
}

say f(5); # 6
say f(5); # 6

say f(5) == f(5); # True
```

Both calls return the same result. Also, the comparison f(5) == f(5) is True. This program may already be considered a program written in functional style.

Introducing a variable does not break the principle:

```
sub f($x) {
    return $x + 1;
}

my $a = 5;

say f($a); # 6
say f($a); # 6

say f($a) == f($a); # True
```

The $a variable only gets the value once during its initialization. It is never changed after that.

Now, let us modify the argument of the function (you need to use the is rw trait):

```
sub f($x is rw) {
    $x += 1;
    return $x;
}
```

The first call of the function with the same original value of `$a` returns the same result as before. Although, after the function call, the value of `$a` is changed, and the second call `f($a)` cannot return the same result. The condition `f($a) == f($a)` is not `True` anymore:

```
my $a = 5;

say f($a); # 6
say f($a); # 7

say f($a) == f($a); # False
```

Here, the function created a side effect of modifying its argument, which due to declaring it as a read-and-write parameter, changed the value of the variable in the main code.

Another way of having side effects is using global variables inside functions. Examine the following function:

```
my $step = 0;

sub f($x) {
    $step++;
    return $x + $step;
}
```

The argument of the function has not changed now but the function returns different results when it is called twice.

Now, look carefully at the three variants of the `f` function. In the first variant, there were no assignments involved in the body of the function. In the second and the third examples, either a function argument or a global variable were re-assigned. While no = operator was used explicitly, the constructs `$x += 1` and `$step++` are equivalent to the following assignments:

```
$x = $x + 1;
$step = $step + 1;
```

In both cases, this is the root of breaking the `f($a) == f($a)` condition.

The function itself does not necessarily change a global value. The value can be modified by other code between the two calls of the function:

```
my $step = 1;

sub f($x) {
    return $x + $step;
}
```

```
say f(5); # 6
$step = 2;
say f(5); # 7
```

Although the function seems to be predictable, its environment influences its work. In some sense, variable re-assignment introduces the concept of time in the program. At different times the same call of f(5) returns different results:

```
my $t1 = f(5);
$step = 2;
my $t2 = f(5);

say $t1 == $t2; # False
```

Perl 6 does not forbid setting new values of the variables but when writing programmes in functional style, you should only initialize the variables once and should avoid any new assignments. In the next section, you will see how traditional programs can be modified to follow the principles of functional programming.

Using recursion

Our next program in this chapter is a simple loop that prints the numbers from 10 to 15 and calculates their sum. Let us first print in numbers. As we've seen in Chapter 5, *Control Flow,* there are different ways of making a loop in Perl 6. Choosing between them can lead us already in the direction of functional programming.

The loop cycle needs a loop counter:

```
my $sum = 0;
loop (my $n = 10; $n <= 15; $n++) {
    $sum += $n;
}
say $sum; # 75
```

There are two variables that change their values in this program—$n and $sum. It is very easy to get rid of the $n counter, and thus re-assigning it a value:

```
my $sum = 0;
for 10..15 {
    $sum += $_;
}
say $sum;
```

Now, we are using the $_ variable instead of $n and actually the for loop can use an explicit loop variable:

```
my $sum = 0;
for 10..15 -> $n {
    $sum += $n;
}
say $sum;
```

The difference between this code and the program with loop is that now the variable $n only exists within one loop iteration. It is assigned before entering the body of the loop and withdrawn after it is run. In the first example, it is being incremented on each iteration.

One of the assignments is gone. How can we avoid modifying the $sum variable then? It looks unavoidable because of its nature—it should accumulate the sum while looping over the numbers. The answer is—use recursion. Recursion gives us the same trick as we have just seen with the $n variable. Instead of having a single global $sum variable that keeps the state of the program, create a new variable each time the sum is changed. Even more, it is possible to completely get rid of that variable, as shown in the next example:

```
sub sum($min, $max) {
    if ($min == $max - 1) {
        return $min + $max;
    }
    else {
        return $min + sum($min + 1, $max);
    }
}

say sum(10, 15); # 75
```

Let us look carefully at this program. First of all, there are no variables that keep the state here—no loop counter $n, nor the $sum variable keeping intermediate results. Instead of creating an instruction on how to calculate the sum—*start at this number, assume this is a sum; increment the number, add it to the previous sum;* we describe what the summation actually means—*sum is the current number plus the sum of all the previous numbers.*

The sum function calls itself, each time with different arguments. It is, of course, important to stop recursion at some point, this is why there is test $min == $max - 1, which becomes True when the values are the two last values that we want to add up.

This program is already a functional program: it encodes the definition of a sum, it does not keep the state and it uses functions to achieve the goal.

Finally, let us involve some Perl 6 syntactic elements to make the program more compact:

```
sub sum($min, $max) {
    return $min == $max - 1
        ?? $min + $max
        !! $min + sum($min + 1, $max);
}

say sum(10, 15);
```

Also, the `return` keyword is not needed here as Perl 6 will take the last calculated value in a function. The final semicolon may also be omitted:

```
sub sum($min, $max) {
    $min == $max - 1
        ?? $min + $max
        !! $min + sum($min + 1, $max)
}
```

Another transformation is to move similar parts out of both expressions:

```
sub sum($min, $max) {
    $min + ($min == $max - 1 ?? $max !! sum($min + 1, $max))
}
```

Let us stop here and see what other fascinating options Perl 6 offers us.

Using reduction

In the previous section, we were calculating the sum of the numbers between 10 and 15. The program, after some transformations, became equivalent to the following one:

```
say 10 + (11 + (12 + (13 + (14 + 15))));
```

Each pair of parentheses here corresponds to the recursive call of the `sum` function. Calls of the function are replaced here with its implementation. This is one of the consequences of the restriction of the state-less approach. Would the function depend on the program state, it would not be possible to replace the function call with its implementation without knowing the values reflecting the state at different moments.

As parentheses do not change any order of execution here, let's remove them:

```
say 10 + 11 + 12 + 13 + 14 + 15;
```

What we see here is a list of all the values between 10 and 15 separated by the + operator. We have already met that in the *Reduction meta-operator* section of Chapter 4, *Working with Operators*. The whole construction can be replaced with simple code:

```
say [+] 10..15;
```

This is also a program in a functional style. Compare its size with one of the examples in the previous section.

The reduction operator [+] also works perfectly with arbitrary arrays:

```
my @a = 10, 11, 100, 101, 1000, 1001;
say [+] @a; # 2223
```

We are now coming close to another important concept in functional programming, higher-order functions.

Higher-order functions and lambdas

The [+] reduction operator that we have just seen in the previous section is performing the action of the + operator as many times as needed to add up all the elements of the provided data.

In Perl 6, there is an alternative way of doing reduction operations. There exists a built-in function reduce that expects a code block that will execute the action. First, we will use the function add($a, $b) that we created in Chapter 2, *Writing Code*:

```
sub add($a, $b) {
    return $a + $b;
}

say reduce &add, 10..15;
```

The reduce function takes the reference to a function as the first argument and a flattened list of values. In &add, the ampersand before the name of the function tells Perl 6 that this is not a function call but a code reference to a function.

The reduce function is an example of the **higher-order function**. One of its arguments is another function. In Perl 6, functions are the **first-class objects**, which means that they can be passed as arguments to other functions as easily as you do it with regular variables. The function that is called from the higher-order function is also sometimes called a **callback function**.

As the `add` function is only used in the `reduce` function, it is possible to inline it and create it directly at the place where it is needed:

```
say reduce sub add($a, $b) {return $a + $b}, 10..15;
```

Now it is obvious that the `add` name is not adding any value and can be omitted, thus making the function anonymous:

```
say reduce sub ($a, $b) {return $a + $b}, 10..15;
```

In this context, the anonymous function is also called a **lambda function**. It has all the properties of a regular subs except that it neither has a name nor can be called from other places in the program. The whole function definition is inlined.

Now let us see how can Perl 6 help syntactically to simplify creating lambdas.

First of all, the `sub` block can be replaced with the pointy block:

```
say reduce -> $a, $b {$a + $b}, 10..15;
```

The arguments of the anonymous function are listed after the `->` arrow, and you don't need parentheses to enclose them. Also notice that with a pointy block, the `return` keyword cannot be used (the compiler will generate an error: `Attempt to return outside of any Routine`). Actually, `return` is not needed at all, as all the function has to do is calculate an expression, whose result will be the result of the function.

Furthermore, even the arguments are not the obligatory elements of such a function. They can be replaced by the placeholder variables inside a code block in curly braces (see the *Parameter placeholders* section in `Chapter 6`, *Subroutines*):

```
say reduce {$^a + $^b}, 10..15;
```

There are more built-in functions in Perl 6 that can act as higher-order functions. These are, among the rest—`map`, `grep`, and `sort`. Each of them can optionally take a code block or a reference to an existing function as the first argument. Let us see a few examples.

The `map` function initiates a callback for each element of the sequence. The result is a new list containing individual mapping of each element using the code of the callback function:

```
say map {.uc}, 'a'..'d'; # (A B C D)
```

The `grep` function also calls its callback for every element but only copies those elements, for which the callback returns a `True` value:

```
say grep {$_ > 10}, 1..15; # (11 12 13 14 15)
```

In both cases, the `$_` variable is used: with `map`, it is implicit as `.uc` is the shortcut for `$_.uc`.

With the `sort` function, it is a little bit more complex as the callback function needs two arguments. The easiest is to use placeholders:

```
say sort {$^b <=> $^a}, 10..15; # (15 14 13 12 11 10)
```

The code block allows sorting the numbers in reverse order.

The WhateverCode blocks

Now, as we have used code blocks with `sort`, `grep`, `map`, and `reduce`, it's time to use the so-called `WhateverCode` type in Perl 6. It involves the (*) star and creates a code block that can be used as any code block that we used earlier.

For example, instead of `{.uc}` you can write `*.uc`. The following two lines of code are equivalent:

```
say map {.uc}, 'a'..'d'; # (A B C D)
say map *.uc, 'a'..'d'; # (A B C D)
```

Similarly, this is how the `WhateverCode` block can be used to replace anonymous code block in the examples with `grep` and `sort`:

```
say grep * > 10, 1..15; # (11 12 13 14 15)

say sort * <=> *, <11 12 10 13 15 14>; # (10 11 12 13 14 15)
```

In the second example, there are two stars, which corresponds to the `$^a` and `$^b` placeholder arguments used earlier. With the `*`, no curly braces are needed to create a block.

Piping data and feed operators

The `grep`, `map`, `reduce`, and `sort` functions are so powerful and easy to use that (together with other similar user-defined higher-order functions) they can handle many practical tasks in those areas where traditional imperative programming would organize it via loops.

Often, you will need to call one of the functions on the result that another function returned. Consider an example with the list of houses on a street. Some of these houses have to be painted, but you need to choose only those on the even side of the street, which has red facades, which were renovated more than five years ago. The task is to know how much paint you need.

Let us assume that the information about the properties of the house is contained in a data structure like this:

```
my @street = (
    {
        number           => 1,
        renovation_year  => 2000,
        storeys          => 4,
        colour           => 'green',
        width            => 20,
    },
    {
        number           => 2,
        renovation_year  => 2014,
        storeys          => 6,
        colour           => 'red',
        width            => 10,
    },

    #  . . .
);
```

It is obvious that some kind of filter should be created. Either it should check each house and decide if it passes all the conditions, or it can step by step filter the houses that match one condition at a time. Let us start, for example, with selected houses on the even side of the street:

```
my @houses-to-paint = grep {$_<number> %% 2}, @street;
```

The `grep` function receives, one by one, all the elements of the `@street` array. In each iteration, the element is accessible via the `$_` topic variable. Only those elements that return a non-zero result after calculating the `$_<number> %% 2` condition are passed to the `@houses-to-paint` array.

Similarly, filtering based on the color and renovation year can be added:

```
my @houses-to-paint =
    grep {$_<renovation-year> < 2012},
    grep {$_<colour> eq 'red'},
    grep {$_<number> %% 2},
    @street;
```

Do not be confused by the coincidental pair of > < in the first `grep`. Each angle bracket has its own function, and the compiler understands it perfectly.

Finally, we need to calculate the area of the facade to understand how much paint is needed. Let's assume that for each square meter you need 0.7 liters of paint, and the height of one storey is 3 meters:

```
my $paint-volume = 0.7 * [+] map {$_<width> * $_<storeys> * 3}, @houses-to-
paint;
```

The `map` function is used here to *convert* a house to the area of its facade. The [+] reduction operator adds up all the values to get the total result.

We can now combine all the code in one statement:

```
say
    0.7 *
    [+]
        map  {$_<width> * $_<storeys> * 3},
        grep {$_<renovation-year> < 2013},
        grep {$_<colour> eq 'red'},
        grep {$_<number> %% 2},
    @street;
```

You may come up with your own style of indentation here.

It is even better if the houses are stored in objects rather than in hashes:

```
class House {
    has $.number;
    has $.renovation-year;
    has $.storeys;
    has $.colour;
    has $.width;

    method area {
        return $!width * $!storeys;
    }
}
```

```
my @street = (
    House.new(number          => 1,
              renovation-year => 2000,
              storeys         => 4,
              colour          => 'green',
              width           => 20),
    House.new(number          => 2,
              renovation-year => 2014,
              storeys         => 6,
              colour          => 'red',
              width           => 10),
    . . .
);
```

In this case, the code blocks of the map and grep functions may look simpler:

```
say
    0.7 *
    [+]
        map  {.area * 3},
        grep {.renovation-year < 2013},
        grep {.colour eq 'red'},
        grep {.number %% 2},
    @street;
```

Now it looks done. In a minute we will make it even better but for now notice once again, that there are no assignment operators that change the values of the variables. Actually, there are not many variables in the whole program.

The data flow in the last example with chained map and grep happens from bottom to top. First, the @street is filtered to find the houses with even numbers, then red houses are picked, then only old ones and then the areas of their facades is calculated. Perl 6 allows us to organize the code in such a way that you read it from top to bottom using the ==> and <== feed operators. Feed operators were briefly introduced in the *Data pipe operators* section of Chapter 4, *Working with Operators*. This is how you can re-write the chain using them:

```
say 0.7 * (@street ==>
    grep {.number %% 2} ==>
    grep {.colour eq 'red'} ==>
    grep {.renovation-year < 2013} ==>
    map {.area * 3} ==>
    reduce {$^a + $^b});
```

The reverse <== operator changes the flow of data.

In this example, the result of the chain is a number. In case you get arrays, you can even define the variable at the end of the chain. For example, instead of traditional assignment (parentheses are needed here):

```
my @even-red-houses =
    (@street ==> grep {.number %% 2} ==> grep {.colour eq 'red'});
```

Put the my declaration at the end:

```
@street ==> grep {.number %% 2} ==>
grep {.colour eq 'red'} ==> my @even-red-houses;
```

To reduce the number of braces, the whatever blocks can be used:

```
@street ==> grep *.number %% 2 ==>
grep *.colour eq 'red' ==> my @even-red-houses;
```

As we've seen, Perl 6 offers many different ways to express your ideas the best possible way.

Again, you see that there are no variables involved, but that does not mean that variables are forbidden in the functional style of programming. What is not desired is only modifying them. In the next section, we will talk about what else we can do with variables.

Manipulating the scope

In this section, we will learn three techniques that can change the scope of variables. These are closures, currying, and dynamic scoping.

Closures

In Perl 6, lexical variables exist within their scope. Closures are functions that can extend that scope and let you access the lexical value, which were available at the place where the closure was defined. Let us consider an example of the counter that keeps the current state in a variable.

First, no closures are involved. The counter value is kept in a global variable:

```
my $counter = 0;

sub next-number() {
    return $counter++;
}
```

```
say next-number();  # 0
say next-number();  # 1
say next-number();  # 2
```

Each time the `next-number` function is called, an increasing integer number is returned.

Now, the goal is to hide the `$counter` variable so that it is not accessible directly to the user of `next-number`. Here comes a closure. First, both the variable and the function are put inside another function, which creates a lexical scope for them:

```
sub new-counter() {
    my $counter = 0;

    sub next-number() {
        return $counter++;
    }
}
```

It is now not possible to access the `$counter` from outside the `new-counter` function, while it is still accessible inside the `next-number` sub. Both the `$counter` variable and the `next-number` sub are local and their scopes are equal to the body of the `new-counter`.

Although, the `new-counter` sub returns the `next-number` sub and it can be saved in a variable:

```
my $c = new-counter();
```

The type of the content hosted in `$c` is `Sub`:

```
say $c.WHAT;  # (Sub)
```

This means that `$c` is callable and can be used as a function:

```
say $c();  # 0
say $c();  # 1
say $c();  # 2
```

Each call changes the `$counter` variable that is captured inside the closure, and thus the call of `$c()` returns incrementing numbers as expected.

You can create another independent counter, which will internally contain another container for its $counter:

```
my $a = new-counter();
my $b = new-counter();

say $b(); # 0
say $b(); # 1
say $a(); # 0
say $b(); # 2
say $a(); # 1
```

As you see, the $a and $b counters keep their state between calls and do not affect each other.

In the previous code, the subs were saved in scalar variables, prefixed with the $ sigil. If you do so, you always have to add parentheses to indicate a function call. Without them, an address of the function in memory will be printed:

```
my $c = new-counter();
say $c;
```

This is what you get in the output:

sub next-number () { #`(Sub|140645269514272) ... }

As you know, it is possible to omit empty parentheses with regular functions, say with new-counter:

```
my $cntr = new-counter;
say $cntr(); # 0
say $cntr(); # 1
```

Perl 6 has a separate sigil, &, for containers that keep values that implement the Callable interface. We will not go into detail here, if you are interested, please refer to the documentation at https://docs.perl6.org/type/Callable. Variables with the & sigil are treated by the compiler as objects that you can call, so empty parentheses and even the sigil itself can be omitted, as is shown in the next program:

```
my &d = new-counter();
say &d(); # 0
say d();  # 1
say d;    # 2
```

Both bare d and d() and the full-formed &d() are the same calls.

The final note is about how the sub is returned from the new-counter function. To be more strict, it can be returned implicitly using a reference as shown in the next fragment:

```
sub new-counter() {
    my $counter = 0;

    sub next-number() {
        return $counter++;
    }

    return &next-number;
}
```

The ampersand is used here to denote that this is not a function call but a sub itself.

Currying

Currying is a technique to reduce the number of argument of a function by creating a wrapper function that substitutes some predefined values of the original function.

Let us see that in an example of a simple function taking two arguments:

```
sub greet($type, $name) {
    return "$type, $name!";
}
```

Assume now that we want to choose a default greeting; the function calls will contain repeated arguments:

```
say greet('Hello', 'Liza');
say greet('Hello', 'John');
say greet('Hello', 'Carl');
```

It is possible to solve the issue by creating a separate function hello, which just calls greet with the needed argument:

```
sub hello($name) {
    return greet('Hello', $name);
}
```

Perl 6 gives us simple syntax of doing that:

```
my &hello = &greet.assuming('Hello');
```

The assuming method creates a new callable sub that is actually a `greet` sub with the given first argument. Now, `hello` is a name of a new callable object that takes one argument and can be used as a function:

```
say hello('Liza');
say hello('John');
say hello('Carl');
```

Currying is somehow similar to using default arguments of subs but there are two main differences. First, default arguments can only appear in the end of the signature. Second, with currying, it is possible to create more than one default. For example, another alternative greeting can be created from the same greet function:

```
my &hi = &greet.assuming('Hi');

say hi('Liza');
say hi('John');
say hi('Carl');
```

Let us now see how to deal with a function with a named argument. Here is a modified version of the greet function:

```
sub greet(:$type, :$name) {
    return "$type, $name!";
}
```

Creating a specified `hello` version is easy:

```
sub hello($name) {
    return greet(:type('Hello'), :$name);
}
```

So, the `:$type` argument gets the predefined value—`:type('Hello')`, while the second argument `:$name` is passed directly using its original name. The result is a concatenated string with a greeting:

```
say hello('John'); # Hello, John!
```

Finally, let us see another way of extending the scope of variables.

Dynamic scope

Dynamic scope is utilizing the * twigil, for example, a dynamic scalar variable $*a. Unlike regular local variables, dynamic variables can be used in functions, which are called from the current scope of a variable. Consider an example:

```
sub f() {
    $*a++;
}

my $*a = 1;
f();
say $*a; # 2
```

Here, $*a is a dynamic variable in the main program. It is initialized with the value of 1. The f function, when it is called, changes the value of the same variable, thus the program prints 2. The thing is that the $*a is not declared inside the f function. The compiler will search for this name looking at the scopes, in which the function is called.

In the preceding example, a simple global variable could be used instead of a dynamic variable:

```
my $a = 1;
f();
say $a;

sub f() {
    $a++;
}
```

With dynamic variables, you can access different containers in different contexts. For example, what if the f function is called from another function?

```
sub g() {
    my $*a = 10;
    f();
    say $*a; # 21
}
```

In this case, f will modify the variable initialized in g. The same will happen to any other call that contains a dynamic variable in that scope:

```
sub f() {
    $*a++;
}

sub g() {
```

```
    my $*a = 10;
    f();
    say $*a;
}

sub h() {
    my $*a = 20;
    f();
    say $*a;
}

g(); # 11
h(); # 21
g(); # 11
```

In the next section, we will talk about creating higher-level functions such as iterators.

Creating and using iterators

Iterators are a powerful technique that provide data on demand and avoid manual counters. These are functions that return the next element of some sequence each time you call it. In the previous section, we already created the iterator `new-counter`, which generates incrementing integer numbers. Let us make something more complex:

```
sub make-iter(@data) {
    my $index = 0;

    sub {
        return @data[$index++];
    }
}

my &iter = make-iter(<red green blue orange>);

say iter; # red
say iter; # green
say iter; # blue
say iter; # orange
```

The `make-iter` function gets an array, installs the `$index` position to zero and returns a sub that will be used as an iterator. Next time the `iter` object is called, it returns the value at the current position and moves the internal pointer to the next element. After the data is exhausted, `Nil` will be returned.

Iterators can also generate sequences according to certain rules. For example, here is an iterator that returns the next factorial number each time it is called:

```
sub make-factorial-iter() {
    my $n = 1;
    my $f = 1;

    sub {
        $f *= $n++;
        return $f;
    }
}

my &iter = make-factorial-iter();
say iter for 1..5;
```

The program prints five numbers—factorials of 1 to 5. Notice that the algorithm does not use recursion or loops, and only minimal required actions are done to calculate the next value. It always uses the previously calculated value of $n - 1$.

And now we come to another topic, lazy evaluated data.

Lazy and infinite lists

The example with a factorial can generate numbers as long as the memory limitations of the computer allow. Although we may want to calculate, say a factorial of 100, the program will not do that until we really need the value. No computational resources are spent if the result is not needed yet. This is the idea behind lazy calculations.

In Perl 6, the ... operator creates a sequence. The simplest case looks similar to how the range is created. A regular array will be created in the next example:

```
my @a = 1...100;
say @a.elems;
```

The `@a` array is created immediately and it gets all the `100` elements, which are integers from `1` to `100`:

```
say @a[0];  # 1
say @a[1];  # 2

say @a[98]; # 99
say @a[99]; # 100
```

Contrarily, a lazy sequence created with the `lazy` keyword, will not populate the array:

```
my @b = lazy 1...100;
```

An attempt to get the size of it by calling `@b.elems`, incurs an error:

Cannot .elems a lazy list

It is possible though to get the element of this array:

```
say @b[0]; # 1
say @b[1]; # 2
```

Requesting elements at the end of an array will also generate the corresponding values:

```
say @b[98]; # 99
say @b[99]; # 100
```

Finally, when the array is over and an extra element is requested, the empty value `Any` is returned. At this point, an array is not lazy anymore and the `elems` method returns the size. To check if an array is lazy, use the `is-lazy` method:

```
say @b.is-lazy; # True

say @b[100];    # (Any)
say @b.elems;   # 100

say @b.is-lazy; # False
```

Perl 6 also allows us to create sequences, whose upper border is infinite:

```
my @c = 1 ... Inf; # or 1 ... ∞

say @c[0];    # 1
say @c[1000]; # 1001
```

As it is not possible to reach the end of such a sequence, `@c.is-lazy` will always remain `True`.

The `. . .` sequence operator can generate more complicated sequences when you supply it with an example of an arithmetic or geometric progression:

```
my @arithm = 1, 3 ... 11;
say @arithm; # [1 3 5 7 9 11]

my @geom = 2, 4, 8 ... 256;
say @geom; # [2 4 8 16 32 64 128 256]

my @float = 3.14, 3.15 ... 3.19;
say @float; # [3.14 3.15 3.16 3.17 3.18 3.19]
```

To create an infinite sequence, use `Inf` or `*` as the right end of the sequence:

```
my @inf = 1, 2 ... Inf;
say @inf[0..5]; # (1 2 3 4 5 6)
```

This program prints its result immediately without waiting until the array is filled with an infinite list.

Finally, it is possible to use a custom generator to calculate the next value:

```
my @cubes = {state $n; $n++; $n ** 3} ... Inf;
say @cubes[0..5]; # (1 8 27 64 125 216)
```

The generating code block is using the `state` variable to keep track of the numbers generated.

Summary

In this chapter, we were talking about functional programming. Perl 6, while not being a functional programming language, includes elements that can implement many features of such languages. We talked about recursions and reduction, about higher-order functions, lambda functions and the `WhateverCode` code blocks (those that use the `*` to ask Perl 6 to do what you want). We created a number of examples that use data piping, closures, currying, and dynamic scopes. And finally, we talked about infinite and lazy lists, and how to generate them.

The subject of the next chapter is reactive programming, which is another paradigm of programming that Perl 6 supports.

15
Reactive Programming

In the previous chapter, we talked about functional programming. Perl 6 is a multi-paradigm language that has built-in support for that. In this chapter, we talk about reactive programming, also known as functional reactive programming or event-driven programming. Again, Perl 6's core supports programming using this style out of the box.

The following topics will be covered in this chapter:

- Concepts of reactive programming
- On-demand and live supplies
- Filtering and transforming data streams

What is reactive programming?

In procedural programming, the program lists instructions of which and when the variable gets a particular value, or when a block of code is executed. For example, a variable gets its value as a sum of two other integer variables:

```
$z = $x + $y;
```

If either $x or $y has been changed after that assignment, nothing changes with the value of $z. Another example—a value returned by a function is assigned to a variable:

```
$area = area-of-circle($r);
```

Although it is clearly seen from the code that it calculates the area of a circle with the given radius, if the $r variable is changed, you have to manually update the value of $area.

Reactive programming aims to change that "static" behavior of dependent values. Interactive interfaces of many computer programs and web pages are good examples of a reactive approach. Imagine an online calculator, where you type two values and immediately get the result on another place on the page. Or you enter a radius and the area of the circle is recalculated and displayed. Let us see how Perl 6 deals with that.

There are two main classes that handle most of what you need for reactive programming—Supply, which is an asynchronous data stream, and Supplier, which is a factory for one of the variations of supplies, namely **live supplies**. There also exists **on-demand supplies**, which will we cover first.

On-demand supplies

The data flow of supplies contains two parts—the supplier that emits data and the tap that receives it. Perl 6's reactive programming model is a thread-safe implementation of the Observer design pattern.

Let us create our first on-demand supply using the supply keyword:

```
supply {
    emit($_) for 'a'..'e';
}
```

The supply is here but it does not emit any data yet because there is no demand. You can easily see this if you add a print instruction to the loop:

```
supply {
    for 'a'..'e' {
        emit($_);
        say "Emitted $_";
    }
}
sleep 2;
```

The program just silently quits after 2 seconds.

To make the supply generate data, we need to create a **tap**. The supply block returns a value of the Supply type, and you can call the tap method on it to pass the code that will be executed in response to the data emitted:

```
supply {
    emit($_) for 'a'..'e';
}.tap({
    .say;
});
```

This time, the program prints a few lines with the letters from a to e. Let us open a tap in our "debugger" program to see that it really executes the emitting block:

```
supply {
    for 'a'..'e' {
        say "Emitting $_";
        emit($_);
    }
}.tap({
    say "Tap received $_";
});
```

Indeed, both say functions are called now:

```
Emitting a
Tap received a
Emitting b
Tap received b
Emitting c
Tap received c
Emitting d
Tap received d
Emitting e
Tap received e
```

It is not a problem to attach more than one tap to a supply. Each of them will receive the same data:

```
my $supply = supply {
    emit($_) for 'a'..'e';
}

$supply.tap({
    say "Tap 1 got $_";
});
$supply.tap({
    say "Tap 2 got $_";
});
```

Unlike channels (see Chapter 13, *Concurrent Programming*), taps do not compete to get the value sent. A supply can feed any number of taps, as you need them. Notice that this also means that taps do not work as parallel processes. This is clearly visible if you add a small delay to the first tap:

```
$supply.tap({
    say "Tap 1 got $_";
    sleep 0.5;
});
$supply.tap({
    say "Tap 2 got $_";
});
```

In the output you will see that all the values from a to e will first arrive to the first tap, and then the second one will be served:

```
Tap 1 got a
Tap 1 got b
Tap 1 got c
Tap 1 got d
Tap 1 got e
Tap 2 got a
Tap 2 got b
Tap 2 got c
Tap 2 got d
Tap 2 got e
```

Generating data with supplies

In the previous section, values were sent to a supply using the emit method. For each data item, a separate call is done. Supplies can generate data themselves. The interval method of the Supply class emits data with the given interval. In the next example, it generates increasing numbers every 300 milliseconds:

```
Supply.interval(0.3).tap({
    say $_;
});
sleep 5;
```

Every time a tap is triggered, it gets an increasing integer number. The first value is 0. Thus, the program above will print numbers from 0 to 16.

Calling the sleep function is needed here to see a few of the first results that the tap received. Without it, the program immediately stops.

By the way, if you want to use a named variable instead of $_, use a pointy block with an argument:

```
Supply.interval(0.5).tap( -> $x {say $x});
sleep 2;
```

The `interval` method also accepts the second argument, which is the delay in seconds before the first data item will be emitted:

```
Supply.interval(1, 2).tap({
    .say;
});
sleep 4;
```

Now the program starts printing numbers after 2 seconds. The initial delay does not affect the sequence that the supply generates. This program also starts printing from 0 (and ends at 1, as the sleep function allows 2 seconds when the program has a working tap).

The tap can be closed at any time. Taps are objects of the `Tap` class, which has the `close` method. Its usage is demonstrated in the following program:

```
my $supply = Supply.interval(0.3);
my $tap = $supply.tap({
    .say;
});

sleep 1;
$tap.close;
sleep 2;
```

After printing the first few numbers during the first second, the tap is closed, after which the program just waits another couple of seconds printing nothing.

If there are no taps, the supply does not generate new data. Let us see that behavior in the following example with a pause before creating the tap:

```
my $supply = Supply.interval(0.3);

sleep 2;
my $tap = $supply.tap({
    .say;
});
sleep 2;
```

The delay before the tap connection is longer than the interval between potential data generation. During 2 seconds, there could be some numbers generated but the program still prints the numbers starting from 0.

This principle also works when a tap is connected to the supply which is already generating data for another tap:

```
my $supply = Supply.interval(0.5);

say "Tap 1\t| Tap 2";
say '_' x 15;

$supply.tap({
    say "$_\t|";
});

sleep 2;

$supply.tap({
    say "\t| $_";
});

sleep 3;
```

The two taps work independently here. This is what the output of the program looks like:

```
Tap 1    | Tap 2

0        |
1        |
2        |
3        |
         | 0
4        |
         | 1
5        |
         | 2
6        |
         | 3
7        |
         | 4
8        |
         | 5
9        |
```

Both taps receive sequences starting from zero.

The `interval` method is a factory method that creates on-demand supplies:

```
my $supply = Supply.interval(10);
say $supply.WHAT; # (Supply)
```

There is an alternative syntax for creating supplies—we will discuss it in the next section.

The react and whenever keywords

In Perl 6, there are special keywords for woking with on-demand supplies. Instead of explicitly creating objects of the Supply class, use the `react` keyword. Creating a tap is replaced with the `whenever` block in this case:

```
react {
    whenever Supply.interval(0.5) {
        .say;
    }
}
```

The program prints number every 0.3 seconds. Notice the major difference with the previous examples. With `react`, there is no need to call `sleep` or somehow control the lifecycle of the program after creating a tap. The program runs infinitely until you break it with `Ctrl+C`, for example.

To break the loop programmatically, call the `done` function:

```
react {
    whenever Supply.interval(0.5) {
        .say;
        done if $_ > 3;
    }
}
```

This time, the program prints the numbers only for a couple of seconds.

Using lists as the source of the supply data

The `Supply` class offers a special method, `from-list`, that takes a list and sends elements from it as emitted data items:

```
my $supply = Supply.from-list('a'..'e');
$supply.tap({
    .say;
});
```

Alternatively, a `react-whenever` construct can be used:

```
react {
    whenever Supply.from-list('a'..'e') {
        .say;
    }
}
```

In both cases, the program immediately streams all the elements to the tap, which prints them.

Similar to the `interval` method, `from-list` creates a supply object:

```
my $supply = Supply.from-list(1..10);
say $supply.WHAT; # (Supply)
```

Now it is time to talk about another type of supplies, live supplies.

Live supplies

Live supplies generate data regardless of the number of taps. Unlike on-demand supplies, if there are no taps open, emitted data is still generated and it simply disappears. As soon as the tap is open, it starts receiving data from that moment; all the history is lost.

To create a live supplier, call a constructor of the `Supplier` class. A tap must be connected to the supply, returned by the `Supply` factory method. This is all shown in the following example:

```
my $supplier = Supplier.new;

$supplier.Supply.tap({
    say $_;
});

$supplier.emit($_) for 'a'..'e';
```

You may be a bit confused by the presence of both the `Supply` and `Supplier` classes. The `Supplier` class is a factory to generate live supplies.

Let us see how live supply streams data and what happens when no taps are open. In the program below, a live supply generates data in a separate thread created by the `start` keyword. Actually, start creates a promise (see `Chapter 13`, *Concurrent Programming*), and thus it is accompanied by the `await` keyword to wait until all is done:

```
my $supplier = Supplier.new;

my $emitter = start {
    for 'a'..'e' {
        sleep 1;
        $supplier.emit($_);
    }
}

sleep 3;
$supplier.Supply.tap({
    say $_;
});

await $emitter;
```

The `$emitter` promise publishes its data from the `'a'..'e'` range every second after the beginning of the program. The tap is created 3 seconds later. At that moment the tap starts getting values from the supply, and the program prints c, b, and e. The first three data pieces are lost (there was no tap open to take them). Notice that neither the supply nor the tap queues the history.

Live supplies, as well as on-demand supplies, distribute data equally if there is more than one tap connected:

```
my $supplier = Supplier.new;
my $supply = $supplier.Supply;

$supply.tap({
    say "Tap 1 got $_";
});
$supply.tap({
    say "Tap 2 got $_";
});

$supplier.emit(10.rand);
$supplier.emit(10.rand);
```

This program emits two random numbers, both of which will land in both taps:

```
Tap 1 got 3.49754022030442
Tap 2 got 3.49754022030442
Tap 1 got 0.196464185630715
Tap 2 got 0.196464185630715
```

Reactive programming in Perl 6 is thread-safe. For example, let's create a program where all the supplies and taps are executed in their own threads:

```
my $supplier = Supplier.new;

start {
    $supplier.Supply.tap({
        say "Tap 1 got $_";
    })
}

start {
    $supplier.Supply.tap({
        say "Tap 2 got $_";
    })
}

start {
    sleep 1;
    $supplier.emit(42);
}

sleep 2;
```

It works perfectly—both taps receive the value emitted by the supplier:

```
Tap 2 got 42
Tap 1 got 42
```

As soon as we have threads and they work in parallel, the output of the program may be different, depending on which tap got its data first:

```
Tap 1 got 42
Tap 2 got 42
```

To learn more about the methods of the `Supply` and `Supplier` classes, refer to the documentation on the `docs.perl.org` site.

Filtering and transforming data streams

Objects of the Supply class have the grep and map methods, which can be used to filter the data of the stream similar to how the built-in functions with the same names do. Both grep and map methods create a new Supply object, to which you can connect a tap.

Consider the following example:

```
my $supply = Supply.interval(0.3);

my $filtered = $supply.grep(* %% 2);

$filtered.tap({
    .say;
});

sleep 3;
```

We had a similar program in the *On-demand supplies* section earlier. This time, another supply, $filtered, is embedded in the data flow. It is created by the grep method called on the original $supply.

The filter itself is implemented by the WhateverCode block * %% 2. Only odd numbers pass from $supply to $filtered now.

For the rest, both $supply and $filtered objects are regular on-demand supplies, and you can attach as many taps to them as you need:

```
my $supply = Supply.interval(0.3);
my $filtered = $supply.grep(* %% 2);

$supply.tap({
    "Unfiltered tap got $_".say;
});

$filtered.tap({
    "Filtered tap 1 got $_".say;
});
$filtered.tap({
    "Filtered tap 2 got $_".say;
});

sleep 3;
```

The program generates the following output containing reactions from all three taps:

```
Filtered tap 1 got 0
Unfiltered tap got 0
Filtered tap 2 got 0
Unfiltered tap got 1
Unfiltered tap got 2
Filtered tap 1 got 2
Filtered tap 2 got 2
Unfiltered tap got 3
Unfiltered tap got 4
Filtered tap 1 got 4
Filtered tap 2 got 4
Unfiltered tap got 5
Unfiltered tap got 6
Filtered tap 1 got 6
Filtered tap 2 got 6
Unfiltered tap got 7
Unfiltered tap got 8
Filtered tap 1 got 8
Filtered tap 2 got 8
Unfiltered tap got 9
```

As you can see, the emitted numbers are incrementing, and the filtered supplies only take even values.

Another method, map, transforms the data and returns the new supply with the transformed stream. Consider the following example, where all the numbers generated by the interval supply are converted into cubes:

```
Supply.interval(0.3).map(* ** 2).tap(*.say);
sleep 2;
```

Here, two *s are used for brevity. If you prefer a more verbose style, use the $_ variable:

```
Supply.interval(0.3).map({
    $_ ** 2
}).tap({
    .say
});

sleep 2;
```

The program prints squares of the first few integer numbers, as expected.

Summary

In this chapter, we were talking about reactive programming in Perl 6. This paradigm has support in the language core, so no external modules are needed to start programming. The supply is the main character in this chapter—we covered two different types of them, on demand and live supplies. We had many examples of attaching taps to supplies and saw how the data flow is organized and how it can be filtered.

* * *

This was the last chapter of the book. In 15 chapters, we went from the very basics of Perl 6 through an object-oriented approach and concurrent programming to higher order features such as functional and reactive programming. Perl 6 naturally embeds all of that. There is no doubt that more than 15 years of development added value to the quality and maturity of the language in general.

During the process of writing this book, which took about half a year, three major releases of Rakudo appeared. I have to admit that the quality of the compiler is so high that I have never experienced any crashes or weird behavior during the last 2 or 3 years. Talking to the attendees at various Perl conferences, I have noticed that more and more people are interested in Perl 6 and say that everything *just works* now. You can download the compiler and it works out of the box, offering the vast amount of features that Perl 6 has.

The current version of the language itself is 6.c. The letter c stands for Christmas here. For a long time, it was announced that Perl 6 will be ready by Christmas, without mentioning the year in which it will happen. Finally, the 6.c standard became a reality by the Christmas of 2015. Later in 2017 or in early 2018, the new version of the language will be released. You can find more details of it in Larry Wall's keynote that he gave at the Perl Conference in Amsterdam in August 2017— https://youtu.be/E5t8qaAGw9w.

As the author of this book, I hope my readers enjoy the language and start using it in their practice. The more you use the language, the more you understand how huge its potential is. We are now at the very beginning of the new era of Perl.

Index